NEW CALVINISM

COPYRIGHT © 2014 DREW CURLEY

ALL RIGHTS RESERVED.

ISBN-13: 9781799260783

NEW CALVINISM:
HISTORY AND THEOLOGY

DREW CURLEY

TO MY BEST FRIEND, ABY

A special thanks to Dr. Dave Olander for always challenging me, to my proofreaders, Jim Curley, Rodney Phillips, Dr. Bill Korver for their time and grace, and to my extended family for all of their support.

TABLE OF CONTENTS

Acknowledgments

Chapter 1 Where Did New Calvinism Come From?

Chapter 2 How Did New Calvinism Develop?

Chapter 3 A Calvinist Soteriology?

Chapter 4 Missionally Flooding Into Cities

Chapter 5 Continuationism

Chapter 6 Fundamental Issues and Conclusion

Appendix 1: Repentance and the 2014 Together for the Gospel Conference

Appendix 2: New Calvinist Reviews of *Future Grace*

Appendix 3: Origins of New Calvinism

Bibliography

CHAPTER 1

WHERE DID NEW CALVINISM COME FROM?

In 2009, David Van Biema published an article describing new Calvinism as one of the "10 Ideas Changing the World Right Now."[1] This article gave worldwide recognition to a theological trend that was previously relegated to relative obscurity. The article itself is a reflection of an earlier effort chronicling a new form of Calvinism[2] emerging among young pastors and seminarians. In this 2008 work by Colin Hansen, *Young Restless, Reformed: A Journalist's Journey with the New Calvinists*, the author identifies many new Calvinists but he does not provide a clear definition of new Calvinism.[3] This may be caused in part by a degree of theological fluidity that exists amongst the group's members.

What will be asserted here is that new Calvinism is not a monolithic entity. It cannot be tracked to a single seminary or institution, but it has been highly influential in several seminaries. Its origin is not found in a particular

---

[1] David Van Biema, "10 Ideas Changing the World Right Now: New Calvinism," (March 12, 2009) *Time*, http://www.time.com/time/specials/packages/article/0,28804,1884779_1884782_1884760,00.html, (1/20, 2012)

[2] What is being observed is what some call "New Calvinism." This form of Calvinism and its relationship to other forms of Calvinism is discussed in greater detail below.

[3] Colin Hansen, *Young Restless, Reformed: A Journalist's Journey with the New Calvinists*, (Wheaton, IL: Crossway, 2008).

theologian, but new Calvinists draw on the influence of several historical persons. In addition to these historical figures, there have been more contemporary voices, while not specifically new Calvinists themselves, have laid the groundwork others have followed. Within the movement, several theologians have attracted a cult-like following that has given prominence to the movement as a whole.[4] With all this established, there remains vagary, producing difficulty when attempting to identify what truly unifies the new Calvinists.[5]

It needs to be clearly stated before continuing: new Calvinists are men of God who are wholeheartedly devoted to serving the Lord. They are brothers in Christ. Their ministries are truly being used mightily by God and are influencing the world. They really are being used of God to change the world. This writer is not attempting to attack anyone personally. Instead, an analysis is to be made of the doctrinal and theological trends that can be observed within the movement. This dissertation, therefore, seeks to be an analysis of the doctrine of this loose confederacy.

The church must be diligent in protecting the biblical gospel. Sproul's words are also appropriate: "an 'inadequate' gospel is not the gospel."[6] The importance of the topic is

---

[4] This movement as a whole may be just as much about people as it is about theology. New Calvinism is synonymous with names like Driscoll, Piper, Keller, but its theology is yet undefined. More detail on this follows.

[5] Many new Calvinists are ardent defenders of the doctrine of grace, but openly reject tradition elements present in reformed theology. These notably include continuationism, infant baptism, Baptist ecclesiology, et cetera. In addition to this there is no uniform definition of the terms of TULIP. Differences are present between how one defines total depravity, perseverance, et cetera.

[6] R.C. Sproul, *Faith Alone: The Evangelical Doctrine of Justification*, electronic ed. (Grand Rapids: Baker Books, 2000), 46.

without question. Paul's admonition to the Galatians must be remembered; there is only one gospel and

> even if we, or an angel from heaven, should preach to you a gospel contrary to what we have preached to you, he is to be accursed! As we have said before, so I say again now, if any man is preaching to you a gospel contrary to what you received, he is to be accursed![7]

Although much of the theological discussion that follows does not flow specifically from Calvin's personal understanding of the gospel, one crucial issue is summarized well by Calvin himself. In commenting on Acts 16:31, he states that to believe in the Lord Jesus "is but a short, and, to look to, a cold and hungry definition of salvation."[8] All too many who have claimed to follow Calvin have built upon this idea. There also remains a necessary call for revision and clarity within new Calvinism. This is a theology that is quickly becoming the consensus opinion of mainstream evangelicalism and will certainly affect the church for many years to come. Any doctrinal deficiencies will certainly be magnified in the next generation.

ORIGINS OF NEW CALVINISM

Since *Time* magazine published its article referencing new Calvinism as one of the 10 Ideas Changing the World Right Now, new Calvinism has garnered a great deal of attention. Most of this attention focuses on the relative merits of the movement. One thing that has not been adequately understood is the origin of new Calvinism. Even though the movement began prior to the publishing of the article, the

---

[7] Galatians 1:8-9, NASB.

[8] John Calvin, *Acts*, electronic ed., Calvin's Commentaries (Albany, OR: Ages Software, 1998), Ac 16:31.

focus here will be limited to its rise in prominence after the 2009 release of the aforementioned article. One major reason for this is the great difficulty in identifying the exact beginning to any theological movement. It is likely that the movement began to build momentum in the 1980s, but many within the movement trace its roots all the way back to Augustine and beyond.

There are several important events that chronicle the more recent developments of new Calvinism. These include, but are limited to, the formation of *The Gospel Coalition* in 2005, *Together for the Gospel* in 2006, Acts 29 in 1998, the beginning of the *Passion Conferences* in 1997, the publication of *Desiring God* in 1986, as well as the election of Al Mohler as president of the Southern Baptist Theological Seminary in 1993, one of the key figures in the Southern Baptist Convention's conservative resurgence.

This leads to another difficulty in clearly identifying new Calvinism's beginning. Did old Calvinism actually become new? When did it become new? How has it departed or developed reformed theology? Who is responsible for instigating or authorizing such changes? Why new Calvinism now? Many simply see themselves in a long continuous line of other like-minded theologians who have just championed the doctrines of grace to a new generation; men like Jonathan Edwards, John Owen, John Calvin, and Augustine. One proposal would then see new Calvinism as Calvinism believed in a new generation instead of a new type of Calvinism. If this is not the case, then how many forms of Calvinism are there?

Much has been written in recent years concerning the relationship between John Calvin and those who are known today as Calvinists. Given that no one attempts to hold Calvin's doctrines exclusively, there are two basic approaches to Calvin and Calvinism. The first is Calvin against the Calvinists as articulated by R.T. Kendall in *Calvin and English Calvinism to 1649*. His basic thesis is that what is called Calvinism today is not the theology of John Calvin, especially in regards to the doctrine of limited atonement. In response to this work, Paul Helm wrote *Calvin and Calvinism,* which sought to refute Kendall and argued for the essential unity between Calvin and Calvinism. In a recent and perhaps more important work, Richard Muller sides with neither Kendall nor Helm.[9] Muller states, "we have no indication from Calvin's correspondence that his theology was viewed as the primary expression of Reformed thought in his generation."[10] The terms Calvinism and reformed theology are not necessarily indicative of Calvin or the Reformation. This point needs to be understood.

If one were to ask new Calvinists, many of them might be inclined to equate reformed theology with Calvin and the acronym TULIP. Although their definitions of the terms may vary, this is the essential basis for the ecumenicalism within new Calvinism. The origin of the concept of the five points of Calvinism most likely arose in response to the Remonstrants, the followers of Jacob Arminius. The five points, articulated in the Canons of Dordt, were developed in response the five protests of Arminius concerning the theology of Theodore Beza. The fact that both men were disciples of Calvin further complicates matters. Which disciple followed more Calvin more closely? Kennedy observes, "there are striking dissimilarities between Calvin's reading of Scripture and that of the later Reformed tradition."[11] It will be shown that much

---

[9] Corresponding to this is another discussion concerning whether the entity referred to as reformed theology is true to the theology of the Reformation.

[10] Richard A. Muller, *Calvin and the Reformed Tradition: On the Work of Christ and the Order of Salvation,* Kindle Edition, (Grand Rapids, MI: Baker Academic, 2012), loc 372-373.

[11] Kevin D. Kennedy, "Hermeneutical discontinuity between Calvin and

of what is known as Calvinism follows in the line of men like Theodore Beza and Johannes Cocceius[12] as much as it does from Calvin. Although Calvin himself was not always consistent in his thinking, others developed his earlier teachings. Ferguson states:

> the interpretation of Beza's thought and his role in the development of Calvinism has caused considerable controversy. His fidelity to Calvin was accepted by contemporaries, but by the middle of the 17th century Peter Heylyn (1600–62) in England and Amyraut on the Continent found Beza responsible for hardening Calvin's theology.[13]

A.H. Strong observes:

> Beza carried Calvin's doctrine of predestination to an extreme supralapsarianism, which is hyper-Calvinistic rather than Calvinistic. Cocceius…made theology centre about the idea of the covenants, and founded the Federal theology.[14]

Likewise, Berkhof describes Cocceius' theology in the following way:

> others, since the days of Coccejus, distinguish two covenants, namely, the covenant of redemption (*pactumsalutis*) between the Father and the Son, and, as based on this, the covenant of grace between the triune God and the elect, or the elect sinner.[15]

---

later Calvinism,"
Scottish Journal of Theology 64.3 (Aug 2011):312.
[12] Cocceius is also spelled Coccejus and Koch
[13] Sinclair B. Ferguson and J.I. Packer, *New Dictionary of Theology* (Downers Grove, IL: InterVarsity Press, 2000), 91.
[14] Augustus Hopkins Strong, *Systematic Theology* (Philadelphia: American Baptist Publication Society, 1907), 46.

> Coccejus and his school maintained that in the counsel of peace Christ became a *fidejussor*, and that consequently Old Testament believers enjoyed no complete forgiveness of sins[16]
>
> Coccejus' theory makes the work of God in making provision for the redemption of sinners dependent on the uncertain obedience of man in an entirely unwarranted way.[17]

This theology, known as federal or more frequently covenant theology provides the basis for reformed theology.[18] Historically federal theology eventually ruled the day in the Westminster Confession and the Three Forms of Unity. These documents are said to be the "north star" of Reformed Theology.[19] Is this the system universally held by new Calvinists? Larsen believes this to be the origin of what is now known as Calvinism, making it more a Bezan theology codified at Westminster.[20]

In addition to this, it must be asked whether the title new Calvinism is even a legitimate conclusion given their

---

[15] Louis Berkhof, *Systematic Theology* (Grand Rapids, MI: Wm. B. Eerdmans publishing co., 1938), 265.
[16] Ibid, 267.
[17] Ibid, 268.
[18] Not all agree on this point. While not all agree on this point (cf. R. Scott Clark, "The History of Covenant Theology," *Tabletalk Magazine,* October 2006 (Lake Mary, FL: Ligonier Ministries, Inc., 2006) more within
reformed theology believe there to be a definitive beginning with Cocceius (cf. A.H. Strong, *Systematic Theology,*
(Philadelphia: American Baptist Publication Society, 1907) or Louis Berkhof, *Systematic Theology,* (Grand Rapids,
MI: Wm. B. Eerdmans Publishing Co., 1938). See below for discussion on the connection between federalism and the federal headship of Adam.

[19] Carl Trueman, Phone Conversation (June 18, 2013).
[20] David Larsen, Phone Conversation, (June 12, 2013).

theology. Muller, in discussing the meaning of the actual terms of TULIP, observes that TULIP is:

> an acronym of questionable pedigree…there is no historical association between the acrostic TULIP and the Canons of Dort. As far as we know, both the acrostic and the associated usage of 'five points of Calvinism' are of Anglo-American origin and do not date back before the nineteenth century.[21]

All too often the acronym TULIP has been equated with not only the Reformation but also Christian orthodoxy in general. TULIP is too vague and imprecise to be the determinative principle by which to judge all post-Reformation soteriology. Even R.C. Sproul, a Calvinist par excellence, does not prefer the terminology of TULIP.[22] This shows the limitations of judging new Calvinism's soteriology exclusively upon the terms and merits of TULIP.

Much of the discussion of whether there is a consistent soteriology within new Calvinism then becomes tied to the question of just how the soteriology of new Calvinism is Calvinistic. Is it Calvinistic in the broadest sense of the word or is it decidedly linked to either Calvin or others like Beza or Cocceius? Thorson's assessment is interesting in that he believed Kendall's view of Calvin and Calvinisms:

> may have done an excellent job clarifying the theological drift of Calvin's followers, he did not begin with the actual complexity of Calvin's thought. Some would put it stronger: Calvin is not simply complex, but inconsistent[23]

---

[21] Ibid, loc 1013, 1081-1083.
[22] Cf. R.C. Sproul, *Grace Unknown: The Heart of Reformed Theology*, electronic ed. (Grand Rapids: Baker Books, 2000).
[23] Stephen Thorson, "Tension in Calvin's View of Faith: Unexamined

If there is disagreement with Calvin, one must ask why? Is it an attempt to clarify his doctrines in light of contemporary challenges or is it an effort to correct or revise his teaching? It may seem counter-intuitive, but it is actually easier to assess the consistency of new Calvinism's soteriology after their continuity (or their relative discontinuity) with the theology of Calvin has been examined.

Overall, there is a difficulty in identifying the movement's origins based on its use of Calvin's name. No one would argue that new Calvinism truly follows the teachings of John Calvin on all matters.[24] When this point is conceded, the term Calvinism itself may become imprecise to the point of being antiquated. As one professor at Westminster Theological Seminary explains, the term Calvinism is a misnomer.[25] He argues that most –isms are the construct of historians and because of this, no definitive form of Calvinism exists. New Calvinism is, therefore, one shade in the spectrum of many Calvinisms. This begs the question of where they may fall on the spectrum. Should they be seen to align with Hodge? Warfield? Edwards? Beza? Calvin? A specific confessional tradition? Are they more Dutch or Scottish reformed?[26]

NEW CALVINISM'S SINE QUA NON

Assumptions in R.T. Kendall's Calvin and English Calvinism to 1649," *Journal of the Evangelical Theological Society* 37/3 (September 1994), 421.
[24] Baptism, ecclesiology and spiritual gifts are noteworthy examples.
[25] Carl Trueman, "Calvin and Calvinism," http://www.youtube.com/watch?v=XZ-kG_r_OSY (Accessed June 12, 2013).
[26] This is not a distinction that many readers of this dissertation will naturally be familiar. An oversimplified answer would be that the Scottish reformed theology is highly confessional while the Dutch (e.g. Kuyper) is more focused on social reform.

Before delving into new Calvinism's *sine qua non*, one must first establish the fact that there is, at the very least, a group of people who comprise the core of the movement. Identifying the new Calvinists, this is the essential first step. Once this has been established, only then can one attempt to classify their doctrines into a working *sine qua non*. In addition to this, one should understand the historical circumstances that helped to fuel the rise of the movement. This will be the focus of chapter 2.

The essentials that will be focused on, as a functional *sine qua non* for the purpose of this work, are built upon one new Calvinist's definition of what differentiates new Calvinism from old Calvinism. He says:

> 1. Old Calvinism was fundamental or liberal and separated from or syncretized with culture. New Calvinism is missional and seeks to create and redeem culture.
>
> 2. Old Calvinism fled from the cities. New Calvinism is flooding into cities.
>
> 3. Old Calvinism was fearful of the Holy Spirit and generally cessationist (i.e. believing the gifts of the Holy Spirit such as tongues and prophecy had ceased). New Calvinism delights in the Holy Spirit and is generally continuationist with regard to spiritual gifts.
>
> 4. Old Calvinism was fearful and suspicious of other Christians and burned bridges. New Calvinism loves all Christians and builds bridges between them.[27]

---

[27] Mark Driscoll, "Time Magazine Names New Calvinism 3rd Most Powerful Idea," *The Resurgence*, *http://theresurgence.com/2009/03/12/time-magazine-names-new-Calvinism-3rd-most-powerful-idea* (Accessed 1/28/2013).

Although this is an imperfect description, until recently, it was the only one produced by a new Calvinist of any significance.[28]

---

[28] More recently Piper has said that there are 12 distinctive features of new Calvinism. (1) The New Calvinism, in its allegiance to the inerrancy of the Bible, embraces the biblical truths behind the five points of Calvinism (TULIP), while having an aversion to using the acronym (or any other systematic packaging) along with a sometimes-qualified embrace of Limited Atonement. The focus is on Calvinistic soteriology but not to the exclusion or the appreciation of the broader scope of Calvin's vision. (2) The New Calvinism embraces the sovereignty of God in salvation and all the affairs of life and history, including evil and suffering. (3) The New Calvinism has a strong complementarian flavor (as opposed to egalitarian) with an emphasis on the flourishing of men and women in relationships where men embrace a call to robust, humble, Christ-like servant-leadership. (4) The New Calvinism leans toward being culture-affirming, as opposed to culture-denying, while holding fast to some very culturally-alien positions on issues like same-sex practice and abortion. (5) The New Calvinism embraces the essential place of the local church: it is led mainly by pastors; it has a vibrant church-planting bent; it produces widely-sung worship music; and it exalts the preached Word as central to the work of God both locally and globally. (6) The New Calvinism is aggressively mission-driven, including missional impact on social evils, evangelistic impact on personal networks, and missionary impact on the unreached peoples of the world. (7) The New Calvinism is inter-denominational, with a strong (some would say oxymoronic) Baptistic element. (8) The New Calvinism includes both charismatics and non-charismatics. (9) The New Calvinism places a priority on pietism or piety in the Puritan vein, with an emphasis on the essential role of the affections in Christian living, while esteeming the life of the mind and being very productive in it, and embracing the value of serious scholarship. (10) The New Calvinism is vibrantly engaged in publishing books, and, even more remarkably, in the world of the Internet, with hundreds of energetic bloggers and social media activists, with Twitter as the increasingly-default way of signaling things new and old that should be noticed and read. (11) The New Calvinism is international in scope, multi-ethnic in expression, and culturally-diverse. There is no single geographic, racial, cultural, governing center. There are no officers, no organization, nor any loose affiliation that would encompass the whole. (As an aside, he adds: I would dare say there are outcroppings of this movement that no one in this room has ever heard of.) (12) The New Calvinism is robustly gospel-centered, cross-

A Calvinist Soteriology

The proper understanding of new Calvinism's relationship to Calvinism can only be fully known after defining new Calvinism's *sine qua non*. Essential to this is answering the question: what makes a new Calvinist a Calvinist?[29] Are they truly Calvinists in any sense of the word? When these questions are answered, their theological heritage can be unfolded. One can then understand whether there is a great divergence from Calvin by the new Calvinists. For example, do new Calvinists largely ignore Calvin's ecclesiology?

For now, it will be sufficient to conclude that the new Calvinists essentially take their definition of Reformed theology from the five-points of TULIP. Crucially important to the task of determining a *sine qua non* is how new Calvinism defines the terms of TULIP, especially total depravity.[30] Chapter 3 will focus on the claim that the movement is distinctly Calvinist and will examine their definitions of common terms.

---

centered, with dozens of books rolling off the presses coming at the gospel from every conceivable angle and applying it to all areas of life, with a commitment to seeing the historic doctrine of justification finding its fruit in sanctification both personally and communally. Cf. Challies, Tim. "John Piper: 12 Features of the New Calvinism." Challies.com- Informing the Reformed. http://www.challies.com/quotes/john-piper-12-features-of-the-new-calvinism (Accessed March 18, 2014). In many ways, these twelve reflect Driscoll's earlier work. The merits of these individual features are discussed through this work.

[29] Are they Calvinists in any sense of the word and if so, in what sense?
[30] Total depravity is the core issue at stake in just about any discussion of soteriology. When one defines total depravity, the definitions of unconditional election, limited atonement, irresistible grace and perseverance of the saints follow. This is because of the great dependence of these other terms have on the theological concept of depravity. Essentially: define depravity the other doctrines will follow.

This will be the first section that deals with a major theological issue present within the ranks of new Calvinism. One of the doctrines that characterize this movement is lordship salvation.[31] For example, one new Calvinist states, "salvation bestowed by the grace of God when a sinner turns from sin...[is a] black and white and non-negotiable" part of Christian orthodoxy.[32] While this is an important doctrine to discuss, others have ably handled it. What is pertinent to this dissertation is an extreme form of lordship salvation known as future grace or future justification. This is a doctrine, espoused by a few new Calvinists, which asserts that a believer is not presently justified by faith, but will one day be justified following the confirmation of their faith evidenced by works. This is not qualitatively different than what Cocceius asserted concerning "the work of God in making provision for the redemption of sinners dependent on the uncertain obedience of man."[33] This reflects the fact that the reformers were not always ready to break with Rome on all matters and doctrinal vestiges of Roman theology have remained.

Missionally Flooding Into Cities

At the outset of this section, one may be confused as to how the new Calvinist's desire to go missionally into cities has anything to do with the gospel. For starters, new Calvinism's gospel is misunderstood to involve social action or cultural redemption. One prominent new Calvinist has even produced a major theological work on politics. An outgrowth of this thinking is to focus on cities as their

---

[31] Cf. Zane Hodges, *Absolutely Free.* Charles Bing, *Simply by Grace.*
[32] Mark Driscoll, *A Call to Resurgence: Will Christianity Have a Funeral or a Future?* (Carol Stream, IL: Tyndale House Publishers, 2013), 96.
[33] Louis Berkhof, *Systematic Theology,* 268.

primary mission field. For them, this is the gospel. Chapter 4 will discuss the movement missionally floods into cities for the purpose of cultural redemption. The word choice of missionally flooding into cities is very specific. They focus their attention very purposefully on cities. This thinking is reminiscent of the Dutch reformed tradition. Cities are now the focus of their efforts. A city is a modern-day Samaria: a place where nice Christian people would not be found. Many promote this modern variation of the social gospel.

The missional aspect of reaching the lost involves contextualizing the gospel. The possible excesses of contextualization have been a point of contention with some evangelical leaders. One should ask: is the contextualization of the gospel taken to unbiblical extremes? How does this affect their view of the sovereignty of God? One may conclude that what is needed to reach the lost in a major city is a properly contextualized gospel, but is this qualitatively different than an understandable gospel?

Continuationism

Continuationism should be an ancillary issue for the new Calvinist movement, but new Calvinism has claimed that openness to the contemporary use of sign gifts is an essential part of its theology. At first it may appear that the new Calvinism's continuationist beliefs are an ancillary issue, especially in regards to their soteriology. This is certainly true to an extent. This is one reason for the placement and length of this section of the dissertation, but the doctrine of continuationism does still bear some importance in understanding the movement of new Calvinism and its theology. The reason for new Calvinism's openness or affinity for the contemporary use of the sign gifts is because their theology is greatly influenced by the charismatic tradition. Although differing from the Roman understanding of justification, which requires other elements to be present for justification (i.e. the sacraments), charismatic theology usually asserts; the Spirit empowers true believers with certain gifts. These gifts include prophecy, healing, and tongues. This is similar in many respects to lordship salvation except the condition for salvation is changed from the necessity of submission to the lordship of Christ to the presence of certain sign gifts. On this point, it is ironic that new Calvinists identify themselves as Calvinists because there is definitive disagreement with Calvin.

Overall, their stance on continuationism betrays a doctrinal shallowness. The aforementioned *sine qua non* identifies as its core a belief in openness to the contemporary use of the sign gifts while not making continuationism a doctrinal qualifier. Put another way, to be a new Calvinist one need not be a continuationist but he or she cannot rigidly be a cessationist. This is an ecumenical theology that betrays its Calvinist heritage. Its ecumenism produces shallowness on doctrinal matters that will be witnessed in the theology of many new Calvinists, especially among many young or lay new Calvinists. Overall, this is seen as the outworking of the ecumenical spirit of new Calvinism. Chapter 5 will discuss these matters.

CONCLUSION

New Calvinists claim to follow the doctrines of grace. Despite this, their errors could be overcome by following a biblical understanding of the gospel of grace. This would eliminate additions to the biblical gospel as well as correct their understanding of the grace of God. The biblical concept of grace eliminates any contingency upon works. Focusing on the true nature of man, the aim of the doctrine of total depravity understands that there is no hope to be found in the will of man. Man desires neither to be saved nor to submit to the lordship of Christ. Even regenerate man is incapable of producing sufficient evidence to confirm his salvation. Nor is mankind commanded to transform society because the unregenerate man's will is in bondage. God saves man for His own glory.

CHAPTER 2

HOW DID NEW CALVINISM DEVELOP?

New Calvinists see themselves in a long line of other Calvinists.[34] While it is not possible here to discuss the origins and development of new Calvinism exhaustively,[35] it is necessary to see some of the theological influences that have come to shape their theology. It is also not possible to discuss their theology exhaustively. Much of their theology is genuine Christian orthodoxy that, for the sake of brevity, does not need not to be discussed. Instead, the focus here will lie with the issues of utmost importance. One example of this is the Reformation doctrine of justification by faith and its relationship to sanctification.

---

[34] As discussed elsewhere it is very difficult to define Calvinism. Like many other –ism, eventually it strays from its original meaning and becomes so vague it becomes difficult to actually define. What then makes one a Calvinist? Is the Westminster Confession? The Canons of Dordt? Predestination? TULIP? Covenantal theology? Et cetera.

[35] Paul M. Dohse Sr. has self-published one of the only works attempting to comprehensively deal with the new Calvinism movement. He traces the origins of new Calvinism to the Australian Forum. The veracity of this claim is not definitive but some theological connections appear to have some merit. (*The Truth About new Calvinism).*See Appendix 4. In addition, Mark Dever ably traces major influence for new Calvinism on The Gospel Coalition's website. See http://thegospelcoalition.org/blogs/justintaylor/2012/08/27/whered-all-these-new-Calvinists-come-from-a-serious-top-10-list-from-mark-dever/

In looking to history, the new Calvinists read the works of Calvin, Edwards, Owen and even Augustine with a renewed interest. Among young people today, whether pastors, theologians or laity, there is an earnest desire to see themselves in a way that transcends the present. It is great men like these whom the young, restless and reformed see as their theological forefathers and who have gifted the church with a godly heritage to follow. Determining the exact time to begin is not an easy task. The new Calvinists trace their theology directly to the apostolic church. What they have failed to understand is that the true genius of the reformers is not a return to apostolic doctrines but to the text of Scripture itself in its original languages. This paper therefore seeks to view their theology in light of Scripture.

The new Calvinists also esteem Augustine and connect their theology directly to him. One new Calvinist describes Augustine in the follow way:

> more than sixteen hundred years since his conversion, Augustine towers over Western history as arguably the most important person outside of Scripture. Augustine's teachings—that God is Trinitarian and holy, that people are evil by the choice of their own free will and born with a sin nature, and that people can only be saved by grace from God that is granted because he predestinated them—are the hallmarks of orthodoxy; what is often called Calvinistic Christian belief is really in many ways Augustinian belief, which is also simply biblical belief. A millennium later, the entire Protestant Reformation exploded in part because of Augustine's lasting influence on men such as John Calvin and Martin Luther, and today we are still benefiting from his teaching.[36]

---

[36] Mark Driscoll, "Augustine on Theology," The Resurgence, http://theresurgence.com/2009/03/17/augustine-on-theology, (Accessed

Like the term Calvinism, Augustinian is vague and imprecise. While Augustine may have been orthodox in many parts, not all aspects of his theology are equally valid. One theologian said:

> a warning needs to be sounded that not everything in Augustine's philosophy or theology can be accepted as biblical. He was a child of his age and some of his views led the church into serious errors. His Neo-Platonism affected his anthropology. His amillennialism and allegorical interpretations were adopted by the medieval church. Premillennialism and dispensationalism have had to fight his influence. He also contributed to the developing power of the Roman Church which led to the medieval papacy.[37]

No one would ascribe to the whole of Augustinian theology. After all, much of what he believed laid the foundation of medieval Roman Catholic theology (i.e. apostolic succession, perpetual virginity of Mary, et cetera.). Why then claim to follow in the line of Augustine? Augustinianism is synonymous with predestinarianism. It is due to the shared interested in predestination that new Calvinists claim to follow Augustine. Therefore, it may be best to look at the time of Reformation to draw more important connection to the true origin of new Calvinist theology.

REFORMATION THEOLOGY

The Lutheran Doctrine of Justification

November 19, 2013).
[37] Edwin A. Blum, "Augustine: The Bishop and Theologian," *Bibliotheca Sacra* 138, no. 549 (1981).

Martin Luther

     Luther, more than any other person, is connected with the renewing of biblical doctrines during the Reformation. This is especially true concerning the doctrine of justification by faith alone. In his own life, Luther saw the shortcoming of attempting to be justified by works in addition to faith. In terms of holiness, the monkish Luther saw himself as unrighteous. By understanding his own lack of holiness, he was able to see that justification must be by faith alone. While justification by faith alone became the rallying cry of the Reformation, Luther's complete understanding of justification is rarely discussed.[38]

     Luther did see an inevitable amount of growth arising from conversion. He stated, "righteousness (justification) precedes works and good works grow out of it."[39] Some have taken this to mean that only those who have an ever-increasing practical righteousness are truly saved. This is not necessarily what Luther taught. While he may have asserted that faith works, he did not go as far as saying that works prove regeneration. He simply recognizes that regeneration produces growth. He observes, "God frequently permits a man to fall into or remain in grievous sin, in order that he may be put to shame in his own eyes and in the eyes of all men."[40] A Christian then can sin grievously and remain in it according to Luther. He also recognizes that justification comes by faith alone and any discussion of works can only come after justification. He states, "a true Christian says: I am justified and saved only by faith in Christ, without any works or merits of my own."[41] Therefore, justification

---

[38] In addition to this, one of the greatest effects of the Reformation was to set aside the Vulgate and return to the original languages of Scripture. This is one aspect of the Reformation doctrine of Sola Scriptura.

[39] Martin Luther, *Commentary on Romans*, trans. J. Theodore Mueller, (Grand Rapids, MI: Kregel Publications, 1954), 41.

[40] Martin Luther, *A Treatise on Good Works*, 33.

precedes experiential sanctification. This is the gospel message. As he succinctly puts it, "little children are saved only by faith without any good works; therefore faith alone justifies."[42] Why have so many who call themselves descendants of the Reformation insisted on putting works in a necessary relation to faith for justification to occur? Modern followers of Luther say:

> good works follow such faith, renewal, and forgiveness. Whatever is still sinful or imperfect in these works will not be reckoned as sin or defect for the sake of the same Christ.[43]

This is an ambiguous definition of faith. It can create confusion by placing an asterisk on faith: "to this we must add that if good works do not follow, our faith is false and not true."[44] This is not the doctrine of justification taught by Luther. If it was, he would not have struggled so mightily with the book of James and called it an epistle of straw. He states, "we always have most certain and sure arguments that necessarily conclude that justification cometh by faith alone."[45] If one follows in this attachment of works with faith, they betray the theology of Luther who said:

> whereby they would bring us into bondage, and force us to say that we are justified, not by faith alone, but by faith formed and adorned with charity. But we set against them the book of the Acts. Let them read this book, and consider the examples contained in it, and they shall find this to be the sum and the argument

---

[41] Martin Luther, *Tabletalk,* trans. by William Hazlitt, (Ross-shire, Great Britain: Christian Focus Publications, 2003), 235.
[42] Martin Luther, *Tabletalk,* 234.
[43] *The Book of Concord the Confessions of the Evangelical Lutheran Church,* ed. Theodore G. Tappert, 315.
[44] Ibid.
[45] Martin Luther, *Commentary on Galatians.*

thereof: that we are justified by faith only in Christ without works, and that the Holy Ghost is given only by the hearing of faith at the preaching of the Gospel.[46]

When one says that faith must be of a certain type, Luther explains he is putting the believer under bondage. It is bondage because they must keep the whole Law and keep it perfectly. Luther does say that good works confirm our calling.[47] This is likely an unguarded statement that is inconsistent with his overall theology of justification. Luther usually ensured that justification by necessity precedes any confirmation or evidences.

Luther also states, "there is not one in a thousand who does not set his confidence upon the works, expecting by them to win God's favor and anticipate His grace."[48] There is no sense in which believers are to live in anticipation of future justification (see further discussion below). Justification has either already happened or not. Neither are works a necessary confirmation of faith. The roots of new Calvinism are not to be found in Luther's theology.

Augsburg Confession

The Augsburg Confession is a product of the Lutheran side of the Reformation. It is of such importance for Lutheran theology that it is contained in entirety in the *Book of Concord.* The Augsburg Confession therefore should be seen as the heart of Lutheran theology, which is why it is discussed here. In addition to this, it is a product of the Reformation period, so it is an accurate representation of overall Lutheran theology of the Reformation. Only one article of the Augsburg Confession describes the Lutheran

---

[46] Martin Luther, *Commentary on Galatians*, 3:2.
[47] Ibid.
[48] Martin Luther, *A Treatise on Good Works,* Kindle Edition. Loc. 344-345.

understanding of the doctrine of justification (Article IV). It lists only one condition of justification, namely faith, that God will in turn regard and reckon as righteousness. Importantly, it is recognized that Paul teaches in Romans 4:5 that it is the ungodly whom God justifies. Justification must occur either before or simultaneously to regeneration. In speaking of the relationship between faith and obedience, the Augsburg Confession simply asserts, "faith should produce good fruits and that we must do all such good works as God has commanded."[49] The Lutheran understanding, therefore, sees the righteous as possibly producing fruit without lessening the obligation for the believer to produce good works.

This teaching is detailed further in its section (XX) entitled "Faith and Good Works." It is notable that this is the longest of the articles of the Augsburg Confession. It sounds surprisingly free grace in its soteriology. It completely distinguishes itself from Roman theology and divorces works from salvation except in saying that works are to be done as expressed in the phrase "that we may do God's will and glorify Him." Additionally, it is repeatedly affirmed that works are not forbidden in the Lutheran theology. Perhaps the most important statement in this section is that, "the conscience cannot come to rest and peace through works, but only through faith, that is, when it is assured and knows that for Christ's sake it has a gracious God." Works cannot give grounds for salvation nor can they truly provide assurance of salvation. It is only through faith in what Christ has done that peace can be obtained in this life. This is an affirmation that Luther's theology and Lutheran theology are the not the origin of new Calvinism.

The Reformed Doctrine of Justification

---

[49] Augsburg Confession, Article VI.

John Calvin

Since nearly all lordship proponents identify themselves as Calvinists, it should be evident in the writings of John Calvin that truly saving faith needs to be accompanied by acts of evangelical obedience, otherwise it is not of the type that God gifts to man. It is said that God imparts only faith of a certain type. This asks the age-old question of how Calvinistic was Calvin. This issue has been discussed ad nauseam elsewhere and is not going to be delved into here.[50] Instead, a general survey and examination will be made concerning Calvin's view of justification. It will be concluded that while Calvin may have had a proper understanding of anthropology, this did not correspond completely and consistently with his understanding of justification. As Enns observes, Calvin taught a type of "double justification."[51] He did champion justification by faith alone through God's grace alone, but his theology was not limited to this.

The biblical understanding of justification is seen in Calvin's rebuke of the sophist's theology. In responding to them, he states "according to them, man is justified by faith as well as by works, provided these are not his own works, but gifts of Christ and fruits of regeneration."[52] He defines those in error as ascribing justification to being based upon anything other than the work of Christ.

In addition to this, the seed of covenantal theology is evident in Calvin's theology. The basis of the covenant of works is seen in his describing:

---

[50] Cf. R.T. Kendall, *Calvin and English Calvinism to 1649*; Paul Helm, *Calvin and Calvinism*; and Richard A. Muller, *Calvin and the Reformed Tradition*.
[51] Paul P. Enns, *The Moody Handbook of Theology* (Chicago, IL: Moody Press, 1989), 451-52.
[52] Ibid, Book 3, XI:14.

a man will be said to be *justified by works*, if in his life there can be found a purity and holiness which merits an attestation of righteousness at the throne of God, or if by the perfection of his works he can answer and satisfy the divine justice. On the contrary, a man will be *justified by faith* when, excluded from the righteousness of works, he by faith lays hold of the righteousness of Christ, and clothed in it appears in the sight of God not as a sinner, but as righteous.[53]

Does Calvin ever assert that works are not a necessary condition of justification? To answer this is to put too much emphasis on modern terminology for someone who is far removed from the contemporary discussion. Many claim that the answer is clear-cut, but Calvin says:

does [Paul] not plainly enough attribute everything to faith alone when he disconnects it with works? What I would ask, is meant by the expressions, 'The righteousness of God without the law is manifested;' 'Being justified freely by his grace;' 'Justified by faith without the deeds of the law?' (Rom. 3:21, 24, 28).[54]

Here he specifically disconnects works from any discussion of justification. Calvin did distinguish between justifying faith and evangelical obedience; "even in his variant presentations of the relation of faith to repentance and regeneration this distinction is carefully maintained."[55] Bromiley concludes:

primarily, justification is acceptance before God through the imputation of righteousness. This comes

---

[53] John Calvin, *Institutes of the Christian Religion,* Book 3, XII:1.
[54] Ibid, Book 3, XI:19.
[55] Samuel E. Waldron, "John Calvin Versus Norman Shepherd on Sola Fide," *Reformed Baptist Theological Review* 02:2 (Jul 2005): 103.

by faith alone. Secondarily and in consequence, however, justification is the declaration or manifestation before men of the righteousness of faith. This is justification by works[56]

The debate has arisen that Calvin has confused the timing of justification. This is the double justification alluded to by Enns. He readily sees justification as an accomplished fact for the believer. In tying justification to the yet future Bema Seat, he places the actuality of justification at a future point. This provides the groundwork for new Calvinist soteriology. It may simply be an inconsistency in Calvin's thinking. While he says, "a man is said to be justified in the sight of God when in the judgment of God he is deemed righteous, and is accepted,"[57] he goes on to explain:

> "nothing can be accepted that is not in every respect entire and absolute, and tainted by no impurity; such indeed as never has been, and never will be, found in man. It is easy for any man, within the precincts of the schools, to talk of the sufficiency of works for justification; but when we come into the presence of God there must be a truce to such talk."[58]

And again:

> Christian humility consists in laying aside the imaginary idea of our own righteousness, and trusting entirely to the mercy of God, apprehended by faith in Christ.[59]

---

[56] Geofferey W. Bromiley, *Historical Theology* (236), qtd. in Paul P. Enns, *The Moody Handbook of Theology*, 452.
[57] Ibid, Book 3, XI:2.
[58] Ibid, Book 3, XII:1.
[59] Ibid, Book 3, XII:6

When a person stands before God, he is never able to produce sufficient evidence for his own justification. If this were so, then his obedience will need to be absolute. What the Christian has instead is the righteousness of Christ that will enable them to be in God's presence. It is only when man gives up on his own efforts that he remains true to the Reformation understanding of justification by faith alone. It is when he gives up on his own efforts and sees the limits of his attempts at righteousness that he relies on Christ alone and trusts in His provision for salvation. This remains true to Calvin's theology.

Those following in the footsteps of Calvin have taken his language of confirmation too far. It is doubtful that Calvin truly means that the believers are meant to produce evidences before God. As he observed:

> [Paul] calls that glorying when we pretend to have anything of our own to which a reward is supposed to be due at God's tribunal. Since he takes this away from Abraham, who of us can claim for himself the least particle of merit?[60]

Instead of confirming it in the sense that he must produce evidences of regeneration in order to be saved, his acts of evangelical obedience do bear witness to regeneration. In this, he has some limited use in assurance. It is not that man can look at himself and know that he is saved because he is not like those awful sinners. Instead, when looking back at his life, man can have assurance based upon an examination of his Christian life in comparison to his previous experience when unregenerate. Works should not be related to justification as a condition of it. Works certainly should not be thought of as bearing any kind of positive judgment before the Bema Seat of Christ. If this were the case, no one

---

[60] John Calvin, *Romans*, electronic ed., Calvin's Commentaries, Ro 4:2.

would have sufficient evidences. This misunderstanding stems from Calvin's view of the Bema Seat. Calvin sees the Bema Seat as a place where believers and unbelievers are separated. He states "he…is justified who is regarded not as a sinner, but as righteous, and as such stands acquitted at the judgment-seat of God, where all sinners are condemned."[61] This is not the function of the Bema Seat. Although Calvin may have missed the mark in describing this aspect of justification, it is clear from his teaching on depravity that he understood justification to be necessarily based upon the grace of God alone. He did not truly view justification as unfolding in the same manner some New Calvinists do.

The Westminster Confession

The Westminster Confession is the standard by which many reformed churches measure themselves. Vance explains "the literary products of the [Westminster] Assembly, however, have continually been used by Calvinists since their inception."[62] This confession also formed part of the basis for the rift between covenantal and dispensational theology with the former accusing the latter of departing from this standard.[63] Some have jokingly stated that dispensationalists view the Scofield Bible as inspired both above and below the line due to the importance many dispensationalists place on Scofield's theology. The same could be said of the Westminster Confession in covenantal circles treat it almost as authoritative as Scripture itself.

Fortunately for the discussion here, the Westminster Confession treats the subjects of soteriology, justification and works at some length. It states,

---

[61] John Calvin, *Institutes of the Christian Religion,* Book 3, XI:2.
[62] Laurence M. Vance, *The Other Side of Calvinism,* Revised Edition (Pensacola, FL: Vance Publications, 1999), 175.
[63] Cf. R. Todd Magnum, *The Dispensational-Covenantal Rift.*

> As God hath appointed the elect unto glory, so hath He, by the eternal and most free purpose of His will, foreordained all the means thereunto. Wherefore, they who are elected . . . are effectually called unto faith in Christ by His Spirit working in due season, are justified, adopted, sanctified, and kept by His power through faith, unto salvation. Neither are any other redeemed by Christ, effectually called, justified, adopted, sanctified, and saved, but the elect only. The rest of mankind God was pleased, according to the unsearchable counsel of His own will, whereby He extendeth or withholdeth mercy, as He pleaseth, for the glory of His Sovereign power over His creatures, to pass by; and to ordain them to dishonour and wrath for their sin, to the praise of His glorious justice.[64]

One of the important stances that this confession makes is in regard to the vicarious law-keeping of Christ. It is said that justification is accomplished "by imputing the obedience and satisfaction of Christ unto them."[65] It is not enough that Christ has paid the penalty for the sins of man by acting as their substitute; He must also impart His own obedience and righteousness to them. In this, it is said that faith ceased to be a dead faith and becomes a living and active one. Good works are "the fruits and evidences of a true and lively faith."[66] Despite this, this same chapter readily admits that man "cannot endure the severity of God's judgment."[67] How can a believer give evidences that will always come up short and cannot withstand the severity of God's judgment based upon Him as the standard of holiness? It must, therefore, be that the witness borne by the fruits of obedience are for the eyes

---

[64] *The Westminster Confession of Faith* (Oak Harbor, WA: Logos Research Systems, Inc., 1996), Chapter 3, Section 5, Point 6-7).
[65] Westminster Confession, Chapter 11:I.
[66] Ibid, Chapter 16:II.
[67] Ibid, Chapter 16:V.

of man and not the eyes of God. If this is the case, then it is in line with the biblical understanding of the justification spoken of by James. Too many modern-day reformed theologians wish to make justification ultimately dependent upon obedience. Sproul asserts, "if it is a true faith, good works will absolutely, immediately, inevitably, and necessarily ensue from that faith…if works do not follow, there was not true faith."[68] In ecclesiology, this gives license for the church to become fruit inspectors, testing the faith of believers based upon the evidence of their life. As Boice states, "if we do not do good works, we are not justified. We are not Christians."[69] Although Sproul doesn't take this understanding as far as Piper does, this characterizes many Calvinists today. In the end, the inconsistency is seen when Christ's obedience has been imputed to man but man still needs his own obedience as proof. This author is simply calling modern Calvinists back to the true understanding reflected in the Westminster confession that "their justification is only of free grace."[70]

The Canons of Dordt

The Canons of Dordt, more than any other place, is where the foundation of new Calvinist theology has been laid. It is said in the fifth article:

> The cause or guilt of this unbelief as well as of all other sins is no wise in God, but in man himself; whereas faith in Jesus Christ and salvation through Him is the free gift of God[71]

---

[68] R.C. Sproul, *Truths We Confess: A Layman's Guide to the Westminster Confession of Faith*. (Phillipsburg, NJ: P &R Publishing, 2007), 2:173.
[69] James Montgomery Boice, *Whatever Happened to the Gospel of Grace?: Rediscovering the Doctrines That Shook the World.* 119.
[70] Ibid, Chapter 16, III.
[71] *Canons of Dordt,* First Head of Doctrine, Article 5.

In the sixth, it states, "some receive the gift of faith from God, and others do not receive it, proceeds from God's eternal decree."[72] It is no longer faith which is the vehicle for salvation, but the decree of God which issues faith to man. As some new Calvinists will state, God "will(s) that sin exists in the world...[and] ordains that a sinful act will come to pass."[73] This understanding is an important part of new Calvinist theology.

This is supralapsarianism. As Cowan explains more fully:

> Sublapsarianism is the orthodox Calvinist view that states that all people stand under the judgment of God for their sin but that God sovereignly chooses to elect some to salvation and actively works in their hearts to bring them to Christ. Those who are not elected are left to perish for their sin. The basis of God's choice is found in his own 'good pleasure' (Eph 1:9) and not in the merit or demerit of the individual, thus repudiating any possibility of boasting. God is free from any charge of injustice in that the unelected are justly punished for their sin and not because they were simply not elected.
>
> Supralapsarianism, on the other hand, teaches that God positively decrees both faith and unbelief, not only working in the elect to nurture faith but also in the reprobate to purposely bring about sin. The basis for God's choice is still his good

---

[72] Ibid, Article 6.
[73] John Piper, "Is God Less Glorious Because He Ordained that Evil Be?" July 1, 1998 at Jonathan Edwards Institute, http://www.desiringgod.org/resource-library/conference-messages/is-god-less-glorious-because-he-ordained-that-evil-be, (Accessed November 12, 2013).

pleasure, but the unelected are punished because of their nonelection rather than for their sin. A disposition toward sin is placed in the heart of the reprobate so as to give God a "reason" to punish them. In this view God is the author of sin and his election is completely arbitrary. As Sproul rightly argues, this is not the view of John Calvin.

This is unadulterated hyper-Calvinism. Sproul insists that

> to understand the Reformed [Calvinist] view ... we must pay close attention to the crucial distinction between *positive* and *negative* decrees of God. Positive has to do with God's active intervention in the hearts of the elect. Negative has to do with God's passing over the non-elect ... He does not create unbelief in their hearts. That unbelief is already there.
>
> Thus Calvinism formulates election in positive-negative terms, while hyper-Calvinism does so in positive-positive terms. Although both of these views are accurately referred to as 'double predestination,' few non-Calvinists understand the fine distinctions between them and subsequently associate the term with supralapsarianism.[74]

The *Canons of Dordt* state:

---

[74] Steven B. Cowan, "Common Misconceptions of Evangelicals Regarding Calvinism, "*The Journal of the Evangelical Theological Society*, 33/2 (June 1990) 191-192.

faith is therefore to be considered as the gift of God, not on account of its being offered by God to man, to be accepted or rejected at his pleasure, but because it is in reality conferred upon him, breathed and infused into him; nor even because God bestows the power or ability to believe, and then expects that man should by the exercise of his own free will consent to the terms of salvation and actually believe in Christ, but because He who works in man both to will and to work, and indeed all things in all, produces both the will to believe and the act of believing also.[75]

Summary

In summary, in the context of the Reformation, the reformed doctrine of justification had a tendency to wrongly emphasize that while faith alone that justifies, it is not alone in those who are justified. This was due to the nature of the charges brought on the reformers by the Roman church. This does not mean that any of the reformers themselves saw the conversion of a believer being based in their submission to Christ as Lord (master) in addition to Savior. Granted, they may have drawn an improper distinction between faith and works: they did not assert that it was necessary for a believer to justify (to prove or show) their justification (declared righteous) in order to be justified. This is what those who build upon the reformer's theology have done. In building upon the doctrines of the reformers, many new Calvinists have forsaken the reformed doctrine of justification. Not only this, they have departed from the free grace espoused in the Westminster Confession and replaced it with a costly grace. Grace has ceased to be grace. This is a dangerous teaching pervading the next wave of young pastors and theologians.

POST-REFORMATION THEOLOGY

---

[75] *Canons of Dordt,* Third and Fourth Heads of Doctrine, Article 14.

The Puritans

There has been a great resurgence in the study of the Puritans in recent years. Often relegated to the shelves of history, names like Jonathan Edwards, John Owen and others have become part of the theological mainstream once again. This modern phenomenon is assuredly connected to the movement of new Calvinism. It is new Calvinism that has brought about a renewed interest in the American Puritan heritage, but the issue that must be addressed here concerns why this has occurred in new Calvinism? First, much of what has been passed on to the new Calvinism through the Puritans is genuine Christian orthodoxy. Therefore, it would not be beneficial to discuss at length the many points of agreement between Puritans and modern-day new Calvinism. Practically speaking, there is a general attitude shared by the Puritans and new Calvinism. Both groups share zeal and a genuine desire for spiritual growth. The seriousness with which the Puritans approached Christian living truly speaks volumes to this generation, but just because the movement has been correct in calling out the church's lack of focus on sanctification does not mean that the solution to this deficiency lies in combining sanctification with justification. In light of this, it is also beneficial to see where the Puritan's theological shortcomings may be reflected in the theology of the new Calvinism.

Conversion

The doctrine of preparationism has often been the focus of many Puritan studies. This is the concept that there are specific things that must precede conversion. Beeke and Jones, the writers of a massive new work on Puritan theology, do not believe much of what has traditionally been taught about Puritan soteriology. On the other hand, R.T. Kendall's earlier work *Calvin and English Calvinism to 1640* has been highly influential in showing that the Puritans diverged significantly from Calvin's theology. Beeke and Jones highly esteem the Puritans and revolt against the notion that "there is said to be a degeneration from pure Reformed theology in the Puritan movement, a degeneration driven by preparationism."[76] There is disagreement over whether the Puritan concept of preparationism is really true to Puritan theology as a whole, but as Beeke and Jones recognize, "certain Puritans taught aspects of preparation that most other Puritans, indeed most other Christians, rightly reject."[77] The issue does not center on preparation itself per se, but in their understanding of conversion. It is not necessary to get into the specifics of this debate here, but no matter which side one chooses, the Puritan understanding of conversion is highly flawed. Despite this, it remains influential today in new Calvinism.

In Puritan theology, conversion is not seen as a singular event whereby the sinner believes and is saved. Beeke and Jones even recognize "the Puritan belief that conversion is a process."[78] It is not punctiliar and "some Puritans rigorously developed and painfully applied sequences of steps in conversion."[79] This is understood through the Calvinistic lens of predestination whereby God works in the life of the still unregenerate elect to bring them through the process of conversion. They had a definite *ordo salutis* and "the Puritans did not believe in or expect merely 'sudden' conversion."[80] In addition to this, the Puritans are known for understanding that certain preparatory work needed to occur prior to conversion so that conversion could take place. Before conversion, there must be repentance,

---

[76] Joel R. Beeke and Mark Jones, *A Puritan Theology,* (Grand Rapids, MI: Reformation Heritage Books, 2012), 444.
[77] Ibid, 455.
[78] Ibid, 450.
[79] Ibid, 456.
[80] Ibid, 464.

defined as an acknowledgment of sinfulness, and the Puritans believed that one of the major functions of the Law was to convict the sinner. They saw the Law as paving the way to salvation. Somehow this has not caused many red flags to be raised concerning their theology.

The Law

One of the important areas of soteriology where the Puritans struggled to remain biblical is in relation to the Mosaic Law. Like many today, they chose to place the Christian under an obligation to keep the so-called moral law, but not its ceremonial aspects contained within the whole of the Mosaic Law. This does not take into account that the New Testament bears witness to the unity of the Law. While certain moral elements are, in fact, a reflection of God's righteousness, this does not mean that the New Testament saint is under the Law or any portion thereof. This is a common misconception. What is important for the present study of the Puritan's theology is the purpose of the Law. The Law is meant to convict sinners of their unrighteousness by their inability to keep it. Although not seeing the Law as meritorious, "the majority of Puritans spoke freely of obedience to the Law as the way of salvation."[81] This statement comes from someone who unashamedly favors the Puritans. In addition to this, the Puritans saw the convicting aspect of the law practiced through the civil laws of a nation. Their general perspective was that the law convicts sin, it should therefore follow that the enacting of Christian laws helps to convict the unregenerate man of his sin. Kendall accurately observes, "while the law might stir men to seek salvation, for Calvin this 'is but an accidental effect.'"[82] Even Calvin, who

---

[81] Ernest F. Kevan, *The Grace of Law: A Study in Puritan Theology*, (Morgan, PA: Soli Deo Gloria Publications, 1976).
[82] Joel R. Beeke and Mark Jones, *A Puritan Theology*, 452.

established a theocracy in Geneva, did not see the Law functioning in this way. To understand the Law in this way does not properly distinguish between the Mosaic Law and civil laws in general. Civil laws do not necessarily convict sinners of their own unrighteousness. For example, it is sinful to have an abortion but it is legal. In this instance, civil law has the opposite effect, breeding licentiousness. Government has been instituted by God to restrain sin in the world, not to convict the world of sin. This error has led to an undue emphasis on social reform. This remains prominent in many reformed churches, which equate social action with evangelism. This error led in part to the demise of Puritanism. Where did the Puritans go? They were replaced by politics. This still remains a danger today in new Calvinism. All too often today, people equate being Christian with certain political stances.[83]

Union

One of the biggest areas of continuity between modern new Calvinism and the theology of the Puritans involves their understanding of the believer's union with Christ. Union is the key to Puritan soteriology. It may also be the key to the theology of many new Calvinists. Instead of seeing the union of the believer with Christ as a result of the believer's regeneration, they see it as (at least logically) prior to it. The Puritan *ordo salutis* was Union→ Regeneration→ Faith→ Justification. This totally downplays the important role justification plays in salvation and replaces it with union. This doctrine is such a departure from the Reformation that

---

[83] Some of this may be with good reason, but at times this becomes a new twist on Liberation theology or the prosperity gospel applied to nations. For example, if America does X, then God will do Y (usually some form of blessing).

Luther would have hardly recognized it. One consequence of this is that the union, which brings about regeneration, also contains "a righteousness imparted."[84] Beeke and Jones assert, "in the judgment of several significant Puritan theologians, union with Christ, not justification by faith, is the chief blessing a Christian receives from God."[85] Union is the key to the theology of some new Calvinists as well and justification either becomes a vehicle for this union or, more properly, a consequence of it. Owens confirms the latter. He is said to claim, by his admirers, "union with Christ is the cause of all other graces a believer receives."[86] Accordingly, Acts 16:31 must be altered to say, "be united with the Lord and you will be saved." Also, the conclusion is forced in their *ordo salutis* that the unregenerate man is capable of being united with Christ. This all but abandons the doctrine of total depravity. Additionally, the Puritans took the concept of election to its extreme of supralapsarianism, which sees the decrees of God as so pivotal. The union of the believer with Christ has been decided by God's dual decrees of election and reprobation. Owen and Ames even go to the length of saying that God hates the reprobate.[87]

Holiness

The Puritans, perhaps more than anything else, are remembered for their earnest striving for holiness. Charnock especially saw regeneration as not just new life, but a holy life, confusing the capacity for holiness with the actuality of holiness. He said that regeneration involves the whole of man and "produce(s) moral reformation."[88] This underestimates the sinfulness of sin. While there is a new capacity within the

---

[84] Ernest F. Kevan, *The Grace of Law: A Study in Puritan Theology,* 218.
[85] Joel R. Beeke and Mark Jones, *A Puritan Theology,* 483.
[86] Ibid, 485.
[87] John Owen, "The Death that Christ Died," 115; and William Ames, "The Marrow of Theology 156.
[88] Stephen Charnock qtd. in *A Puritan Theology,* 468.

regenerate man whereby he can willingly choose to serve God in his actions, he does not truly live a holy life. Although the believer is commanded to be perfect, by any measure, a believer's sin will exceed his holiness. One can say that there is more sin than righteousness even in the saint's best prayer. Puritan John Preston believed that "Christ will take away not only the guilt but also the power of sin in those to whom He is united."[89] This is close to the truth. Regeneration takes away the enslavement to sin but does not completely remove sin's power. Instead sin's power is broken; its power is no longer absolute. This is why Paul says that he does the very things that he desires not to do in Romans 7.

The Puritans desired a pure church in much the same manner as the new Calvinists. Unfortunately, the former have been known by posterity to have "often spent time pointing out false signs of regeneration"[90] It is only the "holy" who are regenerate. In defending this idea Owens said:

> for there is faith whereby we are justified, which he who has shall be assuredly saved; which purifies the heart and works by love. And there is a faith or believing, which does none of this.[91]

Owens here describes two types of faith. This is something carried forward in many different forms of lordship theology. In abandoning the principles of the Reformation, the Puritans were in some ways a theological return to Romanism. Justification is being made righteous and not simply being declared righteous. Kevan observes, "their general view was that, if it be true that the Gospel is rightly preached without

---

[89] Ibid, 486.
[90] Ibid, 479.
[91] John Owen, *Justification,* in Works, 5:71 qtd in Joel R. Beeke and Mark Jones, *A Puritan Theology,* 493.

any conditions, then neither Jesus nor the apostles ever preached the Gospel."[92] Charnock's straight lines analogy is perhaps the best way to see the folly of this thinking. He describes the regenerate man as a short straight line while God is an infinitely straight line. The difference in holiness is a matter of degree. This author would assert that even at man's most righteous point, his line is crooked in comparison to God's. This is not meant to undermine the work of the Spirit in the life of a believer. A believer can look back at his former way of life and say, "praise God for the change He has brought about in me." When this same man looks at the holiness in his life from God's perspective, he will never be able to say that his line is a small straight line.

Jonathan Edwards

Perhaps more than any other, except Calvin, new Calvinism identifies itself with the theology of Jonathan Edwards.[93] Edwards is arguably the greatest English-speaking Calvinistic theologian, and he is likely admired partly because other modern theologians have been found wanting. Despite this, Edwards fought against the cold orthodoxy of the Old Calvinists of his day, paralleling the present-day agenda of new Calvinism. It has been said:

> Edwards's complaint was that Old Calvinism had gone stale...(his) sympathies lay in the direction of the new Pietism, whose best known English-speaking apostles were John Wesley and George Whitfield.[94]

---

[92] Ernest F. Kevan, *The Grace of Law: A Study in Puritan Theology,* 89.
[93] Jeremy Walker makes an interesting assertion in this regard (cf. Jeremy Edwards, *New Calvinism Considered: A Personal and Pastoral Assessment.* Darlington, England: EP Books, 2013.). He claims that the new Calvinists, especially Piper, read Edwards in light of their own theology rather than truly allow Edwards to speak for himself. An evaluation of the merits of this thesis is beyond the scope of this work.
[94] Douglas A. Sweeney and Allen C. Guelzo ed., *The New England*

Wesley and Edwards are unlikely bedfellows to modern theologians because their current followers are perpetually at odds with one another, but Edwards and Wesley were probably allies because of their support for the Great Awakening and their shared passion for a holy church. Theologically, they both answered that unholy people were not a part of the true church. They simply differed over whether these backsliding persons were originally saved. Edwards specifically was "allied to the assumption that the church must be reserved solely for the pure...[not] 'half-way commitments.'"[95] In pastoral ministry, this led him to support closed communion as well as lean towards including only revived persons into church membership. Edwards, Wesley, and new Calvinism all have a desire for experimental piety determine their theology and in so doing stray from the biblical concept of grace.

Overall, much of Edwards' theology is influenced by philosophical determinism. By this, it is meant that he sees events as occurring by necessity and thereby being able to determine the presence of a cause by viewing its results. Edwards also differentiated his understanding of the sovereignty of God by looking at the will of man. He saw man's will as having the natural ability to repent but not the moral ability. Conversion then becomes a surrendering of the will to the Lord. There are several notable areas where Edwards' soteriology can be seen to influence the new Calvinists. It has been said:

> to an unusual degree, Edwards brought together penetrating insight into religious experience, sophistication in the use of current philosophy, and firm commitment to Calvinistic convictions.... The

---

Theology: From Jonathan Edwards to Edwards Amasa Park, (Grand Rapids, MI: Baker Academic, 2006), 14.
[95] Ibid, 70

major emphases of Edwards' theology were the greatness of God, total dependence upon God for salvation, and the intrinsic value of the holy life.[96]

Salvation is wholly dependent on God and man has no part. It is now necessary to examine the specifics of Edwards' soteriology in greater detail.

Justification as Union

One of the most subtle and gravest of the errors that have gone mostly unnoticed in new Calvinism is its misunderstanding of a believer's union with Christ. The believer does have a union with Christ, but Paul never states that believers are united with Christ in his life. He states "for if we have become united with Him in the likeness of His death, certainly we shall also be in the likeness of His resurrection."[97] Here the believer is said to be united with Christ in His death, and this gives us assurance that the believer will be raised up with Him in the life hereafter. The reformers understood the believer's union with Christ as being an essential part of the act of substitution, but Edwards saw the union of Christ as being identified with Christ in His death as well as His life. This is an error that foresees experiential righteousness resulting from the union with Christ in His life. For Calvin there is a communion with Christ whereby fellowship can be broken, but the relationship does not change.[98] It is more accurate to say that a believer is identified with Jesus in His death alone.[99] This is how the sacrifice works. It is never the righteousness, signified by the unblemished perfection of the animal that is

---

[96] Sinclair B. Ferguson and J.I. Packer, *New Dictionary of Theology*, electronic ed. (Downers Grove, IL: InterVarsity Press, 2000), 458.
[97] Romans 6:5, NASB
[98] John Calvin, *Institutes of the Christian Religion,* Book 4, XV: 12.
[99] A believer is said to be "in Christ," a part of the body, but at conversion it is only Christ's death which is a propitiation.

infused into the one offering the sacrifice. This is not how Christ's sacrifice should be seen. There is a union between the believer and Christ in His death and resurrection. There remains a union after conversion. This union though is not with His life, but the identification through adoption. After conversion believers are related to Him as His children. Believers are not experientially righteous because He was experientially righteous. Instead, God sees His righteousness judicially in the believer's place on account of His sacrifice vicariously. It is through union with Him in Christ's sacrifice that the believer has had his sins paid. Calvin states:

> we must specially remember this substitution in order that we may not be all our lives in trepidation and anxiety, as if the just vengeance which the Son of God transferred to himself, were still impending over us.[100]

Unfortunately, he does not hold to this consistently and says in his commentary that the believer is united with Christ in "a secret union, by which we are joined to him; so that he, reviving us by His Spirit, transfers his own virtue to us."[101] He also explains:

> both of these we obtain by union with Christ. For if we have true fellowship in his death, our old man is crucified by his power, and the body of sin becomes dead, so that the corruption of our original nature is never again in full vigor (Rom. 6:5, 6). If we are partakers in his resurrection, we are raised up by means of it to newness of life, which conforms us to the righteousness of God.[102]

---

[100] John Calvin, *Institutes of the Christian Religion*, Book 2, XVI:5.
[101] John Calvin, *Romans*, electronic ed., Calvin's Commentaries, Ro 6:5.
[102] John Calvin, *Institutes of the Christian Religion*, Book 3, III:9.

For Calvin (here) and Edwards, it is the union with Christ that results in conformity to Christ that makes the believer holy in deed. One could almost say that what Edwards asserts is "the person who is holy in deed is holy indeed." This is the unfortunate doctrine of vicarious law-keeping that many reformed theologians have chosen to follow, and one which Edwards expands upon in his soteriology. Gerstner says:

> in line with Calvin and Puritanism (Edwards) saw union with Christ as the ground of justification. And going beyond his own tradition as he develops 'fitness,' or natural congruity, as the corollary of union with Christ, sharply contrasting it with any 'moral fitness' in faith or obedience. More sharply than any he saw the sense in which justification by faith alone rested ultimately on justification by works- the works of Christ.[103]

This may seem like an insignificant ivory tower discussion, but it is one that has important consequences for practical Christian living. Edwards will make the point that if one is truly united with Christ he or she will have practical holiness as a byproduct or as a result of this union. The outworking of this is seen in Sproul's commenting:

> Christ's mission of redemption was not limited to the cross. To save us he had to live a life of perfect righteousness. His perfect, active obedience was necessary for his and our salvation. He earned the merit of perfect righteousness, not only for his own humanity, but for all those whom he redeems. Christ perfectly fulfilled all demands of the law, meriting by

---

[103] John H. Gerstner, *Jonathan Edwards: A mini-theology,* (Wheaton, IL: Tyndale House Publishers, 1983), 83.

his active obedience the blessing promised in the old covenant.[104]

Sweeney explains that for Edwards "justification is always connected with holiness in the person justified."[105] He was after all a Puritan. This view is based in part on a misunderstanding of Paul's statement, "He made Him who knew no sin to be sin on our behalf, so that we might become the righteousness of God in Him."[106] This righteousness is seen as experiential and not just positional. The union is one of nature and is more than judicial. It is said, in reference to Edwards, "what is real in union between Christ and his people, is the foundation of what is legal."[107] It is also said:

> for Edwards, the question is not, 'how can I become righteous and therefore justified?' but is instead, 'how can I become united to Christ, where righteousness and justification reside?'[108]

The believer is not truly justified by faith but through his or her union with Christ. This union is not being united with Him through his substitution atonement but through personal identification with Christ. It is not surprising then that some of Edwards' followers abandoned the substitution atonement in favor of the governmental theory and people like MacArthur see faith as submission to (i.e. union with) Christ. For Edwards, faith is defined as a union. He even says that salvation is accomplished through "the very act of faith and

---

[104] R.C. Sproul, *Faith Alone: The Evangelical Doctrine of Justification*, electronic ed. (Grand Rapids: Baker Books, 2000), 104.
[105] Douglas A. Sweeney et al, *Jonathan Edwards and Justification*, Kindle Edition, edited by Josh Moody (Wheaton, IL: Crossway Books, 2012), loc 1505.
[106] 2 Corinthians 5:21, NASB.
[107] Douglas A. Sweeney, et al, *Jonathan Edwards and Justification,* loc 301.
[108] Ibid, loc 911.

union."[109] It is claimed by admirers of Edwards that what he taught was "the reason God accepts people who believe is because they are united with Christ. This is not merely legal but real, for the basis of their acceptance (or the foundation) is Christ."[110] What he desires is to see justification as not being a judicial act declaring the one with faith to be positionally righteous, which is the true Reformation doctrine, but is a relational, practical righteousness inevitably resulting in holiness. When one truly examines his holiness in comparison to his sinfulness, man will see that, by any measure, his righteousness is nothing but filthy rags (cf. Isaiah 64:6).

Many since the Reformation have carried the banner of justification as a both active and passive union with Christ.[111] This is a surprisingly diverse group and includes reformed theologians like Michael Horton and John Piper, and also Charles Finney (cf. *Principles of Union With Christ*) as well as the neo-orthodox (esp. Schleiermacher). One theologian has recently stated:

> hav(ing) posited that in Calvin's soteriology – as elucidated in book III of the Institutes–the justification and sanctification of the Christian follow from her union with Christ. And if this interpretation is correct, then Schleiermacher's theology, far from betraying the heritage of the Reformers, both logically and structurally locates the doctrine of justification in exactly the same place as Calvin[112]

It appears that reformed theology and neo-orthodoxy share essential soteriological elements. This same writer asserts:

---

[109] Ibid, loc 1006.
[110] Ibid, loc 333.
[111] This is the more commonly used terminology in reformed theology.
[112] Paul T. Nimmo, "Schleiermacher on Justification: A Departure From the Reformation?" *Scottish Journal of Theology* 66. 1 (Feb 2013): 71.

far from abandoning the soteriological concepts of the Reformation, it seems more likely that Schleiermacher was seeking to translate their meaning and significance into a more contemporary idiom for his own generation.[113]

This is the same thing that new Calvinism wishes to accomplish. Few reading this would argue that Schleiermacher's view represents either the Reformation or orthodox Christianity. One should be suspicious when the theology of Calvin, Edwards, Finney and Schleiermacher all share union with Christ as the central element of their soteriology.

In a world and a church characterized by moral decay, Edwards chose to emphasize the results of justification as an inevitable result of the believer's union with Christ. If one is truly united with Christ, then he will live like Christ. This is not how depravity truly works. Edwards, in his relentless fight against sin, did not see the true joy of *Sola Gratia* and grace as rule of life. Paul says, "you are not under law but under grace."[114] In his opposition to sin, Edwards attempted to place believers under the law, making their final justification contingent upon their obedience to the moral law. It is said that Edwards "even went so far as to say that only holy people are saved, that final justification is granted only to those who persevere in the faith and love that they profess."[115] Edwards is quoted as saying directly "perseverance in holiness is absolutely necessary to salvation."[116] What an unfortunate perversion of the gospel of grace and one that is directly reflected in new

---

[113] Ibid, 72.
[114] Romans 6, 14ff, NASB.
[115] Douglas A. Sweeney et al, *Jonathan Edwards and Justification,* loc 2779.
[116] Jonathan Edwards qtd. In Ibid, loc 2840.

Calvinism. This is not something new to Edwards, but is an ancient misunderstanding of the doctrine of rewards. Tertullian said:

> For all, the righteous and the unrighteous alike, shall be brought before God the Word. For the Father hath committed all judgment to Him; and in fulfillment of the Father's counsel, He cometh as Judge whom we call Christ. For it is not Minos and Rhadamanthys that are to judge (the world), as ye fancy, O Greeks, but He whom God the Father hath glorified, of whom we have spoken elsewhere more in particular, for the profit of those who seek the truth. He, in administering the righteous judgment of the Father to all, assigns to each what is righteous according to his works. And being present at His judicial decision, all, both men and angels and demons, shall utter one voice, saying, 'Righteous is Thy judgment.' Of which voice the justification will be seen in the awarding to each that which is just; since to those who have done well shall be assigned righteously eternal bliss, and to the lovers of iniquity shall be given eternal punishment. And the fire which is unquenchable and without end awaits these latter.[117]

It is this misunderstanding of the judgment of rewards accompanied with man's natural desire and inclination to judge other's actions that the future judgment of believers is falsely understood to be one of rewards and justification.

---

[117] Hippolytus of Rome, "Against Plato, on the Cause of the Universe", trans. S. D. F. SalmondIn , in *The Ante-Nicene Fathers, Volume V: Fathers of the Third Century: Hippolytus, Cyprian, Novatian, Appendix*, ed. Alexander Roberts, James Donaldson and A. Cleveland Coxe (Buffalo, NY: Christian Literature Company, 1886), 222.

Final justification is one thing that has been all too frequently overlooked in the soteriology of many who claim the name of Calvinist. Sweeney says of Edwards:

> in his 'Miscellanies' notebooks, and in the *Blank Bible,* he suggested that the error of those who misinterpret James on the doctrine of justification- particularly the words of James 2:24, 'Ye see then how that by works a man is justified, and not by faith only'- was that they failed to "distinguish...first and second justification. The first justification, which is at conversion, is a man's becoming righteous, or his coming to have a righteousness belonging to him, or imputed to him. This is by faith alone. The second is at judgment, which is that by which a man is proved and declared righteous. This is by works, and not by faith.[118]

This is a return in part at the very least to Romanism. Sanctification becomes an automatic result of justification. This is why one theologian of note has said that the soteriology of Protestantism and Romanism can be brought together by their commonality found in Edwards.[119]

Sproul comments, "Edwards could preach that a pretense of trusting Christ is in vain as long as men live wicked lives."[120] But believers live wicked lives. It is ironic that in his effort to taken sin seriously, he has, in fact, taken sin much too lightly. Even the smallest of sins is such a great violation that it necessitated Christ's death on the cross to bring about reconciliation with God. In an effort to take sin

---

[118] Ibid, loc 2913.
[119] Cf. Anri Morimoto, *Jonathan Edwards and the Catholic Vision of Salvation,*(University Park, PA: Pennsylvania State University Press, 1995).
[120] R.C. Sproul, *Faith Alone: The Evangelical Doctrine of Justification*, 86.

seriously, Edwards and new Calvinism have hardened their doctrine of works (if there is such a doctrine), but taking sin seriously means rejoicing in grace and living in light of already present grace, not by saying that those without works are not saved. He even told people "we can't be saved without being good."[121] Unfortunately, Jesus explains "no one is good except God alone."[122] He was speaking to those who had faith when He explained this to them. Obviously, even the regenerate man is not good unless you are looking at him positionally instead of practically.

Edwards' Social Gospel

The passion driving the ministry of Jonathan Edwards was not too much different from that which gave rise to new Calvinism. Both share a common desire to purge or cleanse the church of professing Christians. Nothing puts off people in the postmodern world more than hypocrisy. The hypocrisy of carnal Christians is a target of this theology. One person observes that Edwards was "chronically frustrated by glib moral laxity in those the Lord has placed under his care, easy-believism and hypocrisy."[123] One could just as easily hear this refrain come from a modern new Calvinist as from the mouth of Edwards centuries prior. Although they would never admit it, it is a desire to rid the church of all those sinners (i.e. professing believers who live in a worldly manner).

The result of this thinking is an eschatologically-based soteriology. This may sound confusing, but what is intended here is to say that the eschatological beliefs of Edwards, and later new Calvinists, drive their soteriological understanding. Essentially, the gospel is not just about

---

[121] Ibid, loc 2970.
[122] Mark 10:18.
[123] Ibid, loc 2775.

personal salvation. It has eschatological features, as well. Personal salvation is one part of a larger gospel. This is why new Calvinists focus so much on the gospel. It is the "whole" gospel that includes not only personal transformation, but also societal transformation. It is said:

> the doctrine of justification is for Edwards of singular importance not only for individual salvation but also for the New England project in terms of its theological priority and its social ramifications...justification came to be associated with a divine social strategy as much as divine and saving balm.[124]

This is mirrored clearly in the Gospel Coalition's statement "men and women.... are both called to move beyond passive self-indulgence to significant private and public engagement in family, church, and civic life."[125] Although not explicitly postmillennial in outlook, Edwards believed that religious revival resulting in societal transformation would help to bring about the kingdom of God. It is especially noteworthy that "international alliances with other churches were (one) of the ways Edwards labored to knit the churches and bring forth the kingdom."[126] This is something that is shared in new Calvinism's usage of *Together for the Gospel*, *The Gospel Coalition*, *Acts 29* and the *World Evangelical Alliance*. Churches are partnering together to bring the gospel (both personal and social) to the world.

Richard Baxter

Richard Baxter has been called "the essence of Puritanism."[127] He is of particular importance to this study

---

[124] Ibid, loc 1511, 1708.
[125] *Foundation Documents* (The Gospel Coalition, 2008).
[126] Ibid, 1714.
[127] Timothy Beougher, *Richard Baxter and Conversion: A Study of the*

because he fought ardently against anything he saw as antinomian. This is something the new Calvinists continually charge against those who espouse free grace theology. It may also be a reason for their stances against dispensationalism.[128] This spirit of Baxter continues to this day in new Calvinism. He saw himself as fighting against the tide of antinomianism and would fellowship with almost anyone in opposition to those he saw as antinomian. New Calvinism is doing the same in its willingness to fellowship with many people (e.g. Rick Warren, T.D. Jakes). This is also one of the reasons why they are willing to fellowship with almost anyone except with dispensationalists.

Like a good Puritan, Baxter believed that you cannot just be saved. Instead, "man has to do something."[129] This is why he fought against free grace theology. In formulating his theology, he echoes Edward's view of future justification that is to occur at the last judgment. Baxter, not unlike some new Calvinists, views there to be two justifications whereby "the first happens when a man believes, but the final justification takes place at the Day of Judgment."[130] In this final justification, the believer has to demonstrate his own obedience to be justified. This flies in the face of truly reformed theology. Beougher asserts, "Calvinists consistently have emphasized that there is only one justification…what takes place at the final judgment is simply a ratification of what took place long before."[131] It is said "for Baxter, the primary reason for good works seems to be because God has ordered us to do them as necessary to our final justification."[132] One wonders why there are not

---

Puritan Concept of Becoming a Christian, (Mentor, 2008), 11.
[128] Dispensationalists are frequently, and falsely, charged with teaching antinomianism.
[129] Ibid, 82
[130] Ibid, 61.
[131] Ibid, 63.
[132] Ibid, 72.

more within reformed theology crying out against this resurgent false teaching. This is said to currently be only a disputed point within reformed theology.[133]

Many of the reformed applaud the work of the new Calvinists, but in terms of justification, free grace theology and dispensationalism share more in common with reformed theology than reformed theology shares with new Calvinism. In fact, new Calvinism here is more like neo-orthodoxy than reformed theology. Hannah says that in neo-orthodoxy:

> fundamentalist literalism, filtered into the Genesis account of creationism, was questioned; an openness to Pentecostal views embraced; a willingness to decentralize eschatological speculation approved; a rejection of the extremes of dispensationalism assumed; a renewal of a social consciousness proposed; a desire to rethink the meaning of biblical infallibility allowed; and a warmness toward ecumenical dialogue engaged.[134]

This could just as easily be a statement concerning new Calvinism as it is about neo-orthodoxy.

MODERN CALVINISM

This section seeks to chronicle the immediate influences upon new Calvinism. It will not attempt to define the many shades of modern Calvinism but will look instead at the prominent persons, institutions and trends that laid the path new Calvinism has followed. It will specifically be limited in time to the events of the past century.

---

[133] Carl Trueman, Phone Conversation (June 18, 2013).
[134] John D. Hannah, *An Uncommon Union: Dallas Theological Seminary and American Evangelicalism*, Kindle Edition, (Grand Rapids, MI: Zondervan, 2009) Loc. 3318-3321.

Fuller Theological Seminary

Although Ladd's influence on new Calvinism is extensive, it is necessary to examine the influence of Fuller Theological Seminary, where Ladd taught and Piper was a student, more broadly. Fuller Seminary's abandonment of its fundamental heritage and its denial of the doctrine of inerrancy is surprisingly well documented. In one generation, the school left the fundamental foundation laid by Charles Fuller and followed the path towards neo-orthodoxy set forth by Daniel Fuller, his son. Marsden documents well the influence the younger Fuller had on the seminary's doctrinal stance following his studies under the prominent neo-orthodox theologian Karl Barth.[135] Marsden, a supporter of Fuller Seminary, affirms the reforming efforts of Daniel Fuller and the direction the school headed under his deanship. While Marsden does not ascribe the doctrinal change to Daniel Fuller primarily, he does believe him to be the linchpin in the progressive change, culminating in the school's decisive "Black Saturday" meeting. It is here that the school's drift towards liberalism became entrenched. The founders sought to create a remade Princeton that was "ecclesiastically positive."[136] Fuller, a prominent fundamentalist, wanted his namesake school to be independent and to abandon the separatism, consciously choosing instead to court the favor of mainline denominations. It must be remembered that, at Charles Fuller's time, the mainline denominations were just moving into liberalism. Fuller Seminary today has continued to court the favor of the mainline denominations, even when they are out-rightly apostate.

---

[135] George Marsden, *Reforming Fundamentalism: Fuller Seminary and the New Evangelicalism*, (Grand Rapids, MI: William B. Eerdmans Publishing Company, 1987).
[136] Ibid, 64.

Ladd himself reflected Fuller Seminary's attempt at integrating fundamentalism with parts of modern liberalism. The former focused on the future aspects of the kingdom while the latter only cared about the present aspects of the kingdom. Ladd's proposal then can be seen now as a compromise between fundamentalism and modern liberalism. It has been observed that Ladd was "torn between his presuppositional critique of modern scholarship and his eagerness to find modern critical scholarship on his side."[137] He wanted to be respected by and contribute to both camps. Compromise in the name of cooperation is a fundamental tenant of Fuller Seminary's theology.

Fuller Seminary's doctrinal understandings are currently reflected in new Calvinism. Their ecclesiology is "a direct repudiation of the dispensationalist view of the church as a refuge in a ruined culture and a consequent affirmation of the Calvinist-Puritan view that the church must play a central civilization-building role."[138] In their understanding,

> modern culture, in (the Reformed theological tradition's) view, is not beyond hope, and Christians have the task of transforming culture to bring it more in conformity with God's Law and will.[139]

> the broadly Calvinistic vision that the Christian's mission involves not only evangelism but also a cultural task, both remaking the mind of an era and transforming society.[140]

As Marsden observes, the desire to stay current with secular academic innovation led the school to pursue certain "innovations including moving away from dispensationalism,

---

[137] Ibid, 250.
[138] Ibid, 63.
[139] Ibid, 76.
[140] Ibid, 79.

taking more positive views of science, scholarship, and social concern, reconsidering the role of the Holy Spirit (in regards to holiness and Pentecostal groups), and reopening discussions about the inspiration of Scripture."[141] Fuller's influence on the trend towards openness, especially concerning continuationism, stems from their commitment to avoid the dogmatic elements of fundamentalism. To some extent these are all carried forth by present-day new Calvinists.

The importance of Fuller is seen in the fact that it was the theological training ground of John Piper. On the Desiring God website, it unabashedly states "Piper attended Fuller Theological Seminary, where he was greatly influenced by Daniel Fuller, a man whose teaching opened new insights into Scripture for Piper."[142] The following survey results indicate how far Fuller Seminary drifted by 1982. The results indicate the views of Fuller's student populous:

> only 15% believed in inerrancy

> barely half believed that the only hope for heaven is through personal faith in Jesus

> 43% speak in tongues

> 21% do not always believe premarital sex is wrong

> only 10% believe that the husband is primarily responsible for the spiritual well-being of the family

---

[141] Ibid, 162.
[142] Tim Ellisworth, "John Piper: God's Glory His Passion," The Southern Seminary Magazine, at Desiring God Ministries, http://www.desiringgod.org/about/john-piper/gods-glory-his-passion, (Accessed 07/15/2013).

80% favor female ordination

37% social reform is just as important as evangelism[143]

It has drifted so far that recently "the nation's first LGBT student club (was) sanctioned by a major evangelical seminary" at Fuller Theological Seminary.[144]

EXCURSUS: THE NORMAN SHEPHERD CONTROVERSY

The connection needs to be shown between the theology of John Piper and the Norman Shepherd controversy. For those not familiar with this, it is a dispute that arose at Westminster Theological Seminary (Philadelphia) over the views of then Professor Norman Shepherd on the issue of justification. This was a highly contentious debate. What is worth noting here is the influence it had on the views of Daniel Fuller. This influence then extended to the students of Fuller Theological Seminary (like Piper and John Frame). Shepherd, Daniel Fuller and Piper are in a line of thinking on justification that is aptly referred to as "neo-legalism."[145] Holding nothing back, Robbins views their understanding of justification as a "rediscovery of the Roman Catholic doctrine of salvation."[146] This is due to with the relationship between faith and works.

---

[143] George Marsden, *Reforming Fundamentalism: Fuller Seminary and the New Evangelicalism*, 302-310.

[144] Sarah Parvini, "Fuller Theological Seminary's Acceptance of LGBT Group, OneTable, Creates Ripples," *Huffington Post,* at http://www.huffingtonpost.com/2013/07/13/fuller-theological-seminary-lgbt-onetable_n_3593237.html, (Accessed September 5, 2013).

[145] It is uncertain the specific origin of this term, but John W. Robbins is its most vocal proponent.

[146] John W. Robbins, "Pied Piper," *Trinity Review* (June, July 2002): 1a.

As VanDrunen summarizes, "Shepherd repeatedly stresses that justifying faith is an active, living, obedient faith."[147]

This controversy began in the seventies. It was at this time that Shepherd, the heir apparent to John Murray:

> set himself to the task of formulating the doctrine of justification in a way that would accommodate the language of James so that the church's presentation of the gospel could just as easily begin with James as with Paul.[148]

Rather than make James be interpreted in light of Paul, he made Paul be interpreted in light of James.[149] It is not too difficult to see how this could quickly result in a return to Romanism. Some within Reformed theology objected to this reformulation of justification. Reid stated that Shepherd's position "seems to link works so closely to faith, not just as the result of faith but as part of faith itself, that he tends to obscure, if not destroy the biblical Reformed doctrine of faith."[150] This is not too different from new Calvinism. It is not just that works come from faith but that they are a part of faith. As Evans explains, "there is an expansive view of faith as including works of evangelical obedience. Shepherd never tires of declaring that the faith that saves is living, active and obedient."[151] Waldron says, "Shepherd is perfectly willing to

---

[147] David VanDrunen, in *Covenant, Justification, and Pastoral Ministry: Essays by the Faculty of Westminster Seminary California,* ed. by R. Scott Clark, (Phillipsburg, NJ: P & R Publishing, 2007), 49.

[148] Ian A. Hewitson, *Trust and Obey: Norman Shepherd &The Justification Controversy at Westminster Theological Seminary,* (Minneapolis, MN: NextStep Resources, 2011), 22-23.

[149] This is not that different than N.T. Wright and the New Perspectives on Paul's approach.

[150] W. Stanford Reid qtd. in ibid, 46.

[151] William B. Evans, "Deja Vu All Over Again? The Contemporary Reformed Soteriological Controversy in Historical Perspective." *Westminster Theological Journal* 72:1 (Spring 2010): 142.

assert that a kind of works is necessary unto (or a condition of) being justified."[152] The motives of Shepherd as with the new Calvinists arise out of a desire to avoiding cheap grace and salvation apart from genuine and deep transformation of life. This in itself is not a wrong motive. In an attempt to correct, they have overcorrected. It is simply not appropriate to see works as a condition for salvation or making it in any way applicable to a discussion of justification. With the passing of time, it unfortunately appears, mild consent to this position has ruled the day within reformed theology.

One of the greatest areas of theological confusion passed on to new Calvinism from the views of Shepherd is a misunderstanding of the substitutionary atonement. There is a tendency to view the atonement as not truly substitutionary. It is more of an exchange atonement. In their view, the believer at conversion is united with Christ. This is not just positional but experiential, as well. Frame states that at conversion "regeneration describes the change God works in us to become like Christ."[153] Having this divine nature, they must act obediently. How much obedience is required is never answered. In looking at Appendix 3, one can see Piper's response to this question; somehow the thief on the cross had enough evangelical obedience or practical righteousness to be confirmed as justified. Apparently, the thief immediately began to live righteously albeit only for a brief period of time. As Shepherd says, God "does not leave the ungodly in their ungodliness."[154] Although this charge is denied, it is Christian perfectionism. What is exchanged then in their theology is the unregenerate sinful life for a new

---

[152] Samuel E. Waldron, "John Calvin Versus Norman Shepherd on Sola Fide," 174.

[153] John M. Frame. *Salvation Belongs to the Lord: An Introduction to Systematic Theology,* Kindle Edition. (Phillipsburg, NJ: P & R Publishing, 2006), Loc. 2732-2733.

[154] Ian A. Hewitson, *Trust and Obey: Norman Shepherd &The Justification Controversy at Westminster Theological Seminary*, 154.

divine life in Christ. In this, he changes how the righteousness of Christ is appropriated. The truly reformed understanding of the substitutionary atonement is that Christ died in the sinner's place as a substitute. It is not the exchange of one life for His that is substituted. This totally redefines the atonement. Imputed righteousness becomes the cause of justification not the result of it. While Shepherd (and Piper) claims to subscribe to the substitutionary atonement, he redefines it. He also redefines faith to mean not one act of faith but a lifetime of faithfulness. Works must play a role in justification for Shepherd. As one supporter states, "according to Shepherd, neither are sinners justified irrespective of anything in them."[155] If one doubts the connection between Piper and Shepherd, their commonality is seen in Shepherd's quote "they (believers) are not simply forensically just, but are covenantally loyal."[156] This could have just as readily come from the mouth of Piper. There is an attempt made to overcome this understanding's obvious deficiency. It is claimed, "the threat of legalism is avoided...because the fulfillment of these covenant obligations is not meritorious."[157] Covenantal obedience is necessary for salvation but not meritorious. It is no wonder that this created a controversy; it is well worth it when someone denies the strictly forensic nature of justification. It is sad that this controversy died out with no apparent condemnation.

John Frame

In his introduction to theology, Frame synthesizes his understanding of justification in a way that is simple for the

---

[155] Ibid, 130.
[156] Norman Shepherd, "The Relation of Good Works," qtd.in ibid, 152.
[157] William B. Evans, "Deja Vu All Over Again?The Contemporary Reformed Soteriological Controversy in Historical Perspective."*Westminster Theological Journal* 72:1 (Spring 2010): 144.

lay reader to understand. It should not be surprising that someone, who is writing a series entitled *A Theology of Lordship,* misunderstands the relationship between works and faith. While maintaining that works have no contributing factor to salvation, Frame believes that they are a necessary condition for salvation. His legalism can be seen in the fact that he exhorts his readers to be fruit inspectors saying, "if you want to know whether someone knows God, look at his or her life."[158] Like so many others he claims to say that complete sinfulness is not possible but still nevertheless desires to claim that a true believer must be characterized by righteousness. He states, "if we see ourselves dominated by sinful patterns, we should ask whether we have really trusted Christ as *Lord* and Savior."[159] One is left wondering how it could be that a person truly recognizes the divinity of Christ and his offer of salvation without realizing His sovereign lordship. He says that the trusting (*fiducia*) element of belief is to "allow (the believer's) knowledge of God's word to govern his thoughts, actions, and behavior."[160] The problem is that no one does this perfectly. He has forgotten the free aspect of grace. How much of one's life must be governed then? His answer to this is that it is simply a "willingness to obey."[161] His *ordo salutis* is off and his attempt to reconcile this issue is a return to costly grace. Shockingly, he asserts plainly:

> some people have taught that anyone who makes a minimal commitment to Christianity-for example, by coming forward, professing faith, and being baptized-will certainly be saved in the end, even if they

---

[158] John M. Frame. *Salvation Belongs to the Lord: An Introduction to Systematic Theology,* Loc. 951.
[159] Ibid, loc. 2703-2704.
[160] Ibid, loc. 2329.
[161] Ibid, loc. 2335.

renounce Christ and live sinful lives. That, of course, is not biblical teaching.[162]

The church cannot consider those sinful people Christians. How sad this is.

The result of his theology will always be to legalism (due to its perfectionist leanings) and Romanism (due to its misunderstanding of justification). One can clearly see this when Frame asserts, "in regeneration and sanctification, God takes away our sinful, disobedient hearts and gives us new hearts, new dispositions, new lives, new desires to obey him."[163] One can also see his connection with Piper in terms of future justification, which results from his understanding of lordship. He states:

> justification is ours already, but one day we will be pronounced righteous before the Father's throne. So, there is a past justification and a future justification.

This is the Laddian concept of an "already/not yet" applied to justification. At its core "saving faith and good works are closely related."[164] One major issue with this is the gospel of John, written so that his reader may believe, never mentions works or even repentance.

PROMINENT CALVINISTS

In the more immediate past, three men specifically have been very prominent in the rise of new Calvinism. These men are R.C. Sproul Sr., John MacArthur Jr. and George Ladd. While they should not be mistaken as new Calvinists, they acted as heralds whose lives and ministries helped to popularize the movement. Whether or not one

---

[162] Ibid, loc. 2802-2803.
[163] Ibid, loc. 2455-2456.
[164] Ibid, loc 2346.

agrees with their theology, these men are three of the theological giants of this time. Ladd's influence has been somewhat restricted to academia, and this will be dealt with later. For now it is necessary to examine the effect MacArthur and Sproul have had on the emergence of new Calvinism

MacArthur's *Grace to You* and Sproul's *Ligonier Ministries* have spread the influence of their founder's theology. By making the most of technology, these ministries have extended the scope of their influence beyond what could have been accomplished in previous decades. There are several factors that have fuel their influence. One is personal dynamism. This is something that continues to be very influential in new Calvinism. Another factor is that these two men and their ministries have gone against the grain of both culture and tradition in standing for what they believe. The message of their ministries speaks volumes to those rooted in the postmodern world desiring to do great things for God. These men are viewed as steadfast upholders of orthodoxy in a world consumed by relativism and immorality. They are not the only theologians of note within the recent past who have stood firm on their convictions and exercised influence, but what separates them from others is that they have helped fuel the rise of new Calvinism in their reformed soteriology and their approach to ministry. Their specific approach involves steeping their theology in the past while making their ministries relevant to the present. This pursuit lies at the very heart of new Calvinism. Their approach, in part, has given rise to the mind-frame that what is needed in the church is a strong theology rooted in history and a model of ministry that is ever-changing to meet the needs of the present time. This is not far from the biblical truth, but it is an extreme form of contextualization that has come to characterize new Calvinism. The new Calvinist philosophy of ministry can be summarized: one should be conservative in doctrine and liberal in praxis. It is not surprising then to see many ascribing to Calvinistic doctrines having ministries that more closely resemble Arminianism in practice (e.g. *Acts 29 Network*). By this it is meant that the church can do anything it wants in trying to reach the lost (some take this very literally) while affirming a belief that there is nothing at all that the church can actually do to reach the lost. It is now necessary to directly examine the beliefs of MacArthur and Sproul to see how they bear influence on the theology of the new Calvinists either directly or indirectly.

John MacArthur

It may be surprising to some that MacArthur is seen as an influence on the movement of new Calvinism because he has at times been outspoken against it. This is especially true in regards to the majority of those within new Calvinism who ascribe to the continuation of the sign gifts in the contemporary church. In addition to this, the issue of over-contextualization characterizing the movement has specifically been the subject of MacArthur's rebuke. In a series of posts, MacArthur even asserts when speaking of new Calvinism:

> evangelicalism's childish fascination with teenage fashions, milk rather than meat, and trivial entertainment rather than serious doctrine is deeply rooted in a pragmatic ministry philosophy. It is not 'Reformed' in any sense but is a classic expression of man-centered free-willism—what Colossians 2:23 refers to as 'self-made religion.'[165]

What MacArthur objects to is not the theology of the movement (for the most part) but its practices. In

---

[165] John MacArthur, "Grow Up Advice for YRR (Part 2)," July 25, 2011, http://www.gty.org/blog/B110725, (Accessed September 5, 2013).

commenting on this verse, MacArthur equates self-made religion with asceticism because it seeks to glory self and not God.[166] He calls this "the antithesis of the Bible's emphasis on the sovereignty of God."[167] What he calls for is consistency within new Calvinism. Essentially, he breaks down the tenant of new Calvinism that asserts that being reformed must mean to be continually reforming. This glorifies in the young and restless aspects of their ministry philosophy. He calls for a practice that is consistent with their theology. He affirms new Calvinism's overall theological understanding, exhorting them "don't squander your good theology and your opportunity to make an impact by selling out to stylishness, self-promotion, or mere popularity."[168] Because of this doctrinal affirmation, too much distance should not be placed between MacArthur and new Calvinism.

Theological Seeds

While MacArthur definitely separates himself from new Calvinism, it is his theological affirmations and not his rebukes that have been heard by those within the movement.[169] It can be seen that there are certain elements of his theology that have, in part, influenced specific elements within new Calvinism's theology. Many of MacArthur's theological seeds have been planted within the field of soteriology and have reached a greater fullness in new Calvinism. New Calvinism, as almost universally ascribing to lordship salvation, has specifically built upon MacArthur in this area. This teaching has reached its fullness in the work *Future*

---

[166] John MacArthur, *Colossians & Philemon,* in "The MacArthur New Testament Commentary," (Chicago: Moody Press, 1992), 123.
[167] John MacArthur, "Grow Up Advice for YRR (Part 2)."
[168] JohnMacArthur, "Keep Reforming," August 29, 2011, http://www.gty.org/blog/B110829, (Accessed September 5, 2013).
[169] In more recent times new Calvinism has begin to distance itself from MacArthur because he has spoken out against some of its practice.

Grace. This wok asserts, "Jesus says that if you don't fight this sin with the kind of seriousness that is willing to gouge out your own eye, you will go to hell."[170] The teachings of Paul Washer are also the product of an extreme position on lordship salvation, albeit not yet as mainstream as others. Commonality between MacArthur and new Calvinism can also be found in their shared understanding and defining of the terms of TULIP.

Lordship Salvation

There has been a great deal of conflict between those within free grace theology (often referred to as easy-believism) and lordship salvation. John MacArthur has been at the center of this debate for more than 25 years. It is not necessary to rehash this debate in detail here because others have ably handled it.[171] Instead, lordship salvation will be shown as it relates specifically to new Calvinism. Not all reformed theologians ascribe to lordship theology; this is one reason why MacArthur can be specifically seen to influencing new Calvinism. Before getting into some of the details concerning MacArthur, it may helpful to first to discuss lordship more generally because of new Calvinism's great abhorrence of free grace theology. Both lordship and the free grace theology agree that justification is distinct but connected to sanctification. Both also recognize that it is Scripture's teaching that the one who truly believes will bear fruit in their life. One of the differences between the lordship position and the free grace position lies in the degree or amount of fruit that will be present. Distinction can also be drawn very easily in the outworking of their understandings

---

[170] John Piper, *Future Grace: The Purifying Power of the Promises of God,* Revised Edition (Colorado Springs, CO: Multnomah Books, 2012), 331.
[171] Cf. *Lordship Salvation: A Biblical Evaluation and Response* by Charlie Bing and *Absolutely Free* by Zane Hodges.

on this matter as it relates to sanctification. Classically, free grace proponents see Scripture as teaching that neither the amount of fruit nor its perceptibility necessarily known. Lordship looks for the fruit to be definitive; i.e. visible and quantifiable. Overall the disagreement originates from very different understandings of total depravity and the perseverance of the saints. Lordship proponents view soteriology through the lens of an improperly defined sense of depravity and perseverance. Rather than saying that the believer will be preserved or kept by God, lordship salvation teaches that those who are not persevering are not truly believers. In this, they stray from the biblical teaching.

Faith

Free grace theology asserts that faith is equivalent to belief. A person who believes places their reliance on Christ and His provision for salvation. Chafer in his affirmation of this divides his understanding of faith (πίστις) by distinguishing between saving faith and serving faith. Saving faith "is the inwrought confidence in God's promises and provisions respecting the Savior that leads one to elect to repose upon and trust in the One alone who can save."[172] It is the object of faith that changes at conversion. The volitional element in saving faith is seen in that the believer relies upon Christ and His work instead of their own effort, or in some other provision that is offered in another religious system. Chafer sees serving faith as "the fact of divinely bestowed gifts and all details respecting divine appointments for service. This faith is always a personal matter."[173] The lordship position confuses saving faith and serving faith. Instead of seeing service as an outgrowth of saving faith, they see it as a necessary part of truly saving faith. It cannot

---

[172] Lewis Sperry Chafer, *Systematic Theology*, 7:148.
[173] Ibid.

be both the outgrowth of salvation and a necessary requirement for regeneration to have previously occurred.[174]

Volition

The lordship position takes the volitional element within salvation to an extreme. Berkhof states, it is "a change of purpose, an inward turning away from sin, and a disposition to seek pardon and cleansing."[175] This causes great confusion in the *ordo salutis*. While all evangelicals assert that man is justified by faith, after all Paul explicitly states δικαιοῦσθαι πίστει ἄνθρωπον (Romans 3:28), but views begin to diverge in describing how justification comes about. A problem is bound to arise when following Berkhof, because in order for someone to be justified, they must first not only have faith, they must have a faith which first turns away from sin. It is then that they will become regenerate, therefore, being justified. The biblical doctrine, following Romans 1, teaches that the unregenerate man is unable to have a faith that turns from sin. This leads to the hypothetical solution proposed by many reformed theologians whereby God imparts regeneration logically prior to faith enabling them to have a faith that desires to turn away from sin.

One shortcoming of this understanding is that there is some point, at least logically, whereby the regenerate man is

---

[174] This is where it will be seen that new Calvinism uses Ladd's already/not yet framework to hold to mutually exclusive ideas. This is necessary because it is the new Calvinist teaching that people are already justified but not yet justified. See below for more detailed discussion of this issue.

[175] Louis Berkhof, *Systematic Theology*, (Grand Rapids, MI: WM. B. Eerdmans, 1941), 486.

in need of justification. What need does a regenerate man have for justification? This thinking introduces the logical impossibility of the regenerate unjustified. The folly of this overall approach will be seen in more detail or in greater fullness later. Needless to say, faith, regeneration and justification should be seen as simultaneous acts. The understanding of the volitional element of faith as it has been proposed by Berkhof and affirmed by MacArthur[176] has paved the way for new Calvinism's misunderstanding.

One more thing needs to be discussed before moving on from here. In commenting on the jailer's question, 'what must I do to be saved?' Paul answers with the simple response Πίστευσον ἐπὶ τὸν κύριον Ἰησοῦν.[177] MacArthur admits that in order for the jailer to be saved, he only needed to believe Jesus was who He claimed to be and to believe in what He did.[178] What he then adds is that truly saving faith contains within it a desire to turn from sin (and submit to Christ as Lord). In this, MacArthur fails to understand Scripture's command for the believer to ἐνδύσασθαι τὸν καινὸν ἄνθρωπον.[179] One must ask how it is that the believer, who has submitted to the lordship of Christ, has not already put on the new man since he has already inwardly turned from sin? Are they to bring their outward actions in accordance with their inward submission? If this is so, then believers should be concerned with their outward actions, where they fall short, rather than the inward desires which have already been turned over to Christ. It appears that this might be the case to a degree.

---

[176] John MacArthur, *The Truth about the Lordship of Christ,* (Nashville, TN: Thomas Nelson, 2012), 100.
[177] Acts 16:31.
[178] John MacArthur, *Acts* in "The MacArthur New Testament Commentary," 326.
[179] Cf. Ephesians 4:24, Colossians 3:10.

MacArthur sees the sin in the life of a believer as that which is done, not by the believers, but by his body/ flesh. According to MacArthur, Ephesians 2:20 references a putting on that "is not a one-time accomplishment but the continual work of the Spirit."[180] At the moment of salvation, the believer has a faith that desires to turn from sin and submit to the lordship of Christ, but this is only fleeting, and the believer will need to continually submit to Christ in their life, thereby seeing the putting on of the new man as necessary for them in the future. This confuses serving faith with saving faith and sanctification with justification. MacArthur is inconsistent in his theology and unable to truly defend his soteriology against the possibility of having carnal or sinful believers in the church, something he so earnestly fights against. For example, if one were to conclude with him that at the moment of salvation that all true believers submit to the Lordship of Christ, but this (a) does not last long and (b) is a continual necessity in the life of a believer, then what prevents the believer from not submitting to Christ's lordship in the future? He would be forced to concede that not all believers are presently submitting to the lordship of Christ thereby nullifying the desired goal of his argument. This is nothing more than a Band-Aid fix to a crack in the foundation of his soteriology. The new Calvinists will attempt to rectify this in various ways.

Depravity

MacArthur's misunderstanding of true biblical depravity is seen in his overestimation of unregenerate man. It is given that the unregenerate man is unwilling to seek God and is in bondage to the power of sin, enslaving him to the desires of the flesh. As MacArthur sees it, God then imparts new life into this man, thereby regenerating him. This act

---

[180] John MacArthur, *Ephesians* in "The MacArthur New Testament Commentary," (Chicago: Moody Publishers, 1986), 178.

enables the man to have faith. Because it is the power of God accomplishing this, it ensures a specific type or quality of faith. Rather than see depravity in all its fullness, he sees it only in a very limited sense, namely as it relates to the inability of man to be saved by his own power. It is this definition of total depravity, rightly called total inability, which has come to be believed by new Calvinism. One new Calvinist defines depravity in part as:

> we Christians were once all 'dead in trespasses and sins.' The point of deadness is that we were incapable of any life with God. Our hearts were like a stone toward God (Ephesians 4:18; Ezekiel 36:26). Our hearts were blind and incapable of seeing the glory of God in Christ (2 Corinthians 4:4-6). We were totally unable to reform ourselves.[181]

He even later describes grace being conditioned upon obedience. MacArthur reflects this understanding of depravity when he asserts, "the unsaved person is a spiritual corpse and consequently is completely unable, in himself, to respond to the things of God."[182] This is certainly true, but the biblical picture of depravity is much greater and MacArthur's narrow picture of depravity and causes him to force other conclusions with regard to his soteriology. This is a natural consequence of focusing on the terminology TULIP.

MacArthur all but eliminates depravity, the capacity to serve sin and self, in the life of a believer. This must be done to maintain the lordship position. Rather than

---

[181] John Piper, "What We Believe About the Five Points of Calvinism." March 1, 1985.
http://www.desiringgod.org/resource-library/articles/what-we-believe-about-the-five-points-of-Calvinism (Accessed September 5, 2013).
[182] John MacArthur, *Romans 1-9,* in "The MacArthur New Testament Commentary," 417.

subscribing to the biblical concept of total depravity, he expounds upon his own version of total depravity. This depravity is limited in its definition as it functions within the TULIP framework. MacArthur asserts, "in Christ we cannot help but be pleasing [to] God."[183] In submitting to the lordship of Christ, the believer is said to have overcome depravity and will lead a life which is pleasing to God. MacArthur claims, "a true Christian not only wears the name of Christ, but he demonstrates the virtue of Christ."[184] One must ask how is it that the church Paul wrote to in Corinth demonstrated the virtue of Christ? One of the errors of Pelagius, as Sproul observes, was a belief that "sin does not change our essential moral nature." This is an excellent understanding of the Pelagian outlook but all too often in Calvinism, both old and new, there is a belief that, after regeneration, the new life has eradicated the old life. This one nature view is applying the same error of Pelagius, in principle, to the life of a believer. The Calvinistic outlook then sees within the regenerate man a change that has occurred in his essential moral nature. No longer, MacArthur says, is the unregenerate man unrighteous, he has replaced the unrighteous sin nature with the righteousness of life. While it is true that the believer has the righteousness of Christ, it is only true positionally, and the old nature remains, not getting exchanged at regeneration.

One Nature View

This misunderstanding of depravity is closely related to MacArthur's view that the believer only has one nature. This stems from his taking Romans 7:18 out of context. This verse states, "so now, no longer am I the one doing it, but sin

---

[183] John MacArthur, *Ephesians* in "The MacArthur New Testament Commentary," 59.
[184] John MacArthur, *The Truth About the Lordship of Christ,* 16.

which dwells in me."[185] In explaining another verse, MacArthur makes his stance:

> the new nature is not added to the old nature but replaces it…biblical terminology, then, does not say that a Christian has two different natures. He has but one nature, the new nature in Christ. The old self dies and the new self lives; they do not coexist. It is not a remaining old nature but the remaining garment of sinful flesh that causes Christians to sin. The Christian is a single new person, a totally new creation, not a spiritual schizophrenic. It is the filthy coat of remaining humanness in which the new creation dwells that continues to hinder and contaminate his living.[186]

He takes this to mean that it is the flesh in the believer that sins and not the believer himself because he is now regenerate. This is a return to the Aristotelian concept of the flesh. The flesh in Aristotle's thinking was the sinful part of man while the spirit (or non-material) part of man does good. The problem is that he completely ignores the plain teaching of the verses immediate prior to and after this verse. It is said in these surrounding verses:

> Κατεργάζομαι (I am doing)
> πράσσω (I am not practicing)
> θέλω (I would like to do)
> ποιέω (I am doing)
> πράσσω (I practice)

It is not the flesh that does these things but Paul himself. This is affirmed through his other writings. He says, "but I say,

---

[185] Romans 7:17, NASB.
[186] John F. MacArthur, Jr., *Ephesians*, MacArthur New Testament Commentary (Chicago: Moody Press, 1986), 164.

walk by the Spirit, and you will not carry out the desire of the flesh."[187] Peter describes "those who indulge the flesh in *its* corrupt desires and despise authority" as "daring, self-willed."[188] It is correct to say it is the flesh that acts in sinful ways, but the believer can desire to follow the flesh. On can conclude from MacArthur's argument: the believer is not the cause of his own sin. For him, regeneration means that the believer only has one desire which wars against the alien flesh outside of them. Scripture teaches that the believer has two natures or desires within them. One is the desire to follow the flesh in rebellion against God, and the other is to follow the Spirit and the desire to please God. The sin nature remains. Whether or not this one nature error is directly carried forward in the new Calvinists, its fruit most certainly are. At the very least, there is tacit agreement by one new Calvinist who explains:

> what is this 'new creation' that counts for everything? The new creation is what exists when the old mindset is crucified with Christ. ...so I would infer that the 'new Paul' who is created when the "old Paul" is crucified with Christ is a Paul who lives by faith which works through love.[189]

Confession

An essential element to MacArthur's soteriology is the believer's confession of Jesus as the Lord of his life at the time of his conversion. He states, "we must confess Him as Lord. That's a part of salvation, not a subsequent act."[190] Jesus is Lord of everyone's life whether they admit it or not,

---

[187] Galatians 5:16
[188] 2 Peter 2:10ff, NASB
[189] John Piper, "Only a New Creation Counts," August 28, 1983, http://www.desiringgod.org/resource-library/sermons/only-a-new-creation-counts, (Accessed October 16, 2013).
[190] Ibid, 13.

whether one is saved or not. MacArthur equates confession of Christ as Lord with making Him the ruler of one's life. The problem is that one cannot make Jesus Lord because He already is Lord. This understanding forces MacArthur to make certain assertions about the nature of confession. He comments upon Scripture:

> 'whoever confesses Me before men, him I will also confess before My Father who is in heaven.' When the heat is on, when the pressure and the persecution are bearing down and the world is attacking, the true believer will openly confess Christ. He won't bail out. He won't deny his faith.[191]

It would be greatly saddening to share this message with fellow believers in Iran or China who recant under torture. As Moyer explains concerning confession, "whether or not one confesses Christ does not determine whether or not one possesses Christ. One possesses Christ the moment one has trusted Him as personal Savior."[192] MacArthur's is the wrong perspective to take on perseverance, and it is the reason why many have chosen to utilize the word preservation instead of perseverance of the saints.

Perseverance

MacArthur sees true believers as limited in number to those who are willing and able to persevere in faith until the end. Any denial of Christ is evidence of insufficient faith. In a way, this makes a denial of Christ, even under torture, an unforgivable sin. The biblical teaching is that the believer will abide due to the power of God. This does not mean that believers can judge people as unsaved because they recanted

---

[191] Ibid, 19.
[192] R. Larry Moyer, *Free and Clear: Understanding & Communicating God's Offer of Eternal Life,* (Grand Rapids, MI: Kregel Publications, 1997), 123.

in the midst of torture. Luther struggled mightily with this. MacArthur fails to see that denying Christ happens in subtle ways in addition to the more dramatic. Do not believers deny Christ in one way or another every day of their lives? By failing to trust him, one denies Christ's faithfulness. By choosing sin, does not the believer deny Christ's sufficiency? Peter is a great example in Scripture to examine. MacArthur, in an attempt to remain consistent, asserts that Peter was not saved until after He denied Christ.[193] This is certainly not true, and most would not try to make this claim. It is recorded that Peter confessed

Christ prior to his recantation (denial) saying:

> Simon Peter answered, 'You are the Christ, the Son of the living God.' And Jesus said to him, 'Blessed are you, Simon Barjona, because flesh and blood did not reveal *this* to you, but My Father who is in heaven. I also say to you that you are Peter, and upon this rock I will build My church.'[194]

Christ would be affirming the faith of an unsaved Peter if one were to follow MacArthur's view. How does MacArthur deal with text? In his commentary, he never mentions the fact that Peter was not saved at this point. Instead, it is assumed that Jesus is commending the faithfulness of Peter. This shows the inconsistency in his theology. Despite this, new Calvinism will carry the lordship torch forward even though this was not the view that Calvin himself held.

Calvin and Depravity

Depravity was not limited to its aspect in the life of the unregenerate in Calvin's theology. The teaching that

---

[193] Ibid.
[194] Matthew 16:16-18, NASB

depravity, often referred to as original sin during the Reformation, is eliminated at conversion, was not held by Calvin who states:

> it is now clear how false the doctrine is which some long ago taught, and others still persist in, that by baptism we are exempted and set free from original sin, and from the corruption which was propagated by Adam to all his posterity, and that we are restored to the same righteousness and purity of nature which Adam would have had if he had maintained the integrity in which he was created.[195]

Baptism here can be seen to analogous with conversion (i.e. the baptism of the Spirit). Calvin says that it is a false doctrine to believe that the corruption of original sin, and depravity, ends with conversion resulting in righteousness lives. This is the very error that lordship proponents wish to make. MacArthur says:

> some teach that when a person becomes a Christian, God gives them something new in addition to his old sin nature. But according to the Word of God, we don't receive something new-we ourselves become new.[196]

For him, the sin nature is eradicated after conversion. It is exchanged for a new nature, "the image of God lost in Adam, is more gloriously restored."[197] Lordship proponents long to see the true believer as the one who is righteous, like Adam before the fall. One must ask how and why does the believer sin? It is the flesh (σάρξ), the body that sins, they would assuredly say. Paul refutes this idea stating that ἡ οἰκοῦσα ἐν

---

[195] John Calvin, *Institutes of the Christian Religion*, Book 4, XV:10.
[196] John MacArthur, *The Truth About the Lordship of Christ,* 73.
[197] John MacArthur, *Ephesians* in "The MacArthur New Testament Commentary," 178.

ἐμοὶ ἁμαρτία is what does evil.[198] MacArthur attempts to explain:

> Paul's new **I**, his new inner self, **no longer** approves of the sin that still clings to him through the flesh. Whereas before his conversion his inner self approved of the sin he committed, **now** his inner self, a completely new inner self, strongly disapproves… After salvation, sin, like a deposed and exiled ruler, no longer reigns in a person's life, but it manages to survive. It no longer resides in the innermost self but finds its residual dwelling in his flesh, in the unredeemed humanness that remains.[199]

This is confusing because MacArthur attempts to argue his way out of saying that depravity remains in the believer, while asserting sin remains as an influential part. If he remained consistent and true to the definition of biblical depravity, he would see that this is what Paul is referencing here. While the sin nature no longer enslaves the believer, it has not lost its power. This is all too evident in practice. One must also ask that if the "old self dies" as MacArthur believes, then why command the believer ἐνδύσασθαι τὸν καινὸν ἄνθρωπον.[200] This would be illogical. A new Calvinist carries this forth saying "God doesn't want to simply improve the old you."[201] Calvin elsewhere separates himself from this theory of the eradication of the depraved nature asserting:

---

[198] Romans 7:17
[199] John MacArthur, *Romans 1-9* in "The MacArthur New Testament Commentary," 386.
[200] Ephesians 4:24, Colossians 3:10.
[201] Mark Driscoll, "I am New: Sermon Recap," March 26, 2013, http://pastormark.tv/2013/03/26/i-am-new-sermon-recap, (Accessed October 17, 2013).

> another point is, that this corruption never ceases in us, but constantly produces new fruits—viz. those works of the flesh which we previously described, just as a burning furnace perpetually sends forth flame and sparks, or a fountain is ever pouring out water. For concupiscence never wholly dies or is extinguished in men, until, freed by death from the body of death.[202]

Salvation does produce fruit. Free grace theology does not deny this fact. What it, Scripture, and Calvin all deny is that one can judge someone based upon their fruit and make the determination whether or not they are truly saved. Thank the Lord that a person's salvation is not dependent upon their continual perseverance in good works. The believer can rest assured that they are saved as a free gift of grace apart from any anticipated obedience or the promise thereof. Paul explains that the believer once saved is always saved, despite the presence of sin in their life. Calvin explains that Paul:

> teaches that those whom the Lord has once admitted into favour, and ingrafted into communion with Christ… though they may be beset by sin and thus bear sin about with them. If this is the simple and genuine interpretation of Paul's meaning, we cannot think that there is anything strange in the doctrine which he here delivers.[203]

The presence of sin or denying Christ does not nullify faith or prove the non-existence of saving faith. This is the true teaching of "Calvinism." The teaching of lordship as it relates to confession, perseverance and depravity, whether they originated with MacArthur, Jonathan Edwards, Theodore Beza or anyone else were not those held by Calvin

---

[202] John Calvin, *Institutes of the Christian Religion*, Book 4, XV:11.
[203] Ibid.

and are not those evidenced in Scripture. Luther also affirmed "the old Adam is not entirely dead as yet."[204] The new Calvinists have almost universally taken up the mantle of the lordship position.

Trust

It has been said that the reformers save within justification an element that they referred to as *fiducia*. This concept adds to:

> a personal trust and reliance on Christ, and on him alone, for one's justification. *fiducia* also involves the affections. By the power of the Holy Spirit the believer sees, embraces, and acquiesces in the sweetness and loveliness of Christ. Saving faith loves the object of our faith, Jesus himself. This element is so crucial to the debate over justification. If a sinner relies on his own works or on a combination of his righteousness and that of Christ, then he is not trusting in the gospel.[205]

A personal trust and reliance on Christ and him alone for one's justification is the clarion call of free grace theology. Free grace theology is the only system that holds to *Sola Fide* with consistency. The lordship view's misunderstanding is caused by its attempt to put restrictions on who is justified by making submission part of belief by seeing depravity overcome at regeneration. This is unbiblical. Free grace theology is equally concerned about the potential for licentiousness as lordship proponents are, but the solution to this lies in a proper definition of faith. If faith is seen to be trusting in Christ for salvation, then this great display of

---

[204] Martin Luther qtd.in R.C. Sproul, *Grace Unknown,* 74.
[205] R.C. Sproul, *Grace Unknown: The Heart of Reformed Theology*, (Grand Rapids: Baker Books, 2000), 72.

grace will motivate the believer to serve God out of thankfulness. Assurance must always be grounded in the work of Christ. Calvin explains, "believers are taught to examine themselves carefully and humbly, lest carnal security creep in and take the place of assurance of faith."[206] This shows that assurance based in works only produces carnal security and not biblical assurance. Those who make a practice of sin (which is all believers) are still justified by faith alone. Any questioning of their salvation should be related to whether the Spirit is present, indwelling the believer and convicting them of their sin. It is in his concern for the possibility of licentiousness that MacArthur develops the concept of submission to the lordship of Christ. Even when he preaches grace, his theology of lordship is such that it maintains that there are some people who are living too sinfully to be considered saved. There are two possible responses to the question of what to do about all these sinners within the church. First, these people may be saved but they are grieving the Spirit of God. The other response is to say that they may not be saved if they have not trusted in Christ alone for their salvation.

Sanctification

MacArthur does recognize the inherent sinfulness of the believer. He also sees that any increase in holiness (sanctification) in the believer is truly an increased awareness of one's sinfulness. This results in righteous action rather than seeing the practice of righteousness in and of itself as sanctification. This is an area where later new Calvinism has departed from his understanding of sanctification. Although this part of his view of sanctification is commendable, MacArthur confuses discipleship's relation to conversion. Rather than seeing discipleship as an outgrowth of conversion, he sees conversion as contingent upon

---

[206] John Calvin, *Institutes of the Christian Religion*, Book 3, II:11.

discipleship. This is something that, as mentioned, new Calvinism holds too. Although MacArthur may not wish to use the word contingent, and instead frequently opts to refer to it as a necessary, it still remains a part of true conversion. He states, "you cannot be a disciple apart from a life of obedience and a desire to follow Christ as lord."[207] This is at the very least a seed of MacArthur's that has been implanted into others. More often than the new Calvinists, MacArthur uses softened words like the willingness of a believer to live a life of obedience rather than looking more explicitly at the practical righteousness of the believer in action. In this, he is choosing to look at motivation of the action over and above the actual practice of the action. This helps him in part to temporarily avoid the charge of teaching legalism. Notably, one new Calvinist changes the word choice of willingness to desire, thus moving the motivation from the will to the heart.

One major way new Calvinism is related to the theology of MacArthur is that they continue to blur the lines of distinction between conversion and discipleship. While MacArthur takes the stance that discipleship is an inevitable outcome of conversion, the new Calvinists will tend to take this even further. They will overlap positional sanctification and experiential sanctification. Eventually, they will reverse the order of sanctification and justification. It must be remembered that salvation (justification) is the free gift of God. This is apart from merit as well as requiring no obligation. An obligation is defined here as a promise of commitment not the expectation of commitment. While salvation is a free gift from God, there are resultant expectations placed on the believer, but there are no promises required for salvation.

Definition of Sanctification

---

[207] John MacArthur, *The Truth About the Lordship of Christ,* 48.

Overall, sanctification in MacArthur's understanding is defined as being set apart from sin.[208] Adding the words from sin takes the concept of sanctification too far when it functions within his theological system. What MacArthur is attempting to say, by defining sanctification in this way, is that the believer, at conversion, is set apart specifically from sin (positional sanctification). In practice, the believer is being set apart from sin in their life (experiential sanctification). In the end, the believer will be completely set apart from sin (ultimate sanctification). The problem in this understanding is that the experiential aspect of sanctification states that the believer will grow in Christlikeness. In so doing, they are actually becoming set apart from sin in their life, which implies an inevitable increase in practical righteousness. It is more accurate to state, in experiential sanctification, the believer is being set apart from the world (instead of sin). This choice implies that there is no necessary increase in practical holiness. This aligns well with the biblical teachings concerning depravity, carnality and the grieving of the Spirit. MacArthur shows that it is his desire to see an inevitable experiential sanctification as a requirement for salvation. By his choice of definition, sanctification "continues in increasing degrees of practical holiness in one's life and behavior."[209] He lays the foundation for a view that sees the inevitability of experiential sanctification in this life. This virtually eliminates the concept of a backsliding Christian because their actions show that they were never saved due to a lack of practical holiness. MacArthur would assuredly deny this, and it is not the purpose here to thoroughly examine his theology but to show that there are tendencies within it that the new Calvinists pick up on and develop further. This section is attempting to show how his theology lays the groundwork for new Calvinism.

---

[208] Ibid, 69.
[209] Ibid, 66.

Sanctification as an Obligation for Justification

In addition to this, MacArthur lays the foundation for a misunderstanding of justification. He claims that the believer is justified only when he submits to Christ as Lord saying, "when we trust Christ for salvation we settle the issue of who is in charge."[210] This statement is not as far from the truth, but Christ is in charge no matter what anyone says. What gets settled is not one's willing submission to Him, but the content of his or her faith. It is the recognition that Jesus is God. To put submission into the equation is to force a work upon conversion. If one sees the believer as exchanging self-control over his life for God's control, then he betrays the truth. God is in control of every life already, even the unregenerate person's life. This exchange mentality is not far from a works-based salvation. What changes in conversion is that the believer is actually justified through their faith as a free gift of God apart from works whether actual or anticipated. MacArthur affirms that the free gift of God "refers to that which is given completely apart from human merit" but then says that it is not apart from certain obligations.[211] Believers do have obligations (expectations of commitment), but the promise of commitment does not align with the nature of grace as a gift of God. Paul states:

τῇ γὰρ χάριτί ἐστε σεσῳσμένοι διὰ πίστεως· καὶ τοῦτο οὐκ ἐξ ὑμῶν, θεοῦ τὸ δῶρον· οὐκ ἐξ ἔργων, ἵνα μή τις καυχήσηται.[212]

Salvation is a gift and not ἐξ ἔργων (from works). BDAG defines ἔργον as "that which displays itself in activity of any kind."[213] Salvation that is accompanied with a promise of any

---

[210] Ibid, 65.
[211] John MacArthur, *Romans*, in "The MacArthur New Testament Commentary," 302.
[212] Ephesians 2:8–9, UBS⁴.
[213] William Arndt, Frederick W. Danker and Walter Bauer, *A Greek-*

kind is a salvation which displays itself in an activity. Salvation must be gifted apart from submission, even if it is only a willingness to submit. MacArthur contends in his commentary that "human effort has nothing to do with (salvation) and thus, **no one should boast**, as if he had any part. All boasting is eliminated in salvation."[214] Somehow in his view, submission is not a cause for boasting because he does not consider it a work. If submission is not considered a work, then why should one not consider obedience in the same way? New Calvinism will carry this line of thinking forward.

R.C. SPROUL

R.C. Sproul's contribution to the movement of new Calvinism has not been discussed in great detail. This is due in great part to their assumed commonality, but the theology of new Calvinism is not synonymous with the more traditional, covenantal Calvinism of Sproul. If this were not the case, then there would be nothing new about new Calvinism. Additionally, if those who are called new Calvinists have the same theology as R.C. Sproul, then new Calvinism is no longer an accurate title for the movement, and it would be more accurate to refer to them as young Calvinists. The new Calvinists are not simply young Calvinists, and they have departed from the traditional Calvinism of Sproul and others in significant ways. This would clearly include things like paedobaptism (for some), continuationism (in reference to spiritual gifts) and emergent ministry approaches. Perhaps most notable is the understanding that reformed theology does not actually need

---

English Lexicon of the New Testament and Other Early Christian Literature, 3rd ed. (Chicago: University of Chicago Press, 2000), 390.
[214] John MacArthur, *Ephesians* in "MacArthur New Testament Commentary," 61.

to be connected to the covenantal system. Platt laments this deficiency saying:

> there is also a growing need for covenant theology to be strongly reaffirmed in contemporary Reformed circles. In recent decades, many newer advocates of Reformed theology have neglected covenant theology.[215]

It is here the new Calvinists depart from Sproul, who is the contemporary traditional Calvinist par excellence. Sproul today could be considered the populous benchmark of Reformed theology despite the fact that today's young reformed theologians have grown up in a world which stands in opposition to the concept of a benchmark or ultimate standard.

It is not surprising then that they have departed from traditional confessional Calvinism and embraced the doctrines of grace in their own unique way. Rather than seeing the Westminster Confession (or another confession) as the shared heritage of all those who are truly reformed, today's new Calvinists see TULIP as unifying their theology.[216] New Calvinism is actually then an eclectic group of Calvinisms. This superstructure is what Sproul has provided to new Calvinism, provided a standard for their understanding of Christian orthodoxy and basis for their ecumenicity. This superstructure is more precisely Sproul's definitions of the terms of TULIP.[217] For him and the new

---

[215] Richard L. Pratt, Jr., "Reformed Theology Is Covenant Theology," in *Tabletalk Magazine*, 16.

[216] Although the Canons of Dordt are reflected in TULIP, the Canons include other doctrines. For example, article 17 states that only the children of believers are "holy."

[217] This is not to say that Sproul's definitions are definitive. Others, including Boettner, Steele and Packer, may be equally or even more valued.

Calvinists, total depravity is truly total inability; unconditional election is sovereign election, the atonement is limited in its application and in its provision, and preservation of the saints is perseverance of the saints.

It is interesting that new Calvinism abandons Sproul's covenantal structure but takes up TULIP as the unifying element of their dogmatic theology.[218] In this, they connect their theology to the authority of Sproul, Owen, Edwards, Calvin, and Augustine. This sense of authority is crucial for post-moderns struggling in a world that embraces relativism and denies absolute truth. Many have taken this ecumenism based in TULIP to an extreme, judging others based on TULIP as a test of orthodoxy. This is especially prevalent in the theologically diverse Southern Baptist Convention.

On New Calvinism

It is said that God's sovereignty is a uniquely unifying factor within all shades of Calvinism. Sproul states, "its understanding of salvation has as its control factor—its heart—a particular understanding of God's sovereign character."[219] Despite this claim, it is hardly determinative for drawing distinctions because there is no one, not even a full-fledged Arminian, who denies the sovereignty of God. It is often argued that those who ascribe to some system other than Calvinism deny the sovereignty of God in practice. This may be true, but it cannot be claimed definitively that God's sovereignty alone is their unifying factor. Could the

---

[218] By this it is meant that they view TULIP dogmatically. It is essential to their theology and will ardently defend it against all attacks. Other doctrines, like baptism and continuationism are deemed to be of secondary importance. They are not worth dividing over.

[219] R. C. Sproul, "Right Now Counts Forever: Fueling Reformation," in *Tabletalk Magazine, June 2010: The New Calvinism*, ed. Burk Parsons (Lake Mary, FL: Ligonier Ministries, 2010), 6.

determining factor then be God's sovereignty in salvation? This may be closer to what is perceived to be Calvinism, called Calvinist or causes people to self-identify as Calvinists.[220] More specifically God's sovereignty may be the process of salvation passed down through Sproul (and others) where new Calvinists get their shared heritage.

The Process of Salvation

The process of salvation is well defined and well defended by those who ascribe to a full five-point Calvinist soteriology. It is said that man is depraved. This depravity or corruption is total in that it extends to every part of his being. It is not utter depravity in that no man is as evil as he possibly can be; even Hitler was limited in the extent of his depravity. Total depravity simply means that man cannot, in and of himself, will to be saved. He is in bondage to sin and cannot come to Christ apart from the direct work of God. Because of this, God by necessity needs to elect some to be saved. This election must be unconditional because if it is left conditioned on anything in man, then salvation will never happen. Therefore, unconditional election must grow out of total depravity. From these two points comes limited atonement. As Palmer describes, "according to the Calvinist, Christ intended or purposed that His atonement should pay for the sins of only those the Father had given Him."[221] If God had unconditionally elected some, then to them it follows logically that Christ's death is only applicable to some. To declare that the atonement is unlimited is to declare that there is some wasted blood of Christ. If these three premises are true, then it also follows that God must accomplish His purposes in those whom He has elected. If the elect must be saved, then God must work in them in such

---

[220] Carl Trueman of Westminster believes this to be true.
[221] Edwin H. Palmer, *The Five Points of Calvinism,* (Grand Rapids, MI: Baker Books, 1972),42.

a way that He shows His grace to them in an irresistible manner. It also follows from here that if all these premises are true, then the saved person must persevere in faith until the end of their life. As a logical outgrowth of this, regeneration must precede faith. Sproul explains this idea:

> Reformation theology insists that regeneration that changes the heart of the sinner must precede faith. My perception of the value of Christ must change before I will ever embrace him or personally trust him.[222]

This is the philosophical system of TULIP Calvinism that Sproul, although not likely originating with Calvin, which has been passed on to new Calvinism. It is ironic that Sproul himself does not like the acronym TULIP preferring radical depravity, sovereign election, definite atonement, effectual grace, and preservation of the saints.[223]

It is important to remember that TULIP Calvinism is a philosophical system and not a biblical one. It works well because its premises can be easily argued by prooftexting Scripture and refuting the five points of modern (Wesleyan) Arminianism. Scripture's view of the doctrines of grace is much larger and more complex than the philosophical system of TULIP Calvinism would have one believe. If one were to rely on TULIP as the logical basis for their soteriology, then they would be forced to conclude, if consistent, that:

> faith is not really a condition for salvation. Rather, regeneration is a pre-condition for faith, which in turn is a consequence of irresistible grace, which is a consequence of unconditional election, and so on[224]

---

[222] R.C. Sproul, *Faith Alone: The Evangelical Doctrine of Justification*, 87.
[223] R.C. Sproul, *Chosen by God*.
[224] George Bryson, *The Dark Side of Calvinism: The Calvinist Caste*

This is not the natural reading of Scripture. It is eisegesis used to support a system. The biblical teaching is complex, and this is especially true when it comes to total depravity. Classical Arminians[225] also ascribe to total depravity, so it is possible to assent to total depravity without also believing in the rest of TULIP. TULIP might not then derive from total depravity by necessity. The key to this discussion revolves primarily around the proper definition of total depravity and secondarily on the proper definition of perseverance.

Regeneration Precedes Salvation

Overall the process of salvation, according to Sproul, is very linear. He sees the process of salvation in the following way:

Regeneration → Faith → Justification → Sanctification → Glorification

It is of crucial importance to make regeneration precede faith because faith is impossible apart from regeneration in their understanding. Sproul states:

> Reformation theology insists that regeneration that changes the heart of the sinner must precede faith. My perception of the value of Christ must change before I will ever embrace him or personally trust him.[226]

He believes "in regeneration, God changes our hearts."[227] It is because of total inability that man must be born again in

---

System (Santa Ana, CA: Calvary Chapel Publishing, 2004), 222.
[225] Cf. Roger E. Olson, *Arminian Theology: Myths and Realities,* (Downers Grove, IL: InterVarsity Press, 2006).
[226] R.C. Sproul, *Faith Alone: The Evangelical Doctrine of Justification*, 87.
[227] R. C. Sproul, *Chosen by God* (Wheaton, IL: Tyndale House

order to be able to believe. This misunderstands the biblical teaching that regeneration proceeds from and does not precede faith. The danger of preaching regeneration prior to faith is that it tends towards hyper-Calvinism. Men are no longer responsible for coming to Him, or believing in Him because they cannot do so apart from the special grace of God.[228] Faith ceases to be what is truly needed. In addition to this, how can God justify the ungodly if they are already regenerate, even if it is only logical?[229] What they fail to see is that they can be simultaneous, even logically. Free grace theology has allowed this biblical difficulty to remain. Sproul recognizes this saying:

> I think is the most serious issue dividing Dispensationalism and Reformed theology. I answered that the most significant difference, at least in the long run because of its impact on theology as a whole, may be the different views of regeneration. According to Dispensationalism when the Holy Spirit regenerates a person, nothing really happens to effect change in the person's constituent nature.[230]

Overall, the reformed view is very linear and ties justification to sanctification. They place importance on assurance, but ultimately one can only have assurance if they are currently persevering in faith and good works. The difficulty then arises concerning how a new believer can know whether he is regenerate because he lacks any evidential works. Their solution to this is to tie in works as an immediate result of regeneration. Sproul explains:

Publishers, 1986), 118.
[228] Iain H. Murray, *Spurgeon Vs. The Hyper-Calvinists: The Battle for Gospel Preaching.* (Carlisle, PA: Banner of Truth Trust, 1995), 113.
[229] Cf. Romans 4:5.
[230] R.C. Sproul, *Grace Unknown: The Heart of Reformed Theology*, electronic ed. (Grand Rapids: Baker Books, 2000), 192.

the fruit of obedience is both inevitable and necessary; it is immediate. Obedience is by no means perfect, nor does it in any way contribute to the ground of one's justification. Its absence, however, points to the absence of regeneration.[231]

The problem with this is assurance cannot be found in good deeds but only in the Spirit's working within.

Charles Hodge is one reformer who has departed from this linear understanding of salvation choosing instead to see regeneration "as a consequence or result of faith. Regeneration occurs because of faith."[232] Murphy expresses the more traditional reformed understanding in Sproul's *Festschrift*, saying "man is so helpless in the matter of eternal salvation that God has to give him faith in order for him to believe."[233] What is then contributed to new Calvinism is the concept that faith is given to man and is given to man is such a way that it will ultimately persevere. What is truly the gift of God then is not faith but faithfulness; an enduring faith.

Total Depravity

Total depravity is all too often seen to be synonymous with total inability. Sproul, and many other reformed thinkers like him, have chosen to see the biblical teaching on depravity as the first integral cog in the mechanism of TULIP's the process of salvation. While it is true that Scripture affirms that man's will is in bondage to sin apart from Christ and this results in the inability of man to be saved apart from the drawing of the Spirit, it is only a limited

---

[231] Ibid, 193.
[232] Charles Hodge qtd.in R.C. Sproul, *Grace Unknown*, 195.
[233] Martin Murphy, "Total Depravity" in *After Darkness Light: Essays in Honor of R.C. Sproul,* edited by R.C. Sproul Jr. (Phillipsburg, NJ: P & R Publishing, 2003), 21.

view of depravity that leads to Sproul's version of Calvinistic soteriology. All too often within Reformed theology, the depravity of man is only mentioned as it relates to the unregenerate man. They overemphasize the new creation that man becomes in Christ and see depravity as being overcome through regeneration. This is not something that Scripture teaches. The doctrine of depravity has a greater fullness than many reformed thinkers give it. Depravity continues in the regenerate man and by neglecting this, many reformed theologians (especially the Puritans) tended towards a perfectionism or legalism to prove regeneration. There also is a tendency to mix sanctification and justification. This is bound to happen when one looks at depravity only as it relates to the process of salvation in TULIP. This shortcoming is seen in the writings of Berkhof, Strong, Dabney and Buswell. Hodge, on the other hand, affirms that original sin "retains its character as sin even in the regenerated."[234] All these great thinkers, Sproul included, no doubt assert man will remain sinful as long as he lives. If this is the case, then why has this doctrine so often been neglected? It is likely due to the reformed demand to see an immediate change in the life of a believer brought about by conversion. Sproul states "the justified person is manifestly a *changed* person who is regenerated and indwelt by the Holy Spirit."[235] He later explains, "the Reformed position argues that fruit begins immediately, because a justified person is a regenerate person and a regenerate person is a changed person."[236] The point of disagreement between free grace theology and Sproul on this matter is whether the fruit of regenerate is visible and immediate. Free grace denies that the fruit of regeneration will necessarily be visible to others

---

[234] Charles Hodge, *Systematic Theology,* (Peabody, MA: Hendrickson Publishers), 2:230.
[235] R.C. Sproul, *Faith Alone: The Evangelical Doctrine of Justification*, 168.
[236] Ibid, 169.

and may not occur immediately in the life of a believer. There is an inward desire within the regenerate man to change, but not necessarily an outward obedience seen in action. The Spirit indwells the regenerate man so inevitably there will be conviction within the newly regenerate man. To not have the conviction of the Spirit casts serious doubt on the authenticity of the faith of one professing belief. Do they really trust in Christ alone for their salvation? This does not give one reason to judge their eternal destinies. Instead, one should be willing to counsel others that without the conviction of the Spirit in their sins, they do have reason to question whether the Spirit indwells them. Sproul's understanding of depravity is limited in that he only relates the doctrine to its implications for TULIP. He states:

> total depravity means that I and everyone else are depraved or corrupt in the totality of our being. There is no part of us that is left untouched by sin. Our minds, our wills, and our bodies are affected by evil.[237]

There is some incongruence in his theology as he approaches Romans 7. He retells the story of his personal struggle with trying to quit smoking and states, "there is no doubt about the abiding sins that mar our lives."[238] He affirms in his exegesis of this passage that the believer is able to have habitual sin in their life but what separates them from the unbeliever is the inward conviction of the Holy Spirit. This is sound, but he elsewhere asserts in reference to Romans 7:

> despite the ongoing struggle and the failures into sin that mark this Christian life, Paul knows that he is a new creature. What God has done with him can be

---

[237] R.C. Sproul, *Essential Truths of the Christian Faith* (Wheaton, IL: Tyndale House, 1992).
[238] R.C. Sproul, *Roman: The Righteous Shall Live by Faiths* in "The St. Andrews Expositional Commentary Series," (Wheaton, IL: Crossway Books and Bibles, 2009), 228.

seen not in the remnants of his old man, but in the triumph that God has given him through his Holy Spirit in the new man.[239]

To him, one's assurance of salvation can be found in works of righteousness. This is a difficult position to hold consistently.

What Sproul and many others fail to see the true enormity of sin in relation to God. This is a minimizing of the holiness of the Lord. Their basic outlook is that man is depraved and then after regeneration he commits sins, but these are relatively minor in comparison to the sins of his past. The unregenerate man is totally depraved, while the regenerate man is only somewhat depraved. Depravity should literally be understood as man's failing the test. Man fails the test of pleasing God. This is what God desires from man, but man is unable to do this because he is willfully in bondage to sin. After conversion, there is a sense in which man is able to please God, but this is miniscule when compared to the magnitude of the violation that sin is in the eyes of the Lord. These sins have been forgiven, but they nevertheless have consequences. There may be temporal judgment or chastisement, and there is definitely a loss of fellowship with God. If it were not for man's continued depravity (failing the test), then confession (in order to restore fellowship) would not be necessary. Man still continues to fail the test of God after conversion. Sproul and the new Calvinists are placing too much focus upon regeneration, and the positive aspects to conversion. They tend to gloss over the continued sinfulness of regenerated man. Sproul even admits, as a Christian, he experienced habitual sin in his life. While Sproul admits the true distinction between the regenerate and unregenerate man can be found in the testimony of the Spirit who dwells within

---

[239] Ibid, 242.

them and convicts them of their sin, those who follow in his theological footsteps are not so careful. For example, the statement; "because if you died to sin, you can't go on living in it. Or to put it bluntly: Dead people don't sin."[240] A rallying cry can be heard that it is faith alone without works that justifies but faith that justifies is not alone. There must be good works to prove, or show evidence of, one's salvation otherwise you are not saved. This leads into perseverance as well. This is the wrong perspective. The biblical teaching is, before salvation men are sinners and after they remain sinful. This truly is *Sola Gratia*. God does not take into account that the believer's life will still have sin in it after he is saved. Not only this, the believer will have sins too numerous to count. To deny this is to deny the true nature of sin in the eyes of the Lord. What lordship proponents so ardently and continually attempt to do is to show that the true church of God is a righteous one. Christians today should strive for good works, just like their Puritan forefathers. The problem is that by any measurement sinfulness exceeds righteousness, even in the regenerate man. This is what it means to understand the true magnitude of sin. Depravity remains. As Murphy so correctly asserts, "the more we grow in sanctification, the more we understand the depth of our sin, and so the more wretched we seem to be."[241] Why then is there this continual teaching about faith producing works? There is likely a reason why so many young people have been attracted to this theology. This may be due to the shallowness of many within American churches who profess faith in Christ and live unrepentantly sinful lifestyles. This would be poignant to many young people who grew up in the era of seeker-sensitive churches. The answer to this problem

---

[240] John Piper, "Are We to Continue in Sin That Grace Might Increase?" September 10, 2000. http://www.desiringgod.org/resource-library/sermons/are-we-to-continue-in-sin-that-grace-might-increase, (Accessed September 5, 2013).
[241] Martin Murphy, "Total Depravity," 26.

lies in understanding that it is whether someone has trusted in Christ's provision for their salvation, not whether their sinfulness outweighs their righteousness. Sin does not show evidence of an unregenerate state. If true, this would erase the doctrine of assurance. What good is the greatest righteous deed when, as Sproul explains, "even the smallest sin is an act of rebellion against God. Every sin is an act of cosmic treason, a futile attempt to dethrone God in His sovereign authority."[242] It is better to trust in Christ's righteousness alone for assurance rather than his or her own.

Perseverance of the Saints

Sproul sees the practical Christian life as an inevitably victorious one. He says, "this is important to maintain if we are to avoid the antinomian error of assuming that God justifies people who are and remain unchanged."[243] It is certainly true that the Christian life will ultimately be a victorious one. This victory concerns glorification and not experiential sanctification. All too often forgotten is Romans 8:30: "those whom he predestined he also called, and those whom he called he also justified, and those whom he justified he also glorified." The believer is never guaranteed ultimate victory in experiential sanctification. This does not stop Sproul from arguing, "the process of sanctification is a victory. It is a victory because Christians live in the Spirit. A struggle is not an indication of defeat."[244] It becomes clear that, for these theologians, the true believer (the one who experiences victory) conquers sin more often than not. The conclusion becomes unavoidable that the difference between true victory and (hypothetical) defeat is a percentage game or some variation thereof. If sin is not conquered in this way,

---

[242] R. C. Sproul, *Essential Truths of the Christian Faith*.
[243] R.C. Sproul, *Faith Alone: The Evangelical Doctrine of Justification*, 111.
[244] Ibid, 26.

then true faith does not exist. This inevitably ties assurance with perseverance. The result is a lack of assurance.

It must be recognized that it is the Spirit working within the believer that gives one grounds for assurance and not the actions themselves. The problem lies in looking at the actions to give one assurance. Sproul sees this partly and recognizes that the biblical teaching concerning eternal security is better described as preservation and not perseverance. It is all too common in new Calvinist discussions of sanctification, steeped in MacArthur's lordship salvation, to fail to distinguish between perseverance and preservation. In new Calvinism, one falsely believes "I know I am saved because I do good things." How then can one really know that they are saved? Could they not be like the Pharisees who are righteous in deeds but lack faith? Faith must be the sole grounds for justification and assurance. Assurance of salvation can be found in the Spirit's working. Someone can look on their new life (lit. their regenerated life) and compare it with their previous unregenerate life and see the Spirit's work. This working of the Spirit should provide confirmation of regeneration, but salvation should not be judged based on the presence of good works themselves. This would imply that salvation is contingent upon these works. While these works can provide the believer with assurance when contrasted with the works of the unregenerate man this should only be done with self-examination. It is only the legalistic Pharisees who say, "I know I am saved because I am not like the world." This is a grave error to be avoided. Additionally, one should not forget the Spirit's work of conviction in the believer. It is only the believer who has the Spirit within them to convict them in their sin. This is differentiated from the conscience of the unbeliever in that, generally speaking, the conscience makes one feel guilty for wrong actions while the Spirit convicts one of sinful motives.

Social Activism

Most people who have been in a Christian bookstore recently have no doubt seen one of the many books entitled or concerning gospel-centeredness. This can be gospel-centered discipleship, gospel-centered ministry, et cetera. This seems like a good thing at first glance. How can one argue with what appears to be a return to the biblical gospel? In actuality this is something completely different.

Not long ago, there emerged a liberal form of Christianity that saw the church as the enactor of social justice.[245] It is said that the church is to share all things in common and care for the poor and the needy; this is the true gospel message. It does not involve a call to repentance and salvation, but a call to social action. Out of this came perversions like liberation theology that became especially prominent in Latin America. In many respects, gospel-centeredness is a call to action new Calvinism has issued to the church alongside the propositional gospel. It is a merging of the orthodox understanding of the gospel as a call to personal reconciliation to God with the gospel of social justice:

> for centuries, the church understood her task as both to proclaim the saving gospel of the atoning work of Christ and, at the same time, to follow Jesus' example of ministry to the blind, to the deaf, to the imprisoned, to the hungry, to the homeless, and to the poor. The ministry of the church, if it is to be healthy, must always be firmly committed to both dimensions of the biblical mandate, that we may be faithful to

---

[245] This thinking is still present in many church/denominations worldwide.

Christ Himself. If we reject either the ministry of personal redemption or of mercy to the afflicted, we express 'unbelief.'[246]

This concern for social welfare fuels the ecumenicity of the new Calvinism. This is not too surprising since many liberals within Presbyterianism have emphasized the social dimension of their gospel over and above any evangelistic message. Knowing that the social gospel is not the biblical gospel, Sproul and other new Calvinists describe the merging of social gospel with the evangelistic gospel as the gospel in all its fullness. Sproul calls this the whole gospel, insinuating the insufficiency of the evangelistic gospel. It needs to be said that there is only one gospel, and it does not involve a call to social action. Justice is a concern for the church, but it is not the gospel of Christ. Sproul explains the church is not to teach that the gospel is about the offering of salvation made possible through faith, instead:

> we are to teach the gospel of Christ to all nations so that people may be transformed spiritually, but this spiritual renewal is for the sake of extending the lordship of Christ to every facet of culture around the world.[247]

Sproul's work, *Lifeviews: Make an Impact on Culture and Society,* is about the subject of the gospel being about more than life transforming and includes cultural transformation. He includes lessons on how Christians are to transform economics, science, art, literature and government. One is left wondering why Jesus never attempted to correct the

---

[246] R.C. Sproul, *Do We believe the Whole Gospel?* December 1, 2010, http://www.ligonier.org/learn/articles/do-we-believe-whole-gospel/, (Accessed September 5, 2013).
[247] Richard L. Pratt, Jr., "Reformed Theology Is Covenant Theology" in *Tabletalk Magazine, June 2010: The New Calvinism*, ed. Burk Parsons, 17.

social injustices of His day. He chose instead to say, "there will always be poor among you."[248] Jesus not once is recorded as trying to change the culture of His time. According to the social gospel, Paul's exhortation for Philemon to return to his master seems illogical. The new Calvinists that follow Sproul in this endeavor are trying to reform the world through the church, but instead of following liberal proponents of the social gospel movement, they have chosen to walk in the footsteps of Puritans. There is always a tendency within those who espouse this version of the gospel to place any evangelistic message of the gospel as secondary in importance to the social dimension of their gospel. Sproul even believes that the overarching purpose of personal salvation is cultural transformation saying, "this spiritual renewal is for the sake of extending the lordship of Christ to every facet of culture around the world."[249] In examining the core values of a prominent new Calvinist church, virtually nothing is said about personal conversion and most of their values revolve around the concept that Christians are to be agents of cultural change. It is said:

> we believe that the gospel has a deep, vital, and healthy impact on the arts, business, government, media, and academy of any society. Therefore we are highly committed to support Christians' engagement with culture.[250]

If TULIP is what unites new Calvinism theologically, it is the addition of social elements to the biblical Gospel that helps to unite their ministry practices. More will be discussed on this below.

---

[248] Matthew 26:11.
[249] Ibid, 17.
[250] Redeemer Presbyterian Church, "Core Values," http://www.redeemer.com/about_us/vision_and_values/core_values.html, (Accessed September 5, 2013).

George Ladd

The influence of George Ladd on this generation has been tremendous, but it has also often been overlooked. Ladd describes his theological vision succinctly in the thesis of *Jesus in the Kingdom* saying:

> for Jesus, the kingdom of God was the dynamic rule of God which has invaded history in its own person and mission to bring men in the present age the blessings of the messianic age, and which would manifest itself yet again at the end of the age to bring this same messianic salvation to its consummation.[251]

The kingdom of God is already inaugurated but not yet present or consummated. Many have taken the mantle of this already/not yet terminology[252] and applied it to various aspects of soteriology. Various aspects of salvation, like sonship, sanctification and justification, are seen to be a present reality that is yet to be consummated. This author has chosen to describe this trend as post-Laddian soteriology. This is because reformed soteriology after Ladd has seen an increased application of the already/not yet terminology to various aspects of soteriology. New Calvinism also applies this to justification choosing to see a consummation of justification at the Bema Seat of Christ. This is an attempt to have their cake, and it eat it too. This is why there is a growing tendency to hold to mutually exclusive theological concepts simultaneously under the auspices of the already/not yet paradigm. It allows one to assent to virtually

---

[251] George Eldon Ladd, *Jesus and the Kingdom,* (Waco,TX: Word Books, 1964), 303.

[252] It is recognized that Ladd did not originate the "already/not yet" terminology. The terminology likely originated with Gerhardus Vos, but it is ascribed to Ladd because he is the one who popularized this view. This is similar to the way in which Scofield popularized much of the view of Darby.

any orthodox statement on salvation while at the same time departing from it. This, in part, is a fulfillment of what House describes as one of the "dangers of Progressive Dispensationalism."[253] When specifically talking about matters of eschatology, House explains that there is no solid resting place between pretribulational premillennialism and amillennial theology once one begins to abandon the former. When one begins to spiritualize portions of Scripture, who is to determine what is properly allegory and what is literal. When one takes this approach to eschatology, why not use this grammatical-historical-theological hermeneutic more broadly? When one begins to hold the already/not yet paradigm of eschatology, then why not apply it to soteriology?

POSTMODERNISM

Nothing in the recent past has had a greater impact theologically than the shift from modernism to postmodernism. Many different people have characterized this shift at length in a plethora of fields. A concise definition is difficult to come by, but one will be attempted. The term postmodernism is descriptive of a movement that began in the arts, then architecture, English and philosophy before eventually describing culture, especially American culture, as a whole. It is related to the outgoing modern mindset as a specific departure from or reaction to the limitations of modernism. Modernism itself is characterized by rationalism and a belief that a peaceful utopian society is possible with the advancement of science and technology. What unifies these various fields of study is their "rejection of the Enlightenment project and the foundational assumption upon which it was built."[254] While post-modernism's effects and

---

[253] H. Wayne House in *Progressive Dispensationalism: An Analysis of the Movement and Defense of Traditional Dispensationalism,* Ron J. Bigalke Jr., ed., (Lanham, MD: University Press of America, 2005), 328.

duration are still being understood, there has unquestionably been a theological reaction to the rationalism of the modern man.

In a world consumed by the postmodernism, there is an ever-diminishing value being placed on truth claims. Postmodern epistemology has shifted from an attempt to corporately understand the absolute truth to an attempt to find out what works best for the individual. Truth becomes relative, and a situational ethic blossoms. Grenz describes postmodern epistemology in this way:

> the postmodern worldview operates with a community-based understanding of truth. Not only the specific truths we accept, but even our understanding of truth is a function of the community in which we participate. This, in turn, leads to a new conception of the relativity of truth.[255]

It is from this postmodern mindset that the movement of new Calvinism has emerged.[256] In the postmodern worldview, all truth is relative and subjective. While something may be true to one person, it does not necessarily follow that it is true universally. New Calvinism may be seen in part as a reaction to this broader worldview. Rather than offering personal truth, those within the new Calvinist movement have sought to articulate biblical truth in a way that moves beyond the personal. They have, therefore, rooted their theological understanding in history.

---

[254] Stanley J. Grenz, "Postmodernism and the Future of Evangelical Theology: Star Trek and the New Generation," *Evangelical Review of Theology* 18, no. 4, (1994): 328
[255] Ibid.
[256] This should not be surprising since Mark Driscoll, one of the most prominent new Calvinists, was involved in the emerging church, a harbinger of postmodern theology.

Practically speaking, the god of postmodernism is tolerance. The onus placed on tolerance works itself out in new Calvinism. Tolerance produces doctrinal shallowness and a theological hodgepodge. In new Calvinism, there is a great deal of latitude on what they view as ancillary issues. One new Calvinist stated that "debates rage in every direction on a list of secondary border issues...Is Genesis 1-3 to be interpreted literally...was there death of any kind before the fall."[257] Apparently it has yet to be decided within new Calvinism whether death came before the fall (cf. Rom. 5:12-17). At other times, a lack of awareness of potential theological issues is present. The same new Calvinist stated:

> we believe that human beings, created in the image of God the Trinity (who is himself a worshiping community in the Godhead, are unceasing worshipers who continually outpour all they are, all they do, and all they can ever be in Christ.[258]

One is left bewildered about whether anyone has ever been an unceasing worshiper of Christ this side of heaven. If one does not worship Christ at all times, does that make him a non-believer? Elsewhere in new Calvinism, the local church is defined as follows: "the local church is a community of regenerated believers who confess Jesus Christ as Lord."[259] This is a truly perplexing definition. It is also said that "repentance means acknowledging our foolishness, turning to Jesus for help, and leaning into God's grace to do whatever it takes to get out of our situation"[260] How can one who claims to be a Calvinist state such a thing? These statements betray a lack of theological depth. Nowhere is this more

---

[257] Mark Driscoll, *A Call to Resurgence: Will Christianity Have a Funeral or a Future?*, 126.
[258] Ibid, 133.
[259] Ibid, 132.
[260] Ibid, 180.

evident than in eschatology. It has been said by a prominent new Calvinist, "I lean historic premillenial but would not die on that issue, let alone suffer a paper cut for it."[261] While the previous generation grew up with conferences about prophecy, many new Calvinists do not wish to get sidetracked on these unnecessary, and potentially divisive, issues. What they fail to see is the interrelatedness of theology and its various branches.[262] New Calvinism follows postmodern trends in culture and has a pick-and-mix theology. Absolute truth is undermined in favor of an attitude favoring the choosing of individual doctrines someone feels are most biblical. It is far from a systematized theology because, in postmodernism, there is a deep distrust of theological systems. This is in part how new Calvinism can be reformed without being covenantal (or dispensational). As the saying goes: doctrines divide.

---

[261] Ibid, 137.
[262] It is truly surprising the undue emphasis being placed on biblical theology over and above systematic theology.

CHAPTER 3

A CALVINIST SOTERIOLOGY?

Much has been written in recent years concerning the relationship between Calvin and those who are known today as Calvinists (i.e. the various Calvinisms). There are two basic approaches. The first is Calvin against the Calvinists as articulated by R.T. Kendall in *Calvin and English Calvinism to 1649*. His basic thesis: what is called Calvinism today is not the theology of John Calvin. This is especially true in regards to the doctrine of limited atonement. In response to this work, Paul Helm wrote *Calvin and Calvinism,* which sought to refute Kendall, and argued for the essential unity between Calvin and Calvinism. In a more recent work, Richard Muller sides with neither Kendall nor Helm. Corresponding to this discussion is whether the entity referred to as reformed theology is truly the theology of the Reformation. Muller states, "we have no indication from Calvin's correspondence that his theology was viewed as the primary expression of Reformed thought in his generation."[263] The terms Calvinism and reformed theology are not necessarily indicative of Calvin or the Reformation. This point needs to be understood.

Most new Calvinists are inclined to equate Reformation theology with Calvin and TULIP. This forms

---

[263] Richard A. Muller, *Calvin and the Reformed Tradition: On the Work of Christ and the Order of Salvation,* Kindle Edition, (Grand Rapids, MI: Baker Academic, 2012), loc 372-373.

the basis for their ecumenical agreement. Despite this, there remains a great deal of theological development between Calvin's *Institutes of the Christian Religion* and the reformed response to the Remonstrants, known as the Canons of Dordt. As Kennedy observes, "there are striking dissimilarities between Calvin's reading of scripture and that of the later Reformed tradition.[264] It will be shown that much of what is known as Calvinism follows in the line of others like Beza or Cocceius as much as it does from Calvin. No mater their origin, this theology eventually ruled the day in the Westminster Confession and the Three Forms of Unity, which are said to be the "north star" of Reformed Theology.[265] At best, they only resemble Calvin in part.[266]

ARE THEY TRULY CALVINISTS?

Are they truly Calvinists? Is it reformed soteriology? These are similar questions, but not exactly equivalent. What is called Calvinism today is typically equated with reformed theology, but one may examine Calvinism based just upon its divergence from the theology of Calvin. When the new Calvinists refer to themselves as Calvinists, they are not holding to the whole of reformed theology. The former President and Chancellor of Reformed Theological Seminary, Michael Milton, acknowledges that "English speaking Christianity is seeing a great resurgence of Calvinism-it may not look like what we are used to, it may not pass muster with most of our faculty at RTS, or at

---

[264] Kevin D. Kennedy, "Hermeneutical discontinuity between Calvin and later Calvinism,"
Scottish Journal of Theology 64.3 (Aug 2011): 312.
[265] Carl Trueman, Phone Conversation (June 18, 2013).
[266] David Larsen, professor emeritus at Trinity Evangelical Divinity School, believes this to be the origin of what is now known as Calvinistic theology, making it more Bezan theology codified at Westminster. David Larsen, Phone Conversation, (June 12, 2013). This would align well with the theology of New Calvinism.

Covenant or Westminster-but it is surely under the larger umbrella of Calvinistic movements."[267] There is some degree of separation between reformed theology and new Calvinism indicated by this prominent theologian, but there is not a total separation. This epitomizes the view of new Calvinism by those who ascribe to the reformed theology. It is concluded by these Calvinists: new Calvinism is not Calvinism but simply Calvinistic. This is an important semantic distinction made by Milton.

Repentance/Regeneration

One area where there is assumed to be agreement between modern Calvinists and the theology of Calvin appears when discussing the issue of repentance. In the typical Calvinist *ordo salutis,* regeneration is followed by repentance and faith. This stems from their understanding of depravity that asserts that the unregenerate man is incapable of repentance and faith apart from the regeneration brought about by the Spirit. Calvin, on the other hand, insists that repentance must follow faith. He states:

> we obtain by faith, both free reconciliation and newness of life
>
> from faith to repentance
>
> repentance not only always follows faith, but is produced by it, out to be without controversy
>
> those who think that repentance precedes faith instead of flowing from, or being produced by it as the fruit

---

[267] Michael A. Milton, "The Once and Future Calvin," at http://www.monergism.com/thethreshold/articles/onsite/Once&FutureCalvin.pdf, (Accessed September 5, 2013), 8.

> by the tree, have never understood its nature, and are moved to adopt that view on very insufficient grounds
>
> a man cannot seriously engage in repentance unless he knows he is of God[268]

Calvin also said, "in one word, then, by repentance, I understand regeneration, the only aim of which is to form in us anew the image of God."[269] If one holds faith to be the fruit of regeneration, then he is not being true to theology of Calvin. In seeking to differentiate between false and true professions of faith, Calvin introduced, but did not develop the concept of temporary faith whereby any profession of faith and corresponding assurance of salvation is not by necessity true faith. As Thorson explains, "the problem began, Kendall readily admits, with Calvin himself—primarily from Calvin's view of 'temporary faith' in the reprobate. This teaching sprang from Calvin's observation of apparent believers falling away."[270] Arminius and his later followers eventually developed this view.

For new Calvinists, regeneration is the real instrumental cause of salvation because it is this, which ultimately produces faith. It is said:

> if there is true regeneration then these elements of the fruit of the Spirit will be more and more evident in that person's life...genuine love for God and His people, heartfelt obedience to his commands, and the Christlike character traits that Paul calls the fruit of the Spirit, demonstrated consistently over a period of time in a person's life, simply *cannot* be produced by

---

[268] John Calvin, *Institutes of the Christian Religion,* Book 3, III:1-2, XII:1
[269] Ibid, Book 3, III:9.
[270] Stephen Thorson, "Tension in Calvin's View of Faith," 421.

Satan or by the natural man or woman working in his or her own strength[271]

Regeneration, though, does not entirely override the sinfulness of man. Only truly Spirit-filled believers have a heartfelt obedience to the Lord's commands and even the holiest people in Scripture (Jesus excluded) are deeply flawed. The man described above as the true believer is a myth. Even David, a man after God's own heart, would not have qualified as regenerate.

Volition

A great deal of energy has been wasted in an attempt to undermine free grace theology. Its opponents erroneously refer to free grace theology, as teaching that mere assent to Jesus is all that is required to possess a saving faith. This is a straw man argument. The crux of the difference between free grace theology and lordship salvation involves the latter's understanding of the volitional aspect to saving faith. Free grace theology has maintained that to believe in Christ means more than to simply acknowledge His existence. It requires one to place their trust in Him and His offer of salvation. Lordship proponents, of whom new Calvinists comprise in part, believe that man is required to do something in order to really trust in Christ. Their will or volition must be turned completely over to Him. Is this in line with Calvin? He defined faith in the following way:

> we shall now have a full definition of faith if we say that it is a firm and sure knowledge of the divine favor toward us, founded on the truth of a free promise in Christ[272]

---

[271] Wayne Grudem, *Systematic Theology,* 705-706.
[272] John Calvin, *Institutes of the Christian Religion*, Book 3, II:7.

Now, compare this with Sproul, who states, "personal trust and commitment, *fiducia,* is the third element of saving faith."[273] Kendall believes this drift occurred early in the reformed tradition. He says faith can be defined in Calvin's writings as "persuasion, assurance, or apprehension" while, in Beza, it is "applying or appropriating."[274]

There has been a subtle shift from *fiducia* as trust or confidence to also include commitment. For the new Calvinist, those not willing to count the cost and take up their cross are cannot be saved. One wonders, why they do not rest on the view that "*fiducia*, (is) a personal trust and reliance on Christ, and on him alone, for one's justification."[275] Calvin affirms this definition saying, "faith is a knowledge of the divine favor towards us, and a full persuasion of its truth."[276] The Westminster Catechism states, "faith in Jesus Christ is a saving grace, (Heb. 10:39) whereby we receive and rest upon him alone for salvation as he is offered to us in the gospel."[277] This being established; no new Calvinist would affirm Calvin's complete doctrine of faith. In this same section, Calvin explains concerning faith:

> were it not true that many fall away from the common faith (I call it common, because there is a great resemblance between temporary and living, everduring faith), Christ would not have said to his disciples, 'If ye continue in my word, then are ye my disciples indeed; and ye shall know the truth, and the truth shall make you free,' (John 8:31, 32). He is addressing those who had embraced his doctrine, and urging them to progress in the faith, lest by their

---

[273] R.C. Sproul, *Truths We Confess,* 2:123.
[274] R.T. Kendall, *Calvin and English Calvinism to 1649,* 61-62.
[275] R.C. Sproul, *Grace Unknown: The Heart of Reformed Theology*, electronic ed. (Grand Rapids: Baker Books, 2000), 72.
[276] John Calvin, *Institutes of the Christian Religion*, Book 3, II:12.
[277] Westminster Shorter Catechism, Question 86.

> sluggishness they extinguish the light which they have received. Accordingly, Paul claims faith as the peculiar privilege of the elect, intimating that many, from not being properly rooted, fall away…(Paul) compares a good conscience to the ark in which faith is preserved, because many, by falling away, have in regard to it made shipwreck[278]

> In saying elsewhere that the will is not taken away by grace, but out of bad is changed into good, and after it is good is assisted,—he only means, that man is not drawn as if by an extraneous impulse... by the free mercy of God, the will is turned to good... a will which can neither be turned to God, nor continue in God, unless by grace; a will which, whatever its ability may be, derives all that ability from grace.[279]

One can see from these statements where Arminius may have gotten some of his doctrines.

The Westminster Confession explains the volitional element of faith in the following way:

> By this faith, a Christian believes to be true whatsoever is revealed in the Word, for the authority of God Himself speaking therein; and acts differently upon that which each particular passage thereof contains; yielding obedience to the commands, trembling at the threatenings, and embracing the promises of God for this life, and that which is to come. But the principal acts of saving faith are accepting, receiving, and resting upon Christ alone for justification, sanctification, and eternal life, by virtue of the covenant of grace.[280]

---

[278] John Calvin, *Institutes of the Christian Religion*, Book 3, II:12.
[279] Ibid, Book 2, III:14.

Calvin's understanding of depravity is that people who have refused to acknowledge God end up with minds that are disqualified from being able to understand and acknowledge the will of God. Hodge explains that Beza's understanding of total depravity meant man is "incapable of judgment or discernment."[281] This is crucially important for understanding the nature of faith for new Calvinists. New Calvinism's belief that faith is linked to commitment likely originated with Beza and was propagated by the Westminster divines. A new Calvinist affirms this same understanding, saying:

> the approval of the facts of the gospel will also involve a desire to be saved through Christ. But all this still does not add up to true saving faith. That comes only when I make a decision of my will to depend on, or put my *trust* in, Christ *my* Savior. This personal decision to place my trust in Christ is something done with my heart, the central faculty of my entire being that makes commitments for me as a whole person.[282]

It remains obvious that what constitutes Calvinism in not the theology of Calvin. It also appears that Beza, and later Westminster standards may have been equally influential in determining what is referred to today as Calvinism.

The Drawing of God

One specific area where New Calvinism diverges from the theology of Calvin is the way in which God draws

---

[280] Westminster Confession XIV:2
[281] Charles Hodge, *Romans*, Crossway Classic Commentaries (Wheaton, IL: Crossway Books, 1993), 1:28.
[282] Wayne Grudem, *Systematic Theology,* 712.

man to himself. John 6:44 is the linchpin text for this discussion. Here, John uses the Greek word ἑλκύω. It has the following possible meanings according to BDAG:

1) to move an object from one area to another in a pulling motion, draw
2) to draw a person in the direction of values for inner life
3) to appear to be pulled in a certain direction, flow[283]

Sproul argues that drawing (ἑλκύω) "mean(s) to compel by irresistible superiority. Linguistically and lexicographically, the word means 'to compel.' To compel is a much more forceful concept than to woo."[284] Sproul and the new Calvinists define the drawing of God as literally the dragging of God, a word with striking negative connotation that does not align with the character of God. In addition to this, it is not what the word ἑλκύω actually means, but is instead forced upon it to support the author's theological views. One need only look to Jeremiah 31:3, where this word is used in the LXX. "The LORD appeared to him from afar, saying, 'I have loved you with an everlasting love; Therefore *I have drawn* you with lovingkindness'" (NASB)[285] or Song of Solomon 1:4 "Draw me after you; let us run. The king has brought me into his chambers. We will exult and rejoice in you; we will extol your love more than wine; rightly do they love you" (ESV). It is interesting that the ESV, with its reformed leanings, chooses not to translate it in this normative way. The concept of ἑλκύω comes from a loving place and is not forced upon anyone.

---

[283] William Arndt, Frederick W. Danker and Walter Bauer, *A Greek-English Lexicon of the New Testament and Other Early Christian Literature*, 318.
[284] R. C. Sproul, *Chosen by God* (Wheaton, IL: Tyndale House Publishers, 1986), 69.
[285] In the LXX this is Jeremiah 38:3.

Calvin did not define ἑλκύω as the new Calvinists. He viewed this drawing of God as being a wooing. He states:

> (God) continues to visit miserable sinners with unwearied kindness, until he subdues their depravity, and woos them back.[286]

> God is not left without a witness, while, with numberless varied acts of kindness, he woos men to the knowledge of himself, yet they cease not to follow their own ways, in other words, deadly errors.[287]

Elsewhere, Calvin describes the way in which God woos and overcomes the depravity of man's heart is through the enlightening of the mind:

> in order that the word of God may gain full credit, the mind must be enlightened, and the heart confirmed, from some other quarter.[288]

A loving God woos; the deterministic force of deism draws a man through compulsion.

Beza and Calvin

There is a great discussion being had within the reformed community on the relationship between Calvin and Calvinism and much of this is centered on the relationship between the theology of Beza and Calvin. There arose a period of development between the life of Calvin and the confessional reformed tradition. When one examines this period, a conclusion must be drawn on the relationship between Calvin and subsequent Calvinism. It appears from the writings of Calvin and Beza that there was some fairly

---

[286] John Calvin, *Institutes of the Christian Religion*, Book 1, V:7.
[287] Ibid, Book 1, V:15.
[288] Ibid, Book 3, II:7.

major differences between Calvin's soteriology and Beza's, which came to be later codified in the various reformed confessions. Kendall explains:

> while a strong doctrine of predestination tends to characterize the soteriology of Calvin's leading contemporaries in the Reformed tradition on the Continent, it appears Beza was the first of these to make the doctrine of predestination central to his system.[289]

This is something echoed in modern-day new Calvinism which equates true Calvinism with the doctrine of predestination.

Kendall views Beza as being the instigator of limited atonement. This has been a highly controversial conclusion. It appears that Calvin pictured the atonement through the lens of Christ's role as high priest. As the blood of the lamb was shed for all without exception, the sacrifice of Jesus was made for all indiscriminately. As the high priest offered up the actual sacrifice to the Lord and interceded for man, the sprinkling of the blood becomes applicable only for those the priest is interceding for. The blood is spilt for all, but only some of it is applied to the mercy seat. Calvin himself explains:

> in order that the atonement might take effect, he performed the office of an advocate, and interceded for all who embraced this sacrifice by faith[290]

---

[289] R.T. Kendall, *Calvin and English Calvinism to 1649,* Studies in Christian History and Thought Series, (Eugene, OR: WIPF & Stock, 1997), 29-30.

[290] John Calvin, *Isaiah*, electronic ed., Calvin's Commentaries (Albany, OR: Ages Software, 1998), Is 53:12.

yet I approve of the ordinary reading, that he alone bore the punishment of many, because on him was laid the guilt of the whole world. It is evident from other passages, and especially from the fifth chapter of the Epistle to the Romans, that "many" sometimes denotes 'all.'[291]

In looking at reformed thinkers after Calvin, Stewart claims:

the vast majority of older writers surveyed here preferred the language of 'particular atonement' or 'particular redemption' to the acronym's suggestion of an atonement that was 'limited'. But more than this, it is evident that in keeping with Dordt's original insistence that – as to the sheer value of Christ's dying, his death was 'abundantly sufficient to expiate the sins of the whole world' older writers often took pains to spell out the senses in which there were universal benefits in that particular redemption won by Christ.[292]

Importantly for this discussion is the fact that Beza's understanding of faith is based almost entirely upon his doctrines of predestination and assurance. It is said that Beza understands assurance to be based upon self-examination. Many new Calvinists propagate this today:

the doctrine of the perseverance of the saints, if rightly understood, should cause genuine worry, and even fear, in the hearts of any who are 'backsliding' or straying away from Christ. Such persons must clearly be warned that only those who persevere to the end have been truly born again. If they fall away from

---

[291] Ibid.
[292] Kenneth J. Stewart, "The Points of Calvinism: Retrospect and Prospect," *Scottish Bulletin of Evangelical Theology*, 26. 2 (2008): 187-203.

> their profession of faith in Christ and life of obedience to him, they may not be saved- in fact, the *evidence* that they are giving *is that they are not saved,* and they were never really saved. Once they stop trusting in Christ and obeying him (I am speaking in terms of outward evidence) they have no genuine assurance of salvation, and they should consider themselves unsaved[293]

Unfortunately, what Grudem calls a Calvinist and an Arminian "will both counsel a 'backslider' in the same way...'you do not appear to be a Christian now- you must repent of your sins and trust in Christ for salvation'" (Italics removed).[294] One is reminded of the repeated efforts of Luther to find this assurance based upon his outward conformity to Christ. He always lacked this assurance until he saw the biblical doctrine of justification by faith. In addition to this, most Baptists today know of someone who has struggled with assurance and has been baptized 3 times, or is known for repeatedly came forward during the altar call. But "Calvin firmly opposed any such attempt to base our assurance on something within ourselves."[295] Kendall believes this type of Puritan mindset is a departure from Calvin saying:

> while Calvin thinks looking to ourselves leads to anxiety, or damnation, Beza thinks otherwise. Sanctification, or good works, is the infallible proof of saving faith.[296]

This is known in reformed theology as the reflex act of faith. Hodge explains:

---

[293] Wayne Grudem, *Systematic Theology,* 806.
[294] Ibid.
[295] A.N.S. Lane, "Calvin's Doctrine of Assurance," *Vox Evangelica* 11(1979): 34.
[296] R.T. Kendall, *Calvin and English Calvinism to 1649,* 33.

The second objection was answered by distinguishing between the direct and the reflex act of faith. By the direct act of faith, we embrace Christ as our Savior; by the reflex act, arising out of the consciousness of believing, we believe that He loved us and died for us, and that nothing can ever separate us from his love. These two acts are inseparable, not only as cause and effect, antecedent and consequent; but they are not separated in time, or in the consciousness of the believer. They are only different elements of the complex act of accepting Christ as He is offered in the Gospel.[297]

The Canons of Dordt put it the following way:

> assurance of this their eternal and unchangeable election to salvation is given to the chosen in due time, though by various stages and in differing measure. Such assurance comes not by inquisitive searching into the hidden and deep things of God, but by noticing within themselves, with spiritual joy and holy delight, the unmistakable fruits of election pointed out in God's Word-- such as a true faith in Christ, a childlike fear of God, a godly sorrow for their sins, a hunger and thirst for righteousness, and so on.[298]

This is when the effect is drawn from the conclusion. For example, I am not hungry; therefore, I must have eaten. In this situation it is said, "I have the fruit of regeneration, therefore I am saved." This is not logically valid; it begs the question, not to mention the negative conclusion is worrisome. Assurance based in the subjective experience of

---

[297] Charles Hodge, vol. 3, *Systematic Theology* (Oak Harbor, WA: Logos Research Systems, Inc., 1997), 100.
[298] Canons of Dordt, Article 12, "Assurance of Faith".

man is something Calvin was ardently outspoken against. He states:

> if we are to determine by our works in what way the Lord stands affected towards us, I admit that we cannot even get the length of a feeble conjecture: but since faith should accord with the free and simple promise, there is no room left for ambiguity.[299]

> the believer finds within himself two principles: the one filling him with delight in recognizing the divine goodness, the other filling him with bitterness under a sense of his fallen state; the one leading him to recline on the promise of the Gospel, the other alarming him by the conviction of his iniquity; the one making him exult with the anticipation of life, the other making him tremble with the fear of death. This diversity is owing to imperfection of faith, since we are never so well in the course of the present life as to be entirely cured of the disease of distrust, and completely replenished and engrossed by faith. Hence those conflicts: the distrust cleaving to the remains of the flesh rising up to assail the faith enlisting in our hearts[300]

In addition to this, Beza is said to be the originator of supralapsarianism. Rogers states, "Beza was the first supralapsarian among the Reformers who rooted all theological affirmations in God's eternal decrees."[301] This is something that is not to be found in Calvin's theology, but can be seen in new Calvinism.

---

[299] Ibid, Book 3, II:38.
[300] Ibid, Book 3, II:18.
[301] Jack B. Rogers and Donald K. McKim, *The Authority and Interpretation of the Bible: An Historical Approach* (San Francisco: Harper & Row, 1979), 104.

IS THERE A CONSISTENT SOTERIOLOGY?

Answering the question of whether there is a truly consistent soteriology within new Calvinism is easier said than done. Despite this, it is possible to observe some beliefs that are characteristic of the movement. It is especially telling when the doctrinal stances are by new Calvinists are on matters frequently debated among evangelicals. For example, one of the stances taken by new Calvinists involves complementarianism over egalitarianism.[302] In terms of soteriology, it is best to begin with their understanding of sanctification. As discussed extensively later, sanctification is viewed as proving holiness and providing the believer with assurance. These statements are indicative:

> we believe that true Christians born again of God's Spirit will be kept by God throughout their life, as evidenced by personal transformation that includes an ever-growing love of God the Father through God the Son by God the Spirit, love of brothers and sisters in the church, and love of lost neighbors in the culture. [303]

> we also believe that these, the elect of God whom he gave to the Son, will persevere in belief and godly behavior and be kept secure in their salvation by grace through faith.[304]

> good works constitute indispensable evidence of saving grace.[305]

---

[302] This is not an issue that is worrisome, but it is mentioned because it shows that the movement does make telling theological stances at times.
[303] Together for the Gospel, Affirmations and Denials, Article VII.
[304] Acts 29 Network, "Doctrine," http://www.acts29network.org/about/doctrine/, (Accessed September 5, 2013).

Lordship salvation is a necessary part of their soteriology. Calvin though argues:

> in every age there have been some who, under the guidance of nature, were all their lives devoted to virtue. It is of no consequence, that many blots may be detected in their conduct; by the mere study of virtue, they evinced that there was somewhat of purity in their nature... some have not only excelled in illustrious deeds, but conducted themselves most honourably through the whole course of their lives [306]

Calvin admits there are many unregenerate men who appear to be holy based upon the evidences of their outward appearance. They even may excel at this. This may even occur throughout the whole course of their lives. Anyone attempting to understand the truly Calvinist doctrine of total depravity needs to read and understand Calvin's explanation of it. Man, whether unregenerate or regenerate, cannot be experientially righteous.

In addition to this, there is a definitive stance taken on the extent of the atonement. New Calvinists wholeheartedly ascribe to the doctrine of limited atonement. It is said:

> his determination to save his redeemed people[307]

> having set his saving love on those he has chosen and having ordained Christ to be their Redeemer.[308]

This corresponds with their anthropocentric understanding of perseverance of the saints, i.e. "where it (the Gospel) is

---

[305] The Gospel Coalition Confessional Statement, pt. 10.
[306] John Calvin, *Institutes of the Christian Religion*, Book 2, III:2.
[307] Together for the Gospel, Affirmations and Denials, Article VII.
[308] The Gospel Coalition, Confessional Statement, pt. 6.

received, believed, and held firmly, individual persons are saved." [309] When reaching its most consistent conclusion, salvation ultimately becomes dependent upon man's efforts to produce holiness in his life through the Spirit and to hold fast to his faith and repentance until the end of his life. This is not the theology of Calvin. For him, faith is confident in the work of Christ not in the fruits of regeneration or in one's perseverance. Calvin said:

> our faith is not true unless it enables us to appear calmly in the presence of God. Such boldness springs only from confidence in the divine favor and salvation. So true is this, that the term faith is often used as equivalent to confidence.[310]

This is true *sola gratia*, *sola fide* and *solus Christus*. Where these new Calvinists have diverted from Calvin's theology is part of what makes them unique. While the broad nature of the movement and lack of definition does not easily allow for a detailed doctrinal summary there is a degree of uniformity.

CASE STUDY:

Each major section of this work detailing theological trends within new Calvinism will have a corresponding case study. The purpose of these case studies is to show how the specific theological beliefs held by one, several, or all new Calvinists have deficiencies related to the *sine qua non* of new Calvinism. Each of their unique tenants has some troublesome element that need to be dealt with and corrected.

JOHN PIPER

---

[309] Ibid, pt. 7.
[310] John Calvin, *Institutes of the Christian Religion* Book 3, II:15.

In many ways, John Piper is the figurehead or father figure of new Calvinism.[311] Piper's popularity amongst young people, as well as seasoned theologians, is remarkable. What is perhaps surprising to many is that his views do not align well with the traditional reformed faith.[312] It must be asked: is he a wolf in sheep's clothing or has he simply allowed the pendulum to swing too far in one direction?

Red flags should automatically be raised when a well-known liberal seminary produces an outspokenly conservative theologian. It is a challenge to think of any truly biblical theologian who was the product of a seminary after it became liberal. Although he is viewed as a conservative Calvinist, his theology does not correspond with the heart of Calvinism and his view of the gospel, at times, is more in line with Arminianism.[313] Although he never expressly states that one can lose their salvation, he presses the believer to continually produce good works in order to be considered (in the future) as having eternal life. This is an extreme form of perseverance. Piper's general outlook is to see the believer increasing in holiness. This is evidenced by increased righteous behavior instead of an increased awareness of their sinfulness. One author has stated in reference to a theological system:

---

[311] His views are in some sense representative. One may object that his view of future justification is not indicative of New Calvinism as a whole, but an appendix of reviews from major New Calvinists can be seen to show that they are supportive of this controversial work. Cf. Appendix 2.

[312] As discussed above, the Westminster Confession and the Three Forms of Unity define reformed theology. Although not one version of reformed theology is held universally, it is broadly reflected by the covenantal system, which is represented systematically in the Westminster Confession. This is a general confession, which is held by most reformed theologians. This is usually known as Federal Theology.

[313] This is not meant in reference to the theology of Arminius, but as Arminianism is most commonly defined by Calvinists.

> generally, its theology has been marred by a denial of imputed sin and substitution in the cross by affirming a governmental approach (to the atonement). Grace and simple faith have been undermined by adding continuance in works as a condition for justification, which leads to legalism in both salvation and Christian growth. There is also a strong tendency towards sinless perfection.[314]

This could easily characterize Piper's view, but it is actually an evaluation of Arminianism and not Calvinism.

Piper preaches grace, but he betrays the biblical understanding of it in favor of a works-based religion. In this, he not only departs from the great doctrines of the Reformation but returns, in part, to Roman Catholic theology.[315] Nowhere is this more evident than in his view of justification, especially in his teaching on the future aspect of justification. In light of this, it may be best to classify Piper as being in a theological class by himself called limited atonement Arminianism. Other new Calvinists can be classified in the same way.

REDEFINING TERMS

In a theological dispute, it is very possible for two people to hold widely different understandings of Scripture while simultaneously affirming a common statement of faith. What most often differentiates opinions in theological matters involves how a theologian chooses to define terms.[316]

---

[314] C. Gordon Olson, *Beyond Calvinism & Arminianism: An Inductive, Mediate Theology of Salvation,* Third Edition, (Lynchburg, VA: Global Gospel Publishers, 2012), 17.

[315] This will henceforth be referred to as Romanism to distinguish itself from those within the Roman Catholic Church who hold to more evangelical doctrines in opposition to the church's hierarchy.

[316] A more recent new Calvinist supported work, *Stop Asking Jesus Into*

Defining terms is a major part of theology in general. Liberals have often used the redefining of traditional doctrines to show tacit agreement with historic orthodoxy while simultaneously subscribing to unbiblical beliefs. History is replete with examples of this. Piper is no different in this regard. Piper redefines concepts like justification in his own way. In so doing, he is able to affirm a belief in justification by faith alone, while building a theological system around the concept of future justification that inevitably produces justification by works. One must be alert when reading Piper (or anyone), being careful to see the redefining of commonly agreed upon theological definitions. It is the distinction between biblical concepts and Piper's redefinition of these theological terms that make his theology so dangerous. This concern does not even take into account the effect of his widespread popularity.

JUSTIFICATION

The most notable inconsistency in Piper's theology concerns justification. Some may say that a theological straw man will be constructed that misrepresents Piper in order to refute him because of his vociferous insistence that man is justified by faith alone. This is not the case. Instead, it is being argued that Piper has a true system of theological beliefs that are carefully disguised by wording commonly used in historic protestant doctrines. One should be alarmed when Piper makes statements like:

Your Heart: How to Know for Sure You Are Saved, is a great example. Greear's definitions, eternal life: "eternal life is not just a reality we enter into when we die; it is something that comes into us now, and its evidences appear everywhere. Seeing those evidences assures us eternal life is in us" (p. 24), salvation: "salvation is a posture of repentance and faith that you begin in a moment and maintain for the rest of your life" (p. 5), repentance: "repentance is belief in action" (p. 40), and belief: 'belief is the assumption of a new posture toward the Lordship of Christ and His finished work on the cross" (p. 40).

some have so changed the ordinary meaning of the word 'righteousness' that in the act of justification, it no longer refers to anyone's right attitude or right action but only to a courtroom verdict of acquittal.³¹⁷

This statement was made to the Evangelical Theological Society. What Piper is arguing is that being justified is being more than declared righteous; it is being righteous. This is what the Roman Catholic Church teaches.

There are times when Piper articulates an orthodox understanding of justification, but there are often times when he subtly betrays orthodoxy in his theological stances. There remain subtle, telling statements. This is especially true concerning the doctrine of justification. Many applaud Piper for his defense of orthodoxy, specifically related to the doctrine of justification, against the New Perspective on Paul school in his disputation with N.T. Wright. There is still cause for great concern. This is clearly seen in statements about "God's future time of judgment when our justification will be confirmed."³¹⁸ When Piper titles one of his works *The Future of Justification,* he is not simply writing concerning the future of the doctrine of justification within Protestantism but is actually writing from a perspective that believes justification is a future occurrence. This is due to a misunderstanding of δικαιόω, which is believed to occur in the future. It is best not to think of justification in this way because in its biblical usage, δικαιόω only occurs the future

---

³¹⁷ John Piper, "Justification and the Diminishing Work of Christ," November 14, 2007, at Evangelical Theological Society Annual Meeting http://www.desiringgod.org/resource-library/conference-messages/justification-and-the-diminishing-work-of-christ, (Accessed September 5, 2013).
³¹⁸ John Piper, *The Future of Justification: A response to N.T. Wright,* (Wheaton, IL: Crossway Books, 2007), 184.

form when speaking hypothetically about the possibility that a non-believer becoming justified.[319] This happens when one has turned to Christ in faith, not when a believer will be justified in the yet future. What Piper has chosen to do is see justification as an event in the life of a believer that is still to come. This is the crux of the issue.[320] It means that the present possession of justification for the believer is only true in theory. What Piper is arguing against is that justification by faith alone is an accomplished fact. This was the principle on which the Reformation was fought. He diverges from orthodoxy by asserting that the believer's actual justification is accomplished only after this life when works of obedience verifies it. Essentially, this means that one's justification is only true hypothetically until it is verified by his obedience at the end of his life. It is at this point that a believer's previous faith is credited to him, in the past tense, as salvific. This differs only semantically from the Roman teaching of justification by works. The believer then is instructed to live his Christian life in light of the future possibility of justification and the future possibility of God's grace, all in the hope that his obedience will be sufficient to be judged worthy of salvation. God sees a person's works when He looks back on his faithfulness and determines if it is saving faith. Lest the reader think that this is an argument based upon a straw man that has been built, here is a recent quote by Piper, reproduced in its entirety, from the Desiring God National Conference:

> When Paul says 'work out your salvation' the word (Greek *katergazesthe*) means 'produce it,' 'bring it

---

[319] Cf. Mt. 12:37, Gal. 2:16, Rom. 2:13, 3:20, 3:30.
[320] This was also a highly controversial teaching by Norman Shepherd, the former professor of Systematic Theology at Westminster Seminary (Philadelphia). Many within the reformed tradition have taken a stance against Shepherd but have not held Piper to the same standard. Also, cf. Excursus on the Norman Shepherd Controversy.

about,' 'effect it.' Peter O'Brien in his Philippians commentary sums it up with the words, '*continuous, sustained, strenuous effort.*' As dangerous as this language is, it is biblical. 'Bring about your salvation.' 'Produce your salvation.' 'Effect your salvation by continuous, sustained, strenuous, effort.'[321]

The believer produces his salvation through his own effort. This is justification by works. Piper frequently affirms justification by faith, but in following lordship salvation to this extreme, he is forced to make a distinction between salvific faith and non-salvific faith. The believer is said to be justified by saving faith which itself produces sufficient obedience to be judged worthy. This obedience is not simply the effect of justification but the cause of it. In another work on the imputation of Christ's righteousness, Piper looks to William Wilberforce's discussion of the practical errors of Christians in his day. Wilberforce claims that others in his day were "making the fruits of holiness *the effects, not the cause*, of our being justified and reconciled."[322] Piper states that this is a statement with which he "profoundly agrees."[323] It is puzzling how one can say that personal holiness is the cause of justification while maintaining that justification is by faith alone. One should see that one of the errors on which this is based, among other things, is a failure to truly understand the depravity of man. In this part of his system,

---

[321] John Piper, "Act the Miracle: Future Grace, the Word of the Cross, and the Purifying Power of God's Promises," September 30, 2012 http://www.desiringgod.org/resource-library/conference-messages/act-the-miracle-future-grace-the-word-of-the-cross-and-the-purifying-power-of-god-s-promises, (Accessed October 10, 2012). Original quotation can be found in Peter T. Obrien, *Phillipians,* The New International Greek Testament Commentary, Phil. 2:12.
[322] John Piper, *Counted Righteous in Christ: Should We Abandon the Imputation of Christ's Righteousness?* (Wheaton, IL: Crossway Books, 2002), 25.
[323] Ibid.

the gospel no longer remains good news and assurance is all but thrown out the window. It is likely due to the inherent difficulties of this doctrine that Piper glosses over it and does not speak on it as freely and thoroughly as he does other doctrinal matters.

To avoid the charge that this is simply taken out of context, it is necessary to discuss Piper's teaching on the subject of future justification more thoroughly. In a well-known *Christianity Today* article, he says that there is a "final judgment [which] accords with our works."[324] This is itself is not unbiblical if one is referring to believers being judged according to their works and rewarded for their faithfulness based upon the stewardship of what they have been given at the Bema Seat of Christ. This is not what Piper intends. He goes on to say that it is this final judgment according to works where "evidence and confirmation of the true faith and union with Christ" will be brought forth and judged.[325] His focus remains on the efforts of man as opposed to the finished work of Christ. It is not enough to believe in Christ and to trust in the provision He offers for salvation. One must show, produce, be something, but Scripture explains that it is sinners who are justified. Faith, in his definition, is only that which can be confirmed by obedience. How much obedience is enough to confirm faith? Logically, it follows that the believer cannot be justified until after his or her life is completely over. There is no assurance and no justification in this life. This is not biblical. Paul states that δικαιωθέντες οὖν ἐκ πίστεως (we have been justified by faith).[326] Δικαιωθέντες is an aorist participle, a verbal noun identifying the subject as those who have been justified or the justified ones. According to Piper, the

---

[324] John Piper, "The Justification Debate: A Primer," Compiled by Trevin Wax *Christianity Today,* June 2009, 35.
[325] Ibid.
[326] Romans 5:1.

justified one is not actually justified in any real sense. It is not a present possession. This will not happen until the Lord justifies them in the future judgment, which is according to their works. Why need a Reformation at all if this is your teaching? Reconcile with Rome and start judging people according to their level of obedience, the evidence of their righteousness, before considering them saved. Piper concludes one section in his response to N.T. Wright by stating, "without validation transformation, there will be no future salvation."[327] Yes, obedience may demonstrate faith but faith is not contingent upon obedience. Obedience or practical righteousness should always be seen as the outworking of justification, not the grounds for future justification. In this, he moves beyond the traditional lordship position and makes the future justification contingent upon transformation of life.

Piper takes great liberty with theological terms as they are generally understood within evangelicalism. The error in his understanding corresponds with what is called Arminian or Wesleyan theology. Essentially, God is not sovereign, and man is capable of cooperating with God to earn his salvation. As much as Piper proudly asserts that he is a 5-point Calvinist, he does not always believe in divine monergism, valuing the efforts of man to be obedient to Christ. Man, in confirming his justification, works alongside of God and in cooperation with Him to achieve salvation. This is not good news. As mentioned previously, a misunderstanding of depravity causes this and it is not the biblical Gospel. This is one reason why Piper's theology is a case study for this specific section.

In the *Desiring God* statement of faith, it is affirmed:

---

[327] John Piper, "The Justification Debate: A Primer," 35.

we believe that justifying faith trusts in Christ not only for the gift of imputed righteousness and the forgiveness of sins, but also for the fulfillment of all His promises to us based on that reconciliation.[328]

One should look especially towards the later part of this statement and the claim that it makes. It is said that justifying faith trusts in Christ for the fulfillment of all His promises to us. One resulting issue is that there are many promises in Scripture other than the promise of eternal life for those who have faith. Must one believe in all these things in order to be justified? Piper would certainly not say that this is a requirement for faith but it is a true reflection of justifying faith. This is reminiscent of the approach snake-handling churches take to the promises of God. Piper might say, "it is this type of faith that trusts in the promises of God that justifies." To hold this consistently, one would be forced to side with the snake-handlers and say that indeed it is the type of faith that handles poisonous snakes that is truly justifying faith. In his desire to defend the church against licentiousness, Piper ignores that a childlike faith saves. His justification is man-focused. It becomes about what someone has done to prove his or her faith, not Christ-focused in what He has done for, apart from, and even in spite of someone.

Future Grace

The concept of future grace is an important part of Piper's theology. He expounds upon it in depth in his work *Future Grace.* It is here where he reveals his true soteriology. Piper believes that truly justifying faith is future-oriented. It looks forward to the future aspect of God's declaration of righteousness. Piper goes as far as saying, "you can't be a

---

[328] Desiring God Ministries,"Affirmation of Faith," http://www.desiringgod.org/about/our-distinctives/affirmation-of-faith, (Accessed September 5, 2013).

Christian without faith in future grace."³²⁹ What is future grace? This is not a peripheral matter but is central Piper's theology. It is also one of the gravest errors he makes. According to him, the grace, which God shows to the believer, is not a present reality but it will be shown in the future declaration of righteousness by His grace. Piper would say the believer is presently justified but in truth he really argues that he is not justified until a future time when God will look back, affirm the believer's faith and will declare him to be justified in retrospect. Therefore, grace is conditioned on obedience. Piper tries to defend himself against this charge because only a works-based salvation teaches that obedience is a condition of salvation. Nevertheless the salvation of a believer, in his teaching, is depending upon works. What is needed for the application of grace is a "lifetime of obedience."³³⁰ This is not *Sola Fide* in any true sense of the term. Instead it is an "experiential righteousness that is *not* a 'polluted garment'…(that is) evidence of our being justified children of God."³³¹ While it is said that the justified believer is one who has experiential righteousness, Piper never explains precisely how much experiential righteousness is required to be justified. He never defines or qualifies this; instead he simply asserts, "true saving faith is effective in producing practical obedience to God."³³² Faith for him is obedience. It is more than just belief it is faithfulness.

The gospel according to Piper, although orthodox in parts, also involves a justification that is conditioned upon practical obedience that characterizes the life of the believer.

---

[329] John Piper, *Future Grace: The Purifying Power of the Promises of God,* Revised Edition (Colorado Springs, CO: Multnomah Books, 2012), 65.
[330] Ibid, 115.
[331] Ibid, 151.
[332] Ibid, 164.

One can see that he is attempting to answer the question: why are there so many sinners in the church? His answer is a return to the Roman understanding of justification by works, despite the fact that he affirms justification is merely conditioned by works.

When something is said to be an inevitable outcome or a condition, then it logically becomes a requirement for the condition to be met. He states:

> all the forgiveness and help of God are gracious and unmerited. But they are not all unconditional. Our election and our regeneration are unconditional but subsequent blessings like ongoing forgiveness and guidance and help in trouble are conditioned on our covenant-keeping.[333]

Notice that Piper claims a believer's ongoing forgiveness is conditioned on covenant-keeping. It is possible, according to his theology, to have unforgiven sin in the life of a believer. This is due to man's inability to keep this imaginary covenant. He does not always hold to this. At times he states, "the only sin we can fight against successfully is a forgiven sin."[334] It shows at the very least some inconsistency in his thinking.

Piper says in *Future Grace*, "future grace is free, inexhaustible, unmerited, unearned- and conditional."[335] This statement is so inherently contradictory that it borders on the nonsensical. Unmerited grace cannot be conditioned.

---

[333] John Piper, "The Unmerited, Conditional Grace of God," February 2, 1994, http://www.desiringgod.org/resource-library/taste-see-articles/the-unmerited-conditional-grace-of-god, (Accessed September 5, 2013).
[334] John Piper, "God Sanctifies His People Palm Sunday," April, 22, 1992, http://www.desiringgod.org/resource-library/sermons/god-sanctifies-his-people, (Accessed September 5, 2013).
[335] John Piper, *Future Grace*, 251.

Justification conditioned on anything but faith is merited. Faith is not meritorious because it simply accepts the offer of salvation, it does not earn it. The conditions Piper puts forth for justification are extensive. He says:

> the conditions of future grace …are all of a certain kind. The ten conditions (are) loving God, being humble, drawing near to God, crying out to God from the heart, fearing God, delighting in God, hoping in God, taking refuge in God, waiting for God and trusting God. The eleventh condition (is) keeping covenant with God, which I believe is a way of summarizing all the others.[336]

Piper stacks conditions upon conditions. People assuredly will say that this author is misrepresenting Piper's views because to them he represents a bastion of Calvinism and Christian orthodoxy. More examples are available. Piper states explicitly "the future grace of resurrection to life is given to those who have done good deeds."[337] Elsewhere he makes the claim "Jesus says that if you don't fight this sin with the kind of seriousness that it is willing to gouge out your own eye, you will go to hell and suffer there forever."[338] Unfortunately this author knows of no one who has been willing to gouge out his or her eye to prevent sin. Who could possibly be in heaven following this line of thinking? Piper also asserts, "if we don't fight lust, we lose our souls."[339] The chronology of this statement indicates that it is possible to lose your salvation; otherwise Piper might have said if you do not fight lust, you are not saved (whether you agree with this statement or not). Piper summarizes his view in the statement, "the battle for obedience is absolutely necessary

---

[336] Ibid, 251-252.
[337] Ibid, 253.
[338] Ibid, 331.
[339] Ibid.

for our final salvation."[340] If there is no salvation until it is confirmed in the future. The believer can have no assurance. Piper pictures every person as bringing their deeds, which God will judge and determine if they are sufficient to make him worthy of salvation. Notice Piper's teaching in one of the most influential Christian works of recent publication:

> these are just some of the conditions that the New Testament says we must meet in order to be saved in the fullest and final sense. We must believe in Jesus and receive Him and turn from our sin and obey Him and humble ourselves like little children and love Him more than we love our family, our possessions, or our own life. This is what it means to be converted to Christ. This alone is the way of life everlasting.[341]

For one who ardently claims to be reformed in theology, the great Reformation doctrines of *Sola Fide* and *Sola Gratia* are abandoned, resulting in a synergistic view of salvation accomplished through the efforts of man.

EXCURSUS: ROMANS 5:18

NASB

So then as through one transgression there resulted condemnation to all men, even so through one act of righteousness there resulted justification of life to all men.

UBS[4]

Ἄρα οὖν ὡς δι' ἑνὸς παραπτώματος εἰς πάντας ἀνθρώπους εἰς κατάκριμα, οὕτως καὶ δι' ἑνὸς δικαιώματος εἰς πάντας ἀνθρώπους εἰς δικαίωσιν ζωῆς·

---

[340] Ibid, 333.
[341] John Piper, *Desiring God,* 69-70.

This verse is crucial for a proper understanding of justification and therefore needs to be discussed. It is through one transgression, a singular act whereby sin that entered into the world and brought condemnation. It is also through one act of righteousness that justification came. This verse contains ἑνὸς, the numeral one, which denotes the singularity of the action. The usage of δικαιώματος defines this singularity as an event of righteousness. Piper argues in his treatment of this verse that Paul:

> is probably treating the entire life and ministry of Jesus as a single whole – as one great act of righteousness, rather than any one act he did in life. What act would you pick? If you said his death, would you mean the obedience of Gethsemane, or the obedience when the mob took him away, or the obedience when he was interrogated, or the obedience when he was crowned with thorns, or the obedience when he was flogged, or the obedience when he was nailed to the cross, or the obedience when he spoke words of love to his enemies, or the obedience when he offered up his spirit to his Father? So you see, even if you say the 'act of righteousness' is his death, you mean a whole cluster of acts of righteousness. You are treating many acts as one great whole – the death.[342]

This is a straw man argument that he makes. In accordance with Leviticus 17:11, "it is the blood by reason of life that makes atonement." Christ's death provides the propitiation. It is true that one can speak of Christ's death as comprised of many different elements, but it is not His suffering, His being nailed to the cross, or any of these things which matter in

---

[342] John Piper, "Adam, Christ, and Justification, Part 4," August 20, 2000, http://www.desiringgod.org/resource-library/sermons/adam-christ-and-justification-part-4, (Accessed September 5, 2013).

terms of justification. The single act that matters for justification is His death. When Christ dies, he takes upon himself the sins of the whole world. This is the singular act to which Paul refers. Christ's perfect life is unable to provide a provision for salvation. If Piper were consistent in the way he understands ἑνὸς in the book of Romans, he would be forced to make certain theological concessions. Piper defines ἑνὸς using its non-normative sense. It is possible to define ἑνὸς in this way. For example, one could say "give me that one" (pointing to a stack of cards) in reference to the plurality of cards collectively. This person would be referencing the one (stack) as opposed to others (stacks) but this only works when speaking of a collective singularity in reference to another collective singularity. Piper would argue that this verse references Jesus' life in contradistinction to Adam's life. This is not how Paul chooses to use ἑνὸς in other parts of this letter. He uses it in reference to one man (5:12, 15 twice, 16, 17) or one transgression (5:16, 17, 18, 19). In the immediate context, Piper, if he were to understand this word consistently, he would be forced to conclude that Paul is referring to the one lifetime of sin by Adam that resulted in condemnation. Also, if held consistently, the use of ἑνὸς in 3:12 could speak of no one collective group of people who do good.

When examining a biblical word, it is best to see its use within the context to see how the author intended it to be used. Piper makes the assumption of its usage based on his theological presupposition instead of basing it on the natural reading of the passage. What Piper wishes to do is to see Paul's use of the statement διὰ τῆς ὑπακοῆς τοῦ ἑνὸς δίκαιοι (the obedience of the one) as referencing the lifetime of Christ's obedience. Christ's obedience in death, not his lifetime of obedience, provides the grounds for justification. Yes, a lifetime of obedience is required, but this is only because it is qualifies Him to be a sacrifice.

Departure from Reformed Understanding of Justification

Historical reformed theology does not understand justification in the same way as Piper. Berkhof, for example, views justification as a momentary, punctiliar, judicial act that "is completed at once and for all time."[343] Clearly he sees that there is no future element to justification. Berkhof is a great example because he represents the traditional covenantal system of theology. Dabney, as well, views justification as necessarily a past possession of a believer and not to be thought of in a future tense.[344] This goes against Piper's future justification construction. It may be surprising to some, but Charles Hodge asserts that justification "does not produce any subjective change in the person justified."[345] This is because of the distinction he makes between justification and sanctification. He goes on to claim that it is Romanism that views justification as an act of God "making the sinner subjectively holy. Romanists confound or unite justification and sanctification."[346] This is the same charge one could level against Piper from someone within reformed theology. Justification is a past tense occurrence for those in the reformed mainstream and one would be hard pressed to find someone speaking of justification as future.

IMPUTATION

Piper's inconsistent view of justification leads to a view of imputation that inevitably tends towards perfectionism. Although this is a charge that he would undoubtedly reject, it is clear this is the conclusion one

---

[343] Louis Berkhof, *Systematic Theology,* (Grand Rapids, MI: Wm . B. Eerdmans Publishing Co., 1941), 513.
[344] Robert L. Dabney, *Systematic Theology,* (Carlise, PA: Banner of Truth Trust, 1985), 644.
[345] Charles Hodge, *Systematic Theology,* (Peabody, MA: Hendrickson Publishers) 3:117.
[346] Ibid, 3:118.

should reach regarding his understanding of imputed righteousness if it is held with consistency. His view is that the Christian, having received the imputed righteousness of Christ, will live righteously. His understanding of imputed righteousness is more than just judicial and includes an experiential element. His thesis arises from passages of Scripture that are misused or taken out of context. For example, in dealing with Romans 5:18, he states "one righteous act: the totality of Christ's obedience."[347] It is his claim that the singular action of Adam brought condemnation to man but the lifetime of obedience of Christ that brings about justification.

Paul refutes Piper's understanding of imputation. He states, "What shall we say then? Are we to continue in sin so that grace may increase? May it never be! How shall we who died to sin still live in it?"[348] If taken out of context, one could easily conclude that the believer cannot live in sin. This is the teaching of the lordship position classically. Paul here is not talking about whether the believer can or cannot live a life of sin. It is the preceding verse that dictates the context of Paul's teaching. This verse specifically teaches that previously sin reigned (ἐβασίλευσεν ἡ ἁμαρτία) and now it is grace that reigns (ἡ χάρις βασιλεύσῃ). What Paul is explaining in the verse concerns the fact that the believer no longer lives under the dominion of sin. Once saved, sin does not reign; Satan is no longer your father, and your will is not in bondage. The new believer now has the capacity to serve the Lord. It is important to note the shift that occurs in the mood of reigning. Sin ἐβασίλευσεν is in the indicative mood, while graces βασιλεύσῃ is in the subjunctive mood. This is important because the indicative simply pictures the fact that sin is reigning in death while grace, in the subjunctive, indicates the possibility that grace might reign.

---

[347] John Piper, "Justification and the Finished Work of Christ."
[348] Romans 6:1-2, NASB

Additionally, the use of the aorist tense does not truly indicate any time element to the verb. Sin reigning then does not necessarily mean that this is a past tense occurrence. It is best then to see this as stating that sin reigns in death and grace might reign. Death does reign in the life of the unbeliever, but righteousness does not always reign in the life of the believer. If one were to make the declaration that righteousness reigns (without exception) in the life of the believer, then this would eventually lead to some form of Christian perfectionism. A believer is imputed with Christ's righteousness but this involves a change in standing or position, not a complete change in state. To teach that the imputed righteousness of Christ functions this way in practice in the life of the believer is an error with serious repercussions. It flies in the face of John's explicit teaching, "if we say that we have no sin, we are deceiving ourselves and the truth is not in us."[349] This is not to argue that Piper is not saved, but to show the gravity of this error.

What Paul teaches in Romans 6 is that the old self is in bondage to sin until regeneration/conversion. After this believers are freed from slavery and given new life, which enables them to serve God in their lives. Sanctification is therefore progressive in nature, in addition to its punctiliar aspect concurrent with salvation. This provides the context for Paul's statement οἵτινες ἀπεθάνομεν τῇ ἁμαρτίᾳ, πῶς ἔτι ζήσομεν ἐν αὐτῇ. He asks how the believer who has died to sin can live in it. One needs only to look in the mirror to see a Christian who commits sin. It is not that the Christian has died to sinning, but that they have died to the ruling power of sin in their lives. They have been freed and empowered by the Spirit to overcome sin in their life. This does not mean that it must happen. Piper does not seem to remember this important verse. When speaking about Romans 6, he paraphrases Paul as saying "because if you died to sin, you

---

[349] 1 John 1:8, NASB.

can't go on living in it. Or to put it bluntly: Dead people don't sin."[350] In this sermon, Piper explains to his congregation the reasons why dead people don't sin. He gives three reasons summarized in a neat little tautology: (1) When Christ died, believers died in him and with him. (2) When Christ rose, believers in some crucial sense were made alive in him. (3) Therefore, believers are commanded to become in practice what they are in Christ: dead to sin and alive to God. What this tautology really means, when coupled with his misunderstanding of Romans 6, is that a believer's life will be characterized by righteousness because he has died to sin. If one were to examine this belief, apart from any experience with the church of Christ, one would be forced to conclude that unbelievers are sinners and believers are easily identified because they all live righteously. The biblical truth is that the believer's righteousness is primarily judicial; it is true as the saint is seen in the eyes of the Lord. Its truth is found in one's standing and not necessarily in experience. Following Piper's reasoning, by seeing the believer's life one could easily determine the true believer based upon the evidence of their practical righteousness. One is reminded of the Pharisees who bore all the evidence of being righteous but who were whitewashed tombs of unrighteousness. The righteousness of Christ that is imputed to us does not make us sinless righteous people; dead people do sin, otherwise Paul's original question (How shall we who died to sin live in it?) would have been pointless.

Piper claims that Romans support the first premise of the aforementioned tautology. Two passages state, συνετάφημεν οὖν αὐτῷ (6:4) and τοῦτο γινώσκοντες ὅτι ὁ παλαιὸς ἡμῶν ἄνθρωπος συνεσταυρώθη (6:6). There is

---

[350] John Piper, "Are We to Continue in Sin That Grace Might Increase?" September 10, 2000. http://www.desiringgod.org/resource-library/sermons/are-we-to-continue-in-sin-that-grace-might-increase, (Accessed September 5, 2013).

undoubtedly a union that occurs between the believer and Christ because of His death. This is readily apparent. What Piper is arguing is that it is the old sinful self, man's Adamic nature, has been crucified. Previously as an unbeliever, the unregenerate person was endowed with the sinful nature of Adam, but now as a regenerate person, he is given a new righteous nature. It is the very righteousness of Christ in us. The old sinful self, the Adamic nature has been replaced. To see the sinful nature of man suddenly eradicated is a great misunderstanding of depravity. This teaching withstands neither the testimony of Scripture nor the witness of experience. Instead, it should be pictured in the following way. As an unbeliever, the unregenerate person has the old Adamic nature. He has only the capacity to serve sin and self in his life. This does not mean that he is unable to do good things or that he is as sinful as possible, but instead he cannot serve God in his actions. As a regenerate person, the new believer is given the capacity to scrvc God. He is given a new nature, which stands side-by-side with his old sinful nature, and these two natures are at war with each other. The old self remains, but now the regenerate person has been given the power, through the Spirit, to overcome it. This does not mean that this will occur without exception. This is something that the lordship proponents universally fail to recognize.

Paul goes on in Romans 6 to command believers; οὖν βασιλευέτω ἡ ἁμαρτία ἐν τῷ θνητῷ ὑμῶν σώματι (v.12). One is left to wonder why, if Piper is correct, Paul would command believers not to let sin reign if its reign had already been replaced with the reign of righteousness. Piper is thoroughly refuted by Paul's statement "do not go on presenting the members of your body to sin *as* instruments of unrighteousness; but present yourselves to God as those alive from the dead."[351] It is the biblical teaching that believers still continue to sin.

In discussing Piper's view of imputation overall, one is able to see that he views the imputation of Christ's righteousness as something that involves more than just the concept that God looks upon forgiven sinners, and sees the righteousness of Christ instead of sinful creatures. Piper takes this traditional understanding of imputation and redefines it to include not only its positional element, but also has a practical element to the point of nearly being primarily experiential. This is done through an improper connection made with the doctrine of perseverance. Essentially, he claims that since the believer will preserve in faith and will continue to grow in Christlikeness throughout his life as a result of Christ's imputed righteousness. While the sinless life of Christ is important, its true importance lies primarily in the fact that it enables Christ to be a sacrifice for the sins of the world.

VICARIOUS LAW-KEEPING

One major element of Piper's soteriology involves his focus on Christ's perfect life achieving law-keeping vicariously. This is a disputed point within the reformed theology. Essentially, what Piper is arguing is: Christ's life provides the grounds for justification in a sense beyond the fact that it is required to qualify Him as an unblemished sacrifice. Accordingly, Piper believes righteousness stems from the life of Jesus, through union with Him. It would be better not to make this assertion because it inevitably leads to the conclusion that the Old Testament believer could be justified on account of their works. The law would, therefore, be seen as a method of justification, but as Paul explains the law was given that sin may be made known. The law was never a method of justification; salvation has always been through faith.[352] Following this line of thinking, if asked

---

[351] Romans 6:13ff, NASB.
[352] Ryrie has ably handled this issue in Charles C. Ryrie,

during the Old Testament times what a person must do to be justified, then one should say that it was through obedience to the law. But the law was a way to show obedience and faith under the dispensation of law, and was never a means of justification, even for Jesus.

The inconsistency is seen in Piper's argument when he affirms that justification cannot occur by works while believing that it is Christ's work, his active obedience, which provides the grounds for justification. Scripture affirms, "no one is justified by the Law before God."[353] Christ himself is not declared to be righteous by His works of the law, which He obeyed perfectly, but through His faith. His faith was demonstrated, in part, by His obedience to the Law. This is an important distinction between covenantal and dispensational theologies. Following more of a covenantal framework, Piper views the believer as being justified on the basis of his faith, which results in the imputation of Christ's obedience to him. This in turn provides the foundation for the believer's justification. The importance of the resurrection of Christ is minimized. It is more accurate biblically to say that the believer is justified on account of his faith in Christ. Christ was considered justified by His faith, shown perfectly under the Mosaic dispensation. This was the dispensation under which Christ lived and ministered. His righteousness was displayed by His sinless life, but his righteousness was not limited to a strict obedience to the Mosaic Law and included His perfect trust and reliance upon the Lord. The believer is not justified on account of his or her participation in the works of Christ's life but through faith. While the object of faith has changed, faith remains the foundation of justification, as it was for Abraham, as it was for Christ.

Dispensationalism, Revised Edition, (Chicago: Moody Press, 2007).
[353] Galatians 3:11ff, NASB.

HEADSHIP[354]

Connected to both the doctrines of imputation and vicarious law-keeping, is the doctrine of headship of Adam. Covenant theology has traditionally supported the federal headship of Adam. This is of significance to the discussion concerning the new Calvinism for a few reasons. When one supports the concept of the federal headship of Adam, he supports covenant theology by laying the foundation for the covenant of works. There is also an important connection to be made between the believer's relationship to Adam and his relationship to the second Adam. If federal headship were true, then all men after Adam would be responsible for Adam's sins. This is clearly unbiblical. Deuteronomy teaches, "fathers shall not be put to death for *their* sons, nor shall sons be put to death for *their* fathers; everyone shall be put to death for his own sin."[355] It has traditionally been explained that Adam's sin is imputed to his posterity both mediately and immediately. As Gomes explains:

> The immediate imputation of Adam's sin refers to the imputation of the guilt of Adam's actual transgression in the garden to his posterity. Mediate imputation, on the other hand, refers to the imputation of guilt by virtue of the hereditary depravity of heart that inheres in all of Adam's descendants, who derive their corrupt natures from Adam[356]

If federalism were the biblical teaching, then Christ too would have an Adamic nature, since Adam would represent Him on the basis of His humanity. In response to this, federalism has explained that it is the virgin birth of Christ

---

[354] See also Appendix 1.
[355] Deuteronomy 24:16, NASB.
[356] Alan W. Gomes, "Glossary 1" in William Greenough Thayer Shedd, *Dogmatic Theology*, ed. Alan W. Gomes, 3rd ed. (Phillipsburg, NJ: P & R Pub., 2003), 956.

that allowed Christ to be free from the Adamic nature based on his lack of a seminal relationship to Adam. Would not this make Christ less than fully human to avoid being subjected to an imputed sin nature and an imputed guilt? Could not then man say to his Creator, "I sin because of the sin nature imputed to me, but Christ did not sin because He was not imputed with a sin nature?" This is a significant point to fully comprehend. The seminal view of Adam's headship is that man was present, seminally, when Adam ate of the fruit. He then is born with a sin nature because of his participation in the sin of Adam.[357] Hebrews supports this by explaining that Levi paid tithes to Melchizedek prior to his birth. This passage states, "for (Levi) was still in the loins of his father when Melchizedek met him."[358] Likewise, Ezekiel 18:1-4 states,

> then the word of the LORD came to me, saying, 'what do you mean by using this proverb concerning the land of Israel, saying, "the fathers eat the sour grapes, but the children's teeth are set on edge"? 'As I live,' declares the Lord GOD, 'you are surely not going to use this proverb in Israel anymore.'[359]

The Lord holds man accountable only for his own sins. This is why Paul makes the point clearly in Romans 5 that all sinned in Adam.

To hold to federalism makes God the author of sin because, as a result of Adam's sin, man is imputed with a sin

---

[357] Additionally this view is the one which best understands Eve's relationship to sin since Eve at of the sin first. Since she was literally made of Adam, is it Adam who brings sin into the world. When Eve sinned Adam sinned.
[358] Hebrews 7:10, NASB.
[359] What is especially significant about this passage is that it refutes Israel's false idea that they were being punished for the sins of their ancestors.

nature. This sin nature, imputed to man, is the reason that he sins. Man is born in bondage to sin. As Shedd explains:

> the sin of Adam, consequently, is imputed to his posterity in the very same way that the righteousness of Christ is imputed to the believer—namely, undeservedly or gratuitously. The posterity are not guilty in the sense of being inherently and personally ill deserving on account of Adam's sin, just as the believer is not righteous in the sense of being inherently and personally deserving on account of Christ's obedience.[360]

Shedd also goes on to refute this notion saying:

> a mere and simple representative acts vicariously for those whom he represents; and to make the eternal damnation of a human soul depend upon vicarious sin contradicts the profound convictions of the human conscience. To impute Adam's first sin to his posterity merely and only because Adam sinned as a representative in their room and place makes the imputation an arbitrary act of sovereignty, not a righteous judicial act which carries in it an intrinsic morality and justice.[361]

This common sense understanding of God has been confused in the teaching of federalism.

In practice, the distinction between federal and seminal headship is also significant when one begins to view the saint and his solidarity with the second Adam, Christ. It flows naturally from federal theology that when Adam

---

[360] William Greenough Thayer Shedd, *Dogmatic Theology*, ed. Alan W. Gomes, 3rd ed. (Phillipsburg, NJ: P & R Pub., 2003), 435.
[361] Ibid, 448.

sinned, all men became sinners by nature. Likewise, when the second Adam came, He became the representative or federal head of a new people. Man is no longer under the headship of Adam, but under the headship of Christ. As one transition from one head to another it naturally follows that the old imputed nature too has been left behind. This misunderstands total depravity, teaching instead a single nature view of man. Man was a sinner in Adam but becomes righteous in Christ. The new nature completely replaces the old. When Christ becomes the federal head of the born again believer, they will act in with Him. The *Reformation Study Bible* even teaches, "inherent in this teaching is the thought that the restoration provided in salvation must follow the pattern, but reverse the content, of the original constitution of humanity before God."[362] In contradistinction, seminal headship views all mankind as participating in the sin of Adam. Man is born a sinner because he sinned in Adam. Because man is present in the seed of Adam, upon conversion the nature of man is not changed. It is the biblical teaching that the saint remains a sinner by nature, but now has been given a new capacity to act in a way that may please God. He is freed from the bondage to sin but the sin nature remains. If one were to hold to federalism and subsequently a one nature view of man, this would have great consequences. If one's sin nature is replaced, good works must remain. Not only must they have good works, they must persevere in them.

As Romans 5:14 explains, between Adam and Moses men did not sin in the likeness of the sin of Adam. This is because the sin of Adam was a violation of law, a direct command of God and not a violation of the covenant. In federal thinking, man could have eternal life if he obeyed the

---

[362] Luder G. Whitlock et al., *The Reformation Study Bible: Bringing the Light of the Reformation to Scripture: New King James Version* (Nashville: T. Nelson, 1995), Ro 5:14.

covenant of works. After all, this is how the see Christ as meriting eternal life on the saint's behalf. Sin is seen as a violation of the covenant of works. If this is the case then man did sin in the likeness of the sin of Adam from Adam's time until Moses'.

ORDO SALUTIS

Piper's view of the gospel betrays an o*rdo salutis* that is much different from the traditional Protestant understanding of salvation. What is most startling about this conversion process is how regeneration fits the equation. Piper is forced to say that God will only make a believer regenerate after looking back after his life is complete. Regeneration is necessary in order for the believer to live a life of obedience, but they can only be regenerate after their life is completed in good works and perseverance. There is a logical inconsistency in his o*rdo salutis* since regeneration must also occur prior to faith.

Bema Seat of Christ

This error in Piper's *ordo salutis* is forced because of the way that he views the judgment seat of Christ ($\beta\hat{\eta}\mu\alpha$). He sees the Bema Seat as a time when the believer will be judged according to his works, as well as a time when unbelievers will be separated from believers. He

claims that the Bema Seat is intended:

> to declare who is lost and who is saved [whereby] our deeds will be the public evidence brought forth in Christ's courtroom to demonstrate that our faith is real.[363]

---

[363] John Piper, "What Happens When You Die? All Appear Before the Judgment Seat of Christ," August 1, 1993, http://www.desiringgod.org/resource-library/sermons/what-happens-

If one is not declared to be righteous (the biblical understanding of justification) until the judgment seat of Christ, until then one's standing in Christ can only be hypothetical. Regeneration must then be given to the believer in retrospect.

In seeing the Bema Seat as a judgment involving both rewards and salvation, Piper inadvertently equates the Bema Seat with the Great White Throne judgment of Revelation 22. Piper has not spoken directly on the Great White Throne judgment, but his description of the Bema Seat includes aspects of both judgments. He uses several verses to support his understanding of the Bema Seat, and one is Romans 2:5-7. He argues that from this passage that those who do good works will receive eternal life and those who do not will receive condemnation. This is undoubtedly true. While it is true that those who persevere in good works will receive eternal life, it does not automatically follow that those who receive eternal life must persevere in good works. John explains that those who believe already have eternal life.[364] Eternal life cannot be gained or lost at the judgment seat of Christ. Another text where Piper finds support is John 5:29; "those who did the good deeds to a resurrection of life, those who committed the evil deeds to a resurrection of judgment." This is a passage that must be allowed to speak for itself. It is true that those who do good deeds will receive eternal life, but this is based upon their faith. Paul recognizes this in the letter to the Ephesian church, explaining that the believer has been created for good works, which God has prepared for him (cf. Ephesians 2:8-10). Piper also looks to 2 Corinthians 5:10 for support:

---

when-you-die-all-appear-before-the-judgment-seat-of-christ, (Accessed September 5, 2013).
[364] John 5:24.

> for we must all appear before the judgment seat of Christ, so that each one may be recompensed for his deeds in the body, according to what he has done, whether good or bad.

This text explicitly mentions the Bema Seat of Christ, but it only involves rewards. The text never states that the Bema Seat will be a judgment separating the believers from non-believers. The crown of righteousness does not concern salvation but rewards.[365] Commenting on this verse Calvin asserts:

> a man is justified freely through the grace of Christ, and yet that God will render to him the reward of works; for as soon as God has received us into favor, he likewise accepts our works, so as even to deign to give them a reward, though it is not due to them.[366]

This confusion of the Bema Seat and the Great White Throne judgments forces Piper to see the justification as a future event.[367] This leads to confusion about the nature of justification. Piper attempts to explain that the future judgment of Christ will determine whether "we are already enjoying our pardon."[368] It is difficult to image anyone standing before the almighty God attempting to confirm his faith by giving the evidences of his deeds. This underestimates the true holiness of God and the sinfulness of sin. The only thing anyone could likely say to Christ sitting on His throne, if they are able to say anything at all, is "O' wretched man that I am!"[369]

---

[365] 2 Timothy 2:4.
[366] John Calvin, *2 Timothy*, electronic ed., Calvin's Commentaries (Albany, OR: Ages Software, 1998), 2 Ti 4:8.
[367] It may actually be the reverse and he reads these judgments in light of his understanding of the concept of future justification/future grace.
[368] John Piper, "What Happens When You Die? All Appear Before the Judgment Seat of Christ."

INFLUENCES

Where did Piper arrive at such an unusual view? As mentioned earlier, it is not at all common for a liberal seminary to produce a truly conservative scholar. During Piper's studies at Fuller Theological Seminary, Daniel Fuller mentored him. Daniel Fuller's views certainly influenced Piper's theology. In order to emphasize this point, the following quotation will be reproduced in its entirety. Piper states:

> on this particular point, I agree with what [Fuller] wrote in *The Unity of the Bible:* A faith that looks back to Christ's death and resurrection is not sufficient…Forgiveness for the Christian also depends on having, like Abraham, a futuristic faith in God's promises. Thus we cannot regard justifying faith as sufficient if it honors only the past fact of Christ's death and resurrection but does not honor the future promises of God, thus mocking his character and integrity.[370]

One would not go too far in assuming that Piper's view is a reflection of Fuller's since they are so unique. Where there is a departure from the traditional protestant understanding, they are similar.

Another influence on Piper's thinking may be the lordship views of men like John MacArthur. Piper's views are different from other lordship proponents. MacArthur

---

[369] Romans 7:24, KJV.
[370] John Piper, *Future Grace,* 205-206.

argues: true biblical faith is a belief that submits to the lordship of Christ. For MacArthur, faith is belief plus submission. Piper takes this line of thinking one step further in what may be accurately called hyper-lordship salvation. For him, truly saving faith includes not only belief and a life of obedience deemed worthy of salvation at the judgment seat of Christ. One can clearly see why this view could be called hyper-lordship salvation. It is in actuality more difficult to be saved in this system than in lordship salvation.

A third major influence seen in the writings of Piper is Jonathan Edwards. Although many view Edwards as a reformed theologian par excellence, his theology diverged from traditional Reformed theology on several points. More often than not, these divergences from Reformed theology are common to both men. For example, Edwards did not hold to covenant theology as the majority of those within the reformed camp hold. He also put more emphasis on the believer's union with Adam and his subsequent union with Christ. Union with Christ became the essence of faith and not one of the results of it. Salvation is a person's choice to unite himself with Christ. When the distinction between is blurred between justification and sanctification, as it is with federalism, it is not difficult to see how this leads to certain conclusions tending towards Christian perfectionism. Edwards, and Piper subsequently, believed that it is the believer's union with Christ and the imputation of His righteousness that makes the believer live righteously. This will happen with inevitability and the believer will be saved based upon the ultimate fulfillment of these conditions. If the Christian is not living in this way, it is evidence that there is no union with Christ in his life, and he will not partake of eternal life. Fortunately, this is not the biblical teaching. Scripture sees a believer's union with Christ to be the result of salvation. This union is judicial, and it only has practical implications, not necessarily practical results. Edwards and

Piper both downplay the judicial elements in salvation and focus on the practical or real elements associated with it, which some refer to as applied soteriology. Salvation is the means of becoming righteous in deed, which in turn will provide the basis for justification. This is highly circular in nature. How does one avoid the charge of teaching works-based salvation? Evans observes:

> Edwards struggled to formulate his soteriology in such a way that works of evangelical obedience and perseverance in faith stand in a *positive* relation to justification but without making obedience and perseverance the meritorious condition of that justification.[371]

Piper sees himself as one of Edwards' theological descendants. This observation about Edwards is an accurate representation of Piper because he falls prey to this same error. In trying to avoid licentiousness, and ensure that only the worthy are saved, they both make works the grounds of justification. This can be summarized succinctly in Edwards' statement that it is the "righteousness belonging to (man) that entitles him to the reward of life."[372] Luther and Calvin would most certainly object: salvation, which is entitled, cannot be a product of grace alone. To be entitled to something is to merit it. Waldron summarizes these combined influences; "Fuller's assumption is apparently that works were an inextricable part of perseverance and consequently a condition of justification for Edwards."[373] Piper, 300 years later, continues the errors of Edwards.

---

[371] William B. Evans, *Imputation and Impartation,* Studies in Christian History and Thought Series, (Eugene, OR: WIPF & Stock, 2008), 107.
[372] Jonathan Edwards, *Justification by Faith, Works* IV:128 qtd. in William B. Evans, *Imputation and Impartation,* 101.
[373] Samuel E Waldron, "John Calvin Versus Norman Shepherd on Sola Fide." *Reformed Baptist Theological Review* 02:2 (Jul 2005), 145.

FAITH

Piper's misunderstanding of the doctrine of justification causes him to have a wrong definition of faith. As mentioned above, true biblical faith in Piper's theology is comprised of not only belief in Christ but also a union with Him that results in a life characterized by obedience. This is partly a vain attempt to ascribe faith's authorship to God instead of man. Many within Reformed theology attempt to make the faith in Ephesians 2:8-9 the gift of God in salvation, despite the fact that πίστεως is feminine, while τοῦτο is neuter. Faith in this passage refers to salvation as a whole. Calvin describes this false view of faith saying:

> my readers will pardon me if I stay not to dispose of such absurdities; their own weakness, without external assault, is sufficient to destroy them[374]

Zeller observes, "if faith is the gift of God, then why do I need to have faith? A question that (Reformed theology) has never been able to answer."[375] Like others who call themselves by the name of Calvin, Piper falls prey to this error.

The problem arises for Piper that saving faith is not limited to obedience in the eleven categories previously mentioned. Instead, it seems as if he continually adds requirements for salvation. Many of these conditions are highly subjective and others downright impossible. In speaking of his beliefs, Piper states "I say that saving faith must include 'delight'…I think that without it, faith is dead."[376] This should not be too surprising considering the fact that his own ministry and theology revolve around his mantra that

---

[374] John Calvin, *Institutes of the Christian Religion*, Book 3, XVIII:10.
[375] George Zeller, Phone Interview, June 26, 2013.
[376] John Piper, *Future Grace,* 201.

God is most glorified when we are satisfied in him. One is left wondering if there was ever a recording in the New Testament of a person actually delighting in the Lord. The story of Mary and Martha might be the lone exception to this. Delighting in the Lord is not a major point of theology, and it is certainly not a condition of salvation. If this were the case, then people would need to be going around telling others that they are not saved because they do not delight in the Lord. Piper defines what delighting in the Lord is to him, stating "the essence of saving faith is a spiritual apprehension or tasting of spiritual beauty, which is delight."[377] It is certain that the thief on the cross was saved because this fact was recorded in Scripture, but can anyone say with any kind of certainty claim that this man tasted spiritual beauty? One assuredly cannot come to this conclusion without making assumptions and performing eisegesis.

Piper also says, "believing that Jesus is the Son of God means 'embracing' the significance of that truth-that is, being satisfied with Christ as the Son of God and all that God is for us in Him."[378] Piper is not saying that part of believing in Christ means trusting in Him alone for the entire provision of salvation. This is certainly true. If this aspect of Piper's gospel is true, then no one can be saved because no one is able to be satisfied in all that God is for us in Christ. No one is ever completely satisfied because there always remains a part of us, the flesh, which desires to move forward without God. Piper's view of saving faith greatly misunderstands depravity and conversion biblically.

Piper does not limit saving faith to belief and obedience but adds delight or satisfaction along with his other eleven conditions. He needs to heed his own warning that "if we go wrong on the nature of faith, everything in the

---

[377] Ibid, 204.
[378] Ibid, 160.

Christian life will go wrong."[379] His definition of faith is only one symptom of a much bigger problem. Without reserve he claims, "salvation is *owned* by faith... our *salvation* will accord with our deeds."[380] This is a return to Romanism and has no place in Protestantism. One is left wondering how Piper preaches on Acts 16:31 (believe on the Lord Jesus and you will be saved) and if he is really thinking when he preaches that one cannot really be saved now. You must first live an obedient life, and then God will look upon you and see that you have truly believed, only then you will be saved. He denies the punctiliar aspect of conversion. How great this error is.

SANCTIFICATION

Having established that Piper's views contain a great deal of error involving the doctrine of justification by faith stemming in part from a lack of proper understanding of Romans 5, it is not surprising that Piper's views on sanctification are in error resulting in or from a false understanding of Romans 6. Having frequently spoken on this chapter of Scripture, his essential understanding of it is that a believer will prove his union with Christ by demonstrating the righteousness of Christ in his life. Sanctification becomes the basis for future justification and not the result of justification. This is inconsistently held, and Piper recognizes that sanctification must be based on the work of justification, but he does not see this justification as a completed work. His overall view is based on a misguided understanding of God's sovereignty where God is very mechanistic and His creation is run deterministically by His decrees. Man, even regenerate man, is simply the agent of God's actions in His self-glorification. Piper does not see the true spiritual warfare that occurs in the life of a believer but

---

[379] Ibid, 209.
[380] Ibid, 365.

chooses to see practical righteousness as an accomplished fact and an inevitable characterization of the life of a believer. For Jonathan Edwards, this was called experiential piety. Piper confuses the inevitable outcome of the future aspect of sanctification (glorification) and the results of experiential sanctification. As Walvoord observes concerning sanctification, the sin nature defined as "a desire and predisposition to sin" remains alongside of the new nature, which is "a predisposition and inclination to righteousness."[381] A sanctified believer is the one who has an inclination towards sin at war with his new nature, an inclination towards righteousness. Piper totally misses this part of sanctification. He also fails to take into account that it is possible for the justified believer to be carnal or to grieve the Spirit.[382]

His view of sanctification causes a fundamental misunderstanding of Romans 8:13. To begin, σώζω does not always refer to being saved in the spiritual sense. It frequently refers to being saved from physical death. The LXX often uses this term when David speaks of being saved from his enemies in the Psalms. In the same way, ἀποθνήσκω does not always refer to spiritual death. It is not used in this sense in Romans 8:13. Based on this text, Piper claims "if we surrender to the flesh and decide we don't want to make war on sin any more, we will perish. We will show that our sins were never canceled."[383] Instead of seeing the believer as saved, he assumes death is spiritual death and life refers to eternal life. This is not supported by the context. The result is that sanctification is the believer's act of continually persevering in faith to prove his justification.

---

[381] John F. Walvoord, "The Augustinian-Dispensational Perspective," in *Five Views on Sanctification,* (Grand Rapids, MI: Zondervan, 1986), 206.
[382] Cf. 1 Cor. 3, Eph. 4:30.
[383] John Piper, "Act the Miracle: Future Grace, the Word of the Cross, and the Purifying Power of God's Promises."

This is quite a feat of mental gymnastics. One could easily define sanctification in his view as the inevitable conquering of sin in the life of a believer resulting in glorification. This is reflected in the statement "conquering canceled sin is essential if we are to be finally saved."[384] This shows that sanctification is the basis of the believer's future justification. Piper contradicts himself in the very same speech and states, "the pursuit of sanctification can only happen on the foundation of justification."[385] It is this latter statement that is part of the biblical picture of sanctification.

Desiring God Ministries recognizes the possible theological inconsistency and asserts, "final salvation in the age to come depends on the transformation of life, and yet does not contradict justification by faith alone."[386] This statement is incongruent with the Reformation concept of justification by faith alone and extends even further than the commonly repeated phrase "we are saved by faith alone but faith that saves is not alone." In choosing the word depends, *Desiring God Ministries* claims that salvation is determined, based, or contingent upon transformation of life. In the Reformation concept of *Sola Fide*, even amongst strict Calvinists, transformation of life is understood to be a logical outgrowth of saving faith and not dependent upon a transformed life. Calvin himself says:

> the moment you decline from it you have fallen into unrighteousness. Hence it appears, that righteousness is not obtained by a few works, but by an indefatigable and inflexible observance of the divine will. But the rule with regard to unrighteousness is very different. The adulterer or the thief is by one act

---

[384] Ibid.
[385] Ibid.
[386] Desiring God Ministries, "Affirmation of Faith."

guilty of death, because he offends against the majesty of God.[387]

If any obedience is required for future justification, then complete obedience is required. In terms of sanctification, sanctification must always proceed from justification and cannot precede it. Faith must always come first.

Another pitfall of Piper's understanding of sanctification is that he overemphasizes the experiential aspect of sanctification, failing to take into account the positional element of sanctification. Nowhere in his affirmation of faith does he recognize that the believer has been sanctified. He does state, "sanctification, which comes by the Spirit through faith, is imperfect and incomplete in this life."[388] This is definitely true in a limited sense but only as it relates to experiential sanctification. It completely ignores the idea that the believer is sanctified in this life positionally.

Piper does believe in the positional element of sanctification but his error in the overall understanding of sanctification leads to shaky conclusions. For example, in the preaching of 1 Corinthians 1:2, Piper recognizes that believers have been positionally sanctified and because of this are to be motivated by the break they have made with the past.[389] From here, the believer is exhorted to look back at his positional sanctification as well as to look forward to his future justification. This idea is not held with consistency and in most instances he proclaims a more orthodox understanding that sanctification proceeds from justification saying, "without a once-for-all justification through Christ, the only thing that our striving for holiness produces is

---

[387] John Calvin, *Institutes of the Christian Religion* Book 3, XVIII:10.
[388] Ibid.
[389] John Piper, "Sustained by the Faithfulness of God," January 17, 1988, http://www.desiringgod.org/resource-library/sermons/sustained-by-the-faithfulness-of-god, (Accessed September 5, 2013).

despair or self-righteousness."[390] One must ask how he can teach that sanctification is past, justification is future and that sanctification must proceed from justification. One can clearly see that shortcomings of his myopic approach to soteriology. In addition, it is said that an increase in holiness results in an increased awareness of one's sinfulness. It is more accurately said that experiential sanctification results in an increased awareness of one's unrighteousness. This motivates godly behavior. The latter can only come from the former. This is a more biblical portrayal of the experiential aspect of sanctification in practice.

Carnal Christians

Piper views Christians as being on an escalator-like continuum. After conversion, they continue to grow in Christ's likeness until they ultimately persevere in faithfulness at the end of their life. Although there may be missteps along the way, the general trend will be in visible manifestations of obedience. This way of thinking ignores the totality of Scripture, especially as it relates to the carnal Christian. He recognizes the fact that there is a category of believers consisting of those who are called carnal and he even recognizes that Christians can stay in this state for an extended period of time.[391] One is left wondering how the carnal believer's life could be judged and ultimately declared righteous if justification is based upon his works. Judgment that is based upon works will always result in condemnation; to assert otherwise underestimates the sinfulness of man and the sinfulness of sin. Rewards are a notable exception to this in that there is no condemnation, no negative aspect, only the withholding of rewards. Rewards will therefore only be

---

[390] John Piper, "God Sanctifies His People Palm Sunday."
[391] John Piper, "The Danger of Being Merely Human," February 21, 1988, http://www.desiringgod.org/resource-library/sermons/the-danger-of-being-merely-human, (Accessed September 5, 2013).

based on man's stewardship of all that has been entrusted to him.

Grieving the Spirit

Correlating with the doctrine of carnality is the possibility that Christians can grieve the Spirit. Piper does recognize this possibility when preaching, but it is not held with consistency in his theology.[392] BDAG says that grieve is used as severe distress and "in Polyaenus 8, 47 it is used of the severe *humiliation* or *outrage* experienced by a king who has been deposed by his subjects."[393] This is not some light-hearted disappointment experienced by the Spirit due to the imperfectness of man. Instead, it is a strong word describing God's great vexing at man's disobedience. Man is often shown to act in this way.

As noted above, Piper sees the believer as characterized by a lifetime of obedience but he also holds that the believer can have extended periods of rebellion against the Lord when he grieves the Spirit. Where does one draw the line when extended periods of rebellion cause a life to cease being characterized by obedience? Apparently, the placement of the line drawn by Piper is based upon the believer's ultimate perseverance. It is not how much obedience, but whether the believer comes back to faith or remains in faith at the end. More clarity is needed on this issue to say the least. To return to an earlier point, if saving faith is said to be contingent upon obedience to the covenant with God, then this is unfortunate because man is continually shown in Scripture to be unable to keep a covenant with the

---

[392] John Piper, "Make your Mouth a Means of Grace," October 12, 1986. http://www.desiringgod.org/resource-library/sermons/make-your-mouth-a-means-of-grace, (Accessed September 5, 2013).
[393] William Arndt, Frederick W. Danker and Walter Bauer, *A Greek-English Lexicon of the New Testament and Other Early Christian Literature*, 3rd ed. (Chicago: University of Chicago Press, 2000), 604.

Lord. Covenants that are kept are always unconditionally based upon God's faithfulness and not man's obedience. While at times Piper tackles licentiousness by claiming that those whose lives are characterized by sinfulness were never saved, at other times he asserts that it is possible for one to having saving faith despite living a life that falls prey to the desires of the flesh for an extended period.

HERMENEUTICS

Piper's hermeneutic is highly flawed. Anyone who has spent time reading or listening to Piper knows the value he places on the concept of Christian hedonism. In an almost mythical manner, this idea came to Piper. At times this seems like it came to Piper as direct revelation by God himself. This concept is a derivative of the first question of the Westminster Shorter Catechism, which states "the chief end of man is to glorify God and to enjoy him forever." Piper takes this and changes and to by and asserts "the chief end of man is to glorify God by enjoying Him forever."[394] This directly relates to how Piper approaches hermeneutics. This is because this concept that drives his hermeneutics. Many within reformed theology today espouse a version of hermeneutics that is classified as historical-grammatical-theological. Broadly speaking, this method of hermeneutics attempts to use theology and read that general understanding back into Scripture. This is different from the historical-grammatical interpretation in that theology is not derived from exegesis but is one part of the exegetical process. It is this school of thought that Piper falls prey to using in his exegesis. After discovering the principle that God is most glorified when we are satisfied in him, Piper then reads this Christian hedonism back into the Scripture. He finds many places that bear testimony to the truth of his understanding.

---

[394] John Piper, *Desiring God,* (Colorado Springs, CO: Multnomah Books, 2003).

This hermeneutic does not allow the text to speak for itself and remain true to its original context. Piper mentions Christian hedonism so frequently, and in so many different contexts, that it has become a sort of mantra for him and his followers. His hermeneutic could be seen then as mantra-driven theological interpretation.

This approach is seen as well when he forces his understanding of future justification on Scripture. One example is necessary. Paul states:

> therefore I run in such a way, as not without aim; I box in such a way, as not beating the air; but I discipline my body and make it my slave, so that, after I have preached to others, I myself will not be disqualified.[395]

Clearly Paul is speaking here. In the context of this statement Paul is talking about himself possibly being considered disqualified. There is broad agreement, even with reformed thinkers, that Paul is talking about something other than eternal life. To say otherwise would be to clearly be asserting that someone, even Paul himself, could lose his salvation. Piper in his exegesis (or eisegesis) of this passage states that "to be disqualified means that Christ is not in you. The race has been run in vain. It was a sham."[396] According to Piper, Paul would be saying that if he (Paul) had not been disciplining his body, then he would not be saved. Paul's life would be a sham. There is a difference between those who profess something and those who possess something, but clearly Paul is not talking about losing his salvation because of failure in his life. This is the gospel according to Piper.

---

[395] 1 Corinthians 9:26-27, NASB.
[396] John Piper, "Olympic Spirituality Part 1," August 2, 1992http://www.desiringgod.org/resource-library/sermons/olympic-spirituality-part-1, (Accessed September 5, 2013).

DEPRAVITY

Piper's anthropology is interrelated to many of the matters already discussed, especially in regards to his understanding of man's depravity. In an effort to appear conservative and orthodox, Piper attempts to take a Calvinistic approach to the T of TULIP. His view pictures God as overcoming man's sinfulness in an almost mechanical manner. His definition of depravity simultaneously underestimates and overestimates man's ability. Depravity means that man is unable to earn merit in God's eyes and hence is depraved or unable to stand the test. This depravity is total in that it affects all people and all parts of a person. It is also total in that there is absolutely nothing in unregenerate man that can merit him favor in the eyes of the Lord. According to Piper, man is totally depraved in that he is unable to obtain salvation. It is the work of God and this is accomplished through God's imparting of faith in man after regenerating him. This is one of Piper's statements on depravity: "when we speak of man's depravity we mean man's natural condition apart from any grace exerted by God to restrain or transform man."[397] This statement ignores the common grace God shows to man in using His Spirit to restrain evil, but the major issue of his view is that it pictures God as eradicating the old sinful self. While the believer still wars against the flesh, Piper pictures this war as one that must be won in order for the Christian to be ultimately saved. He sees the believer's union with Christ as producing a life characterized by righteousness. He states:

---

[397] John Piper, "What We Believe About the Five Points of Calvinism."

when I embrace Jesus as my savior, I embrace my own death as a sinner. My sin brought Jesus to the grave and brought me there with him. Faith sees sin as murderous. It killed Jesus, and it killed me.[398]

The essence of Piper's argument is that, by union with Christ the believer has died to sin and in dying to sin, depravity has been overcome. In contrast, Paul explains:

For I know that nothing good dwells in me, that is, in my flesh; for the willing is present in me, but the doing of the good *is* not. For the good that I want, I do not do, but I practice the very evil that I do not want. But if I am doing the very thing I do not want, I am no longer the one doing it, but sin which dwells in me.[399]

The old sinful self remains. The believer will at times lose his battle with the flesh, but this does not mean that he has lost his salvation or was never truly saved.

Part of Piper's misunderstanding of depravity comes from using passages of Scripture to proof text his version of TULIP. For example, he claims that Romans 14:23, "whatever is not from faith is sin," asserts that all actions without faith are sin. This is not what the passage speaks of within its original context. When reading the passage as a whole and not simply as one part of a single verse, one can clearly see that Paul is talking about the eating of something that the eater believes (has faith) is inappropriate due to the pricking of his conscience. This is only a small part of Piper's misunderstanding of depravity.

---

[398] John Piper, *The Passion of Jesus Christ,* (Wheaton, IL: Crossway Books, 2004), 79.
[399] Romans 7:18-20, NASB.

SECURITY/ASSURANCE

There is a great deal of difference between the biblical understanding of the eternal security and Piper's doctrine of perseverance. Piper's approach to perseverance is reminiscent of Puritanism. The Puritans attempted to live in strict obedience to God due to the constant fear that their life would be deemed unworthy to prove their salvation. The Puritans were subtly trying to justify their salvation. This is the very error that Piper seeks to avoid. What Piper teaches is that it is the working for God that gives believers ground for His assurance. Piper repeatedly exhorts his congregation to keep working. When the believer works, it is truly God who works in them, and this is to be motivated by the anticipation of future grace they may be shown by God. God graciously honors the earnest efforts of man. At times, Piper preaches that the believer can have assurance but it is grounded in obedience, not based upon the truth of an already present justification. Works must confirm salvation. How are the deeds of those who believe different from the works of those who profess to believe but are not truly saved?

Piper pictures obedience as proof of regeneration, but he fails to take into account that the efforts of the unsaved may give them undue security. Is it simply the motives that separate them? It appears he teaches that a non-believer can work, but they will not persevere in good work and their work does not earn merit in God's eyes. The important distinction for him is the believer's empowerment by the Spirit to work, while the non-believer is not empowered by the Spirit to work. This is certainly true, but it is too subjective to be the grounds for the believer's assurance. Otherwise, one will always be working; never having security and robbed of the great motivation of gratitude in the grace already shown. The Puritans succumbed to this.

One of the things Piper wishes to avoid is the debtor's ethic. This teaches: a debt of obedience is owed to God because of salvation. In this view, it is the repayment of a debt that motivates Christian obedience. What should motivate Christian obedience is not a sense of debt, nor the possibility of future grace, but a thankfulness or gratitude for the grace God has already shown. Gratitude is not the same as the debtor's ethic.

Piper also builds his own straw man while portraying free grace theology. He characterizes free grace theologians, especially Hodges, "as describing faith as intellectual assent."[400] This is a gross misrepresentation of the free grace position. Piper goes on to give tests for determining whether faith is salvific, saying, the "evidence [for our salvation] is that the current of our affection flows toward God, so that God is your delight."[401] This is based too much on an emotional understanding of God and is not necessarily true of all Christians. Paul also says:

> So whether we read Paul or whether we read John the question of assurance is answered in the same way: do we see the evidences of sanctification and belief in the truth? ... So if you obey the commandment to love and to believe, you can have assurance that God abides in you and that you are chosen by God and saved.[402]

---

[400] John Piper, "God Abides in the One Who Loves and the One Who Confesses," May 19, 1985, http://www.desiringgod.org/resource-library/sermons/god-abides-in-the-one-who-loves-and-the-one-who-confesses, (Accessed September 5, 2013).
[401] John Piper, "God Abides in the One Who Loves and the One Who Confesses."
[402] Ibid.

Piper's tests are based in the positive abilities of man. These abilities of man are empowered by the Spirit of God. The problem with this is its subjectivity and an overall outlook that fails to take into account the sinfulness and depravity of man.

When one looks back at the testimony of Scripture, one can see that its pages are replete with those who, while righteous because of their faith, were unrighteous in their actions. Peter denied the Lord. Ananias and Sapphira were judged and immediately put to death due to their rebellion. Abraham repeatedly tried to pass off Sarah as his sister. David, the man after God's own heart, was an adulterer and murderer. What about the church in Corinth? How would these faithful people possibly be declared righteous by showing the evidence of their works? Works continually bear witness to the depth of man's depravity. It is by grace alone that the believer is justified. Fortunately for them, the Old Testament saints were justified by grace through faith apart from obedience. They lived under the same dispensational arrangement as Christ. He did not fulfill the covenant of works. Calvin himself denies this theoretical covenant saying:

> The promise, which gave him hope of eternal life as long as he should eat of the tree of life, and, on the other hand, the fearful denunciation of death the moment he should taste of the tree of the knowledge of good and evil, were meant to prove and exercise his faith.[403]

He also affirms that "full assurance (πλεροφορία) which the Scriptures uniformly attribute to faith."[404]

---

[403] John Calvin, *Institutes of the Christian Religion*, Book 2, I:4.
[404] Ibid, Book 3, II:15.

For Piper, assurance is not something based on the eternal security of the believer, but is a process. It is the "pursuit of assurance."[405] This is the cycle whereby the works of man move him in such a way as to work all the more to keep on persevering. This is the Puritan work ethic, what Piper calls "the fight to maintain the full assurance of hope."[406] It is a desire to put the Christian back under some form of law as a rule of life instead of grace. Paul explains just the opposite; Christians "are not under law but under grace."[407] Piper admits that his congregation struggles not just with the doctrine of assurance but personal assurance, as well. This is not surprising considering his teaching on the subject:

> and here I will only mention the subjective side of the problem, the more pastoral side—namely, the struggle for assurance. Suppose you say to me, what more assurance could a person get from the doctrine of imputation that he doesn't get from the fact that, because of Christ, all his sins are forgiven? My response will be, don't try to be wiser than God. The human soul is a great mystery. Who can understand it? Who are we to say that there are not unique kinds of fear and doubt that, for reasons we may not fully understand, will vanish only before the teaching of Christ's imputed righteousness, but would not budge before the teaching of the forgiveness of sins?[408]

---

[405] John Piper, "The Full Assurance of Hope to the End," October 20, 1996, http://www.desiringgod.org/resource-library/sermons/the-full-assurance-of-hope-to-the-end, (Accessed September 5, 2013).
[406] John Piper, "The Full Assurance of Hope," February 9. 1992, http://www.desiringgod.org/resource-library/sermons/the-full-assurance-of-hope, (Accessed September 5, 2013).
[407] Romans 6:14, NASB
[408] John Piper, "Justification and the Diminishing Work of Christ."

If the imputation of Christ's righteousness could provide Christians with assurance, it can only be accomplished by living righteously and perfectly. As Packer observes, one "destroy(s) assurance by making final salvation depend upon ourselves rather than on God."[409] Praise God that believers are not required to confirm their salvation by their actions. This is pure, undefiled grace.

Excursus: Romans 7:14-25

Piper's treatment of Romans 7:14-25 is very flawed. He recognizes that Paul references the wretched man as himself while a Christian.[410] This is certainly true. He elsewhere asserts, Paul teaches, "*not* that Christians live in continual defeat, but that no Christian lives in continual victory over sin."[411] This is also true. The problem is that it highlights the inconsistency in his theology. According to Piper, in looking forward to the Bema Seat as a judgment, dividing believers from unbelievers, believers at the Bema Seat are justified on account of their obedience. How does one determine when a person's incomplete victory becomes sufficiently complete? Paul characterizes himself in this passage not as obedient, but as ταλαίπωρος. Psalm 137:8 (LXX 136:8) utilizes the same Greek word in reference to the evil daughter of Babylon. Isaiah uses the word in reference to the destroyer Assyria (cf. Isaiah 33:1). This is more than just a believer who occasionally sins. The depth of depravity extends beyond the simple missteps of otherwise righteous people. This is important because as Woods shows, "a post-conversion view of Romans 7:14-25 leads to a dual nature view of the believer."[412] If one were to conclude that Paul is

---

[409] J.I. Packer, *Sola Fide: The Reformed Doctrine of Justification*, Loc. 221.
[410] John Piper, "Who is This Divided Man, Part 2," June 3, 2001, http://www.desiringgod.org/resource-library/sermons/who-is-this-divided-man-part-2, (Accessed September 5, 2013).
[411] Ibid.

speaking of himself as a believer, which Piper follows, it forces certain conclusions. One conclusion is a dual-nature view of the believer. Believers simultaneously have the Adamic nature in addition to a new nature. If this view is held consistently, then it should avoid the pitfalls of Piper's understanding of experiential sanctification.

Two popular translations translate Romans 7:18 very differently.

NASB

For I know that nothing good dwells in me, that is, in my flesh; for the willing is present in me, but the doing of the good is not.

ESV

For I know that nothing good dwells in me, that is, in my flesh. For I have the desire to do what is right, but not the ability to carry it out.

UBS[4]

οἶδα γὰρ ὅτι οὐκ οἰκεῖ ἐν ἐμοί, τοῦτ' ἔστιν ἐν τῇ σαρκί μου, ἀγαθόν· τὸ γὰρ θέλειν παράκειταί μοι, τὸ δὲ κατεργάζεσθαι τὸ καλὸν οὔ·

Paul is clearly speaking of himself in this verse, and it is after his salvation. He recognizes the fact that the flesh, his sinful nature, remains after conversion. Calvin himself affirms this by stating, "both terms, flesh as well as spirit, belong to the soul; but the latter to that part which is renewed, and the former to that which still retains its natural character."[413] Paul laments the fact that he still sins

---

[412] Andy Woods, "Romans 7 and Sanctification," *Chafer Theological Seminary Journal* 14:2 (Fall 2009).

(frequently) after conversion. Κατεργάζεσθαι is defined in BDAG as bringing about a result by doing something, achieve, accomplish, or do.[414] This passage refers to the idea that Paul, while having the desire to do good (ἀγαθός), does not live this out in practice. This is spoken by one of the holiest men ever to live. The reformed leanings of the ESV show an imputation of TULIP into this passage by ascribing to unregenerate man an inability to do good when taken out of context. In reference to this passage, Piper states, "this is a radical confession of the truth that in our rebellion nothing we think or feel is good. It is all part of our rebellion."[415] When this is taken with his view of justification and sanctification, Piper believes man overcomes depravity after conversion. While it is true that man has been freed from the dominion of sin, it is not true that the power or influence of sin in the life of the regenerate believer has been eradicated. Sin still exerts tremendous influence in the life of a believer, as Paul bears testimony.

Piper's vision of man, bringing his works before God at the Bema Seat, underestimates sin and limits the influence of depravity to having power only before conversion. One should applaud him for recognizing the fact that man is in rebellion against God prior to conversion, but even though man has been reconciled positionally to God after conversion, this does not mean that man cannot rebel against God experientially. Just because the regenerate man is now able to do good in the eyes of the Lord, does not mean that he will. Every time believers sin, whether big or small, it is a

---

[413] John Calvin, *Calvin's Commentaries* (Galaxie Software, 2002), Ro 7:18.
[414] William Arndt, Frederick W. Danker and Walter Bauer, *A Greek-English Lexicon of the New Testament and Other Early Christian Literature*, 531.
[415] John Piper, "What We Believe About the Five Points of Calvinism," (Accessed September 5, 2013).

rebellion against God. This is the biblical picture of sin nature.

CONCLUSION

Despite all of his theological flaws, there is one thing of great importance that the young Calvinists see in Piper that is commendable and worthy of careful contemplation. This is the passion that he evidences for God. It is not cold and dead, as some have taken to characterizing many within reformed theology. He is not the typical frozen-chosen predestinarian. He has a vibrant faith that is truly evident whenever he speaks. Authenticity speaks volumes to the postmodern generation. They see his passion and authenticity, and it is something that they desire to emulate. This is an example that many could draw from.

Unfortunately, his gospel is not good news but a call to action. One is left wondering how it is that the just live by faith if they are not yet justified? This gospel is a hopeless one, and it is not good news. There can be no assurance of salvation when the Christian life is one that is lived in hopeful expectation of a future salvation based on future grace in future justification which will be retroactively applied to man. One is left wondering, how this is any different from Roman theology or even Islam? If justification is based on works or is conditioned on obedience, as Piper states, then all will be weighed and be found lacking. It is only on the premise; belief in Christ is trusting in Him, His person and His work, that no one will be found lacking because it centers on Christ, instead of man. Calvin himself asserts:

> let us not suppose, then, that the Holy Spirit, by this promise, commends the dignity of our works, as if they were deserving of such a reward. For Scripture leaves us nothing of which we may glory in the sight

of God. Nay, rather its whole object is to repress, humble, cast down, and completely crush our pride.[416]

Luther translates 1 Corinthians 1:31, to say "he that glorieth, let him glory in the Lord, namely, that he has a gracious God."[417] Works cannot be favorably measured against the ultimate standard of a holy God. New Calvinism, if it continues to follow in the footstep of Piper, will do great harm to the church. Although not all new Calvinists exclusively hold Piper's theology, it remains an important case study for understanding whether new Calvinism is truly Calvinistic in any true sense of the word.

---

[416] John Calvin, *Institutes of the Christian Religion,* Book 3, XVIII:4.
[417] Martin Luther, *Smalcald Articles,* 29.

CHAPTER 4

MISSIONALLY FLOODING INTO CITIES

At the outset of this section, one may be confused as to how the new Calvinist's desire to go missionally into cities has anything to do with the gospel. This is due to the fact that flooding into the cities is a central tenant of their understanding of the gospel. For them, this is the gospel. The words missionally flooding into cities are specifically chosen.[418] The focus of their efforts, at least for some, is what they see as their modern-day Samaria, places where nice Christian people would not be found, paralleling the Jewish sentiment about Samaria. The cities are an unreached mission field, but new Calvinism's theological claims are unfounded. For example, take *The Gospel Coalition's* confessional statement on the kingdom of God. It states:

> living as salt in a world that is decaying and light in a world that is dark, believers should neither withdraw into seclusion from the world, nor become

---

[418] Of Marsden's three major types of Calvinism, this missional Calvinism may be due to the influence of Kuyperian/Dutch Calvinism, which focuses on cultural reformation. This is the branch of Calvinism that would produce a work like Grudem's *Politics-According to the Bible* (Grand Rapids, MI: Zondervan, 2010).George Marsden, "Reformed and American," in *Reformed Theology in America: A History of its Modern Development,* ed. David F. Wells, (Grand Rapids, MI: William B. Eerdman's Publishing Company, 1985).

indistinguishable from it: rather, we are to do good to the city.[419]

In a single page document on theological beliefs, there are few groups who would take the time to mention cities in such a specific way. This is highly telling. For new Calvinism, the gospel is misunderstood to involve social action or cultural redemption. Chapell explains in one of *The Gospel Coalition's* booklet entitled *What is the Gospel?*; "if the King comes to saves sinners and if their salvation includes a renewed heart, an empowered life, and a transformed world, then his purpose and theirs is truly good news."[420] It now becomes necessary to discuss the biblical gospel.

The Biblical Word for Gospel

εὐαγγέλιον-

> 1) God's good news to humans, good news
>
> 2) Details relating to the life and ministry of Jesus, good news of Jesus
>
> 3) A book dealing with the life and teaching of Jesus, a gospel account[421]

This word is actually an amalgamation of the words εὖ meaning good and ἄγγελος meaning messenger. An εὐαγγέλιον then is a message of good news. The verbal form εὐαγγελίζω is to proclaim the message of good news. Spicq

---

[419] The Gospel Coalition, "Confessional Statement," http://thegospelcoalition.org/about/foundation-documents/confessional/, (Accessed June 13, 2013).
[420] Bryan Chapell, *What Is the Gospel?*, Gospel Coalition Booklets, Good News Publishers. Kindle Edition. Loc. 386-387.
[421] William Arndt, Frederick W. Danker and Walter Bauer, *A Greek-English Lexicon of the New Testament and Other Early Christian Literature,* 402.

claims that the news does not have to be unilaterally good, saying, "any kind of news at all, even false news" can be the reference of εὐαγγέλιον.[422] This is certainly true of the biblical gospel because, at its heart, it is an exclusive message. Since it does not proclaim a universal salvation, and the gospel may, in fact, be bad news or condemnation for some.

The LXX uses εὐαγγελίζω in place of בשר. This is not to say that this is the biblical gospel, merely the announcement of good news in a more generic sense. An important distinction needs to be made here. While there is good news that is not the gospel, one should be exercise caution in using gospel in a non-soteriological sense.

The Biblical Gospel

The mission of the church, to proclaim the propositional gospel, has been distorted in recent times by buzzwords like gospel-centered, gospel-based and gospel-focused. Too often, the gospel is seen as something bigger than just the message of the forgiveness of sin and the individual reconciliation to the Lord. That being said, the gospel should be the centerpiece of the message the church carries to the world. Although not all recent publications involving the word gospel hold a specific view, the gospel message should not be confused with its own implications. It is said, "the gospel is not only sufficient for justification but also for sanctification." What is needed today is "people constantly preach(ing) the gospel to themselves."[423] The gospel has too often been replaced with a bigger, missional vision of the gospel. Since missional is a rarely defined

---

[422] Ceslas Spicq and James D. Ernest, *Theological Lexicon of the New Testament* (Peabody, MA: Hendrickson Publishers, 1994), 2:83-84.
[423] Eric Geiger et al, *Transformative Discipleship: How People Really Grow,* (Nashville, TN: B & H Publishing group, 2012), 67.

term, it is used here in reference to the promotion of a specific gospel. This gospel is larger than the simple proposition: believe and live. It is a message of collective reconciliation through the incarnational ministry of the church. It confuses the practical ramifications of the gospel with the gospel itself. The gospel needs to be lived out, but there is no biblical support for this as a specific part of the gospel itself. Stallard traces much of the origin of the contemporary emphasis on the whole gospel to the wording of the Lausanne Covenant (1974).[424] It should not be surprising that in the postmodern world, which abhors propositional statements, there has arisen a movement defining the gospel as experiential in addition to propositional. This may be an outgrowth of the emergent church.

It is necessary to see the biblical usage of the term gospel to truly understand its meaning. Fortunately, there is only a single word that is translated as gospel: εὐαγγέλιον. An examination of this word will help to reveal the biblical concept of the gospel.

The propositional gospel:

The New Testament usage of εὐαγγέλιον falls into three categories.

The gospel of:

>	the kingdom (Mt. 4:23, 9:35,24:14)
>	Jesus (Mk. 1:1)
>	God (Mk. 1:14)

---

[424] Mike Stallard. "Gospel Centeredness, Jesus and Social Ethics" *Journal of Ministry and Theology* 15:2 (Fall 2011): 24.

All of these usages of εὐαγγέλιον appear to be in reference to a specific proposition. This is because of the presence of the definite article. In these instances, the gospel is not referenced as an action (i.e. the gospeling of Jesus) but a specific proposition. Most do not deny the propositional nature of the gospel since it is self-evident. Instead, an experiential aspect to the gospel added alongside of the proposition.

When speaking of the preaching of the gospel, Matthew uses κηρύσσω in the aorist, not present. This indicates that the gospel is being proclaimed (looking at it as a whole action) and not at something which occurs continual (which would necessitate the Greek present tense). The continual aspect of the present must be used if the gospel is to be lived out. What is being proclaimed or preached is not social reconciliation.

The gospel is not in the process of changing the world and reconciling it to God. Mark tells his readers (1:15) to believe the gospel, not live the gospel. The Apostolic fathers universally use the gospel in its propositional sense.[425] The gospel is never the object of any verb that can be translated as to live or to live out (ζαω or κατοικέω). As a result of this understanding, new Calvinism has a tendency towards the social gospel. The social gospel is defined as a corporate obligation to pursue justice in broader society. One new Calvinist states, "ministering to the poor is a crucial sign that we actually believe the gospel" and elaborates, "one aspect of living a holy life is treating the poor with compassion and pursuing justice."[426] These visions of the gospel are

---

[425] Cf. 1 Clement 47:2, 2 Clement 8:2 Ignatius' Letter to Philidelphia 5:1, 2 8:2, 9:2, Ignatius' Letter to Smyrna 5:1, 7:2, Martyrdom of Polycarp 1:1, 4:1, 22:1, Didache 8:2, 11:3, 15:3,4, Epistle of Barnabas 5:9, 8:3, Letter to Diognetus 11:6, and Fragments of Papias 11:4. In Ignatius's letter to the Philadelphians
[426] Kevin DeYoung and Greg Gilbert. *What is the Mission of the Church?*

typically removed from the context of the theocratic kingdom of Israel or based on a misunderstanding of the kingdom. Unsupported claims are often found similar to this, "just as God provided manna for everyone in the wilderness (Ex. 16:18), so the church is to be God's manna equalizer now."[427] Avoiding the term social gospel, the new Calvinists prefer preaching a whole or missional gospel. It is succinctly summarized in a few places. One of the most prominent is Acts 16:31. When asked by the jailer "what must I do to be saved," Paul and Silas respond, "believe in the Lord Jesus, and you will be saved." In giving the purpose statement of his gospel, John states "these have been written so that you may believe that Jesus is the Christ, the Son of God; and that believing you may have life in His name."[428] This is the Gospel.

Becoming the gospel

Notice Paul's statement: "God was in Christ reconciling the world to Himself."[429] The church is to bring the message of reconciliation, but it is another thing to claim that the church is to redeem society. Τὴν διακονίαν τῆς καταλλαγῆς concerns individuals at enmity with God. Paul goes on to say in this verse that God "θέμενος ἐν ἡμῖν τὸν λόγον τῆς καταλλαγῆς." God has committed to the church the word of reconciliation and not the act of reconciliation. The message is concisely stated, "καταλλάγητε τῷ θεῷ."[430] καταλλάσσω occurs in the second person plural since it involves persons and not the third person singular, which could refer to society. Although this may seem to be an insignificant point,

---

Making Sense of Social Justice, Shalom, and the Great Commission. (Wheaton, IL: Crossway, 2011), 174-175.
[427] Ibid, 168.
[428] John 20:31, NASB.
[429] 2 Corinthians 5:19ff, NASB.
[430] 2 Corinthians 5:20ff, NASB.

it is a necessary because there is only one Gospel entrusted to the church.

Acts 20:24

"But I do not consider my life of any account as dear to myself, so that I may finish my course and the ministry which I received from the Lord Jesus, to testify solemnly of the gospel of the grace of God." (ESV)

Although there are very few evangelicals who would deny that the Gospel is all about the grace of God being shown to man, there is only a singular usage in Scripture of the phrase the gospel of grace. This is in the book of Acts and is attributed to the apostle Paul. The gospel of grace is tremendously important as a topic and it has been observed, "one could scarcely summarize the heart of Paul's message better than the 'good news of God's grace.'"[431]

The Greek construct in this passage, το εὐαγγελιον της χαριτος του θεου, has the genitives χαριτος and θεου modifying the accusative εὐαγγελιον. This means adjectival genitives grace and God modify the object, the Gospel.[432] The second genitive identifies the origin of grace, namely from God. It is the Gospel, which is God's, and it is the Gospel that is gracious. Robertson summarizes this well saying, "to Paul the gospel consisted in the grace of God."[433] Likewise, Lenski states, "'the gospel' is the good news, and its contents is 'the grace of God.'"[434]

---

[431] John B. Polhill, vol. 26, *Acts*, The New American Commentary (Nashville: Broadman & Holman Publishers, 1995), 425.

[432] Although these words (grace and God) are nouns in English, in the Greek they are functioning like adjectives.

[433] A.T. Robertson, *Word Pictures in the New Testament* (Nashville, TN: Broadman Press, 1933), Ac 20:24.

[434] R. C. H. Lenski, *The Interpretation of the Acts of the Apostles* (Minneapolis, MN: Augsburg Publishing House, 1961), 843.

The gospel is absolutely free. It is free from merit and free from condition. This does not mean it is free from obligation once received. There is a glimmer of hope in some reformed theologians, so much that one even says:

> it must be noted that the message the apostle preached and all preachers echo is called **the gospel of the grace of God.** The clear emphasis is on grace, the unmerited favor of God by which He forgives undeserving sinners the totality of their sins and freely, mercifully gives them the complete righteousness of Jesus Christ.[435]

Other reformed theologians affirm this statement. For example, "Paul did not preach an easy-believism but rather the necessity of faith in Christ for salvation, which results in a changed life."[436] Others have said:

> the essential feature of the gospel is its declaration of God's free grace to a guilty world, forgiving sins, and imputing righteousness through faith in Jesus Christ. The distinctive work of the ministry is to declare that grace.[437]

Justification is not completed by works; neither is it a condition of it. Precious time and energy has been spent chasing after the wind trying to necessitate works for salvation in a way that is non-meritorious, but grace is free. Unfortunately, "some call their preaching 'gospel' when it does not comply with Paul's description in whole or in part."[438]

---

[435] John F. MacArthur, Jr., *Acts*, MacArthur New Testament Commentary (Chicago: Moody Press, 1994), 326.

[436] R. Kent Hughes, *Acts: The Church Afire*, Preaching the Word (Wheaton, IL: Crossway Books, 1996), 278.

[437] *Acts of the Apostles Vol. II*, ed. H. D. M. Spence-Jones, The Pulpit Commentary (London; New York: Funk & Wagnalls Company, 1909), 146.

EXCURSUS: ROMANS 13:1-7

A believer's relationship to secular government has been an issue of tremendous importance since before the institution of government was created. Many Jews were concerned with achieving independence from the Roman Empire and revolutionaries like Judas Maccabeus and others attempted to make this a reality. Even today, the believer's relationship to secular government remains a significant issue. This is especially true in the United States where a believer simultaneously has the ability to participate in the governmental process while, at the same time, the need to submit to the governmental authorities placed over them. This excursus is included here because it relates to new Calvinism's belief that the church is called through the gospel to be agents of cultural transformation.

The Command

Paul begins his discussion in Romans 13 by giving a command. This imperative serves as the basis of his discourse. This exhortation does not occur in a vacuum. Instead, it is a logical outgrowth of Paul's previous teaching, to "never pay back evil for evil to anyone... [and to] be at peace with all men."[439] Having previously discussed this instruction as it relates to personal interaction with others, Paul now turns his attention to living this out this teaching in relation to civil authorities. This provides the immediate context leading up to the command. Everything that follows this command can be categorized in one of the following three ways: reasons for this command, answers to an objection and practical implications of the command.

---

[438] R. C. H. Lenski, *The Interpretation of the Acts of the Apostles* (Minneapolis, MN: Augsburg Publishing House, 1961), 843.
[439] Romans 12:17-18ff, NASB.

Before getting to Paul's overarching point, it is important first to examine the command itself. First, it is given to every person (Πᾶσα ψυχὴ). One could easily conclude that because of this, the command applies to all humanity, but it is not equally applicable to all. In the context of the passage Paul is clearly talking to believers only. In addition, one should remember that neither Paul, nor Scripture, attempts to regulate the moral behavior of non-believers during the church age. In the command itself, the verb occurs in the present middle imperative (ὑποτασσέσθω). This indicates that the action has the subject acting on himself. Paul is commanding his readers to subject themselves to something. Along with this, the usage of ὑποτάσσω, instead of ὑπακούω, implies that this is to be done willingly by the subject. The believer then is to subject himself to the governing authorities (ἐξουσίαις ὑπερεχούσαις). This is not overly specific in its reference. It does not apply simply to presidents and congressmen, but to all those who have been placed in a position of authority or power over another.

Reasoning

Having just commanded the believer to subject themselves to those in authority over them, Paul now gives his reader the reasoning this. Paul's argument appears like a tautology, which systematically instructs his audience as to the basis for his command. In other places, Paul provides his apostolic office as the authority for a command (e.g. the introductory material an epistle), but this would be counter-productive here. Obedience to authority cannot reasonably be derived from claimed authority, unless speaking of God himself. In addition to this, it is important to remember the highly controversial nature of what Paul was discussing to both his Jewish and Gentile audiences. Not many issues were as hot button as the believer's responsibility to governmental authorities. It is likely because of these circumstances that Paul here gives a more reasonable basis for his instruction.

Paul's argument begins with an assumption. This assumption is that there are people who exercise authority in some way, shape or form over others. This assumption is almost self-evident. If one is going to give a command in regards to governing authorities, then it is logical to conclude that there are in fact governing authorities. It seems like an unimportant point, but this assumption play a role in the logic of Paul's argument. The first major part of Paul's actual argument is that "there is no authority except from God."[440] This clause is interesting in that it has two negative adverbs (οὐ γὰρ ἔστιν ἐξουσία εἰ μὴ ὑπὸ θεοῦ). This type of construct is highly unusual in proper English. It has the effect of being able to say the same thing in positive terms. This could be rendered equally "all authority is from God." This is, in fact, the point that Paul will make in the next clause. The reasoning behind this arrangement is likely because he is guiding his audience in their understanding and building upon an easier, and less controversial, point to comprehend.

There are no exceptions to the rule: all authorities are from God. Exceptions are where people naturally go with any rule, but Paul is breaking the common misconception that there may, in fact, be governing authorities that are put in place by people other than God. Essentially, Paul is stating that while this may be true in a limited sense, it is not true in its ultimate sense because of God's providential control. It is from here that Paul is able to build upon his idea in the positive sense. Having broken the misconception, he is free to state, "those [authorities] which exist are established by God."[441] Paul then brings this thought to a conclusion. Paul then states, if God has established governing authorities, then

---

[440] Romans 13:1, NASB.
[441] Romans 13:2

disobedience to governing authorities is to oppose God himself. This would have struck right at the heart of Paul's contemporaries who, as a whole, were not too fond of being subservient to Rome. If the believer is not to resist authority, what exactly are believers supposed to do? This is the concern of the practical outworking of this doctrine.

Modern ears dull the translation of διαταγῇ as ordinance, as with the NASB. Although the translation is accurate, what Paul is stating is that the resisting authority is opposing "that which has been specifically ordered or commanded" by God.[442] Therefore, Paul equates the commands of man with commands of God. Man's obligation to each is the same. This does not mean that man is obliged to follow ungodly moral commands. This is because, first and foremost, the "responsibility of the Christian is to obey freely and fully, unless to do so would directly violate God's laws" otherwise man's laws would superseded those of God.[443] The result of disobedience to the governing authorities on all other matters is condemnation before both man's governing judicial authorities and God.

Objection

The next section of this reading involves a logical objection to the command, which Paul has given to the believers in Rome. The objection is never explicitly stated. Instead, Paul raises it through a discussion of good behavior

---

[442] Johannes P. Louw and Eugene Albert Nida, vol. 1, *Greek-English Lexicon of the New Testament: Based on Semantic Domains*, electronic ed. of the 2nd edition. (New York: United Bible Societies, 1996), 425.
[443] Charles C. Ryrie, *Dr. Ryrie's Articles* (Bellingham, WA: Logos Research Systems, Inc., 2010), 141.

and fear. Essentially, Paul uses an argument based on the government's use of force. This is not too surprising since Paul has already established the depravity of man in this same letter. Having expounded upon the sinfulness of man, Paul states that if you are evil in your actions you have reason to be obedient to government out of fear of repercussions, this is why government has been given use of the sword. He then turns the table and asks about the believer who does good and obeys his government, but still receives the sword from it. Constable rephrases this in the following way, "if [those who govern] do not but serve the welfare of the people as they should, we have no fear of them and can submit to them fairly easily. What if they are evil?[444] This is the objection; are we to obey a government that persecutes the church? The answer is a resounding yes. The obvious exception to this is always when a believer is forced to choose between obeying the governing authorities and obeying the Word of God.

There are then two reasons given in this passage why the believer is to willingly subject himself to the governmental authorities. The first involves wrath, which the government has been given to enact through the use of force. The government has the power to punish and this should provide the believer with motivation to submit. Paul exemplified this in his own life, repeatedly submitting himself to the force of the government through imprisonment and physical punishment. If this were not enough, Paul previously established that the believer is to submit himself to the governing authorities based on the fact that God has put them there. One must remember that the Lord has ordained the power and force given to government. Additionally, they have been given this power for a reason. Paul earlier asserted in Romans, "God causes all things to

---

[444] Tom Constable, *Tom Constable's Expository Notes on the Bible* (Galaxie Software, 2003; 2003), Ro 13:3.

work together for good to those who love God, to those who are called according to His purpose."[445] Governments have been ordained for man's good, whether they are to be praised or abhorred. Luther explained, governments "do not compel us to do what is evil, but what is good."[446] This is governing in light of depravity. Having answered the most obvious objection, Paul is now free to move on to its practical implications.

Implications

Paul does not usually just give a command and defend it. He also builds upon it and discusses a practical implication of following the command. The practical instruction is meant to challenge his reader. This challenge comes out of the previous verse's conclusion διὰ τὴν συνείδησιν. It is because of conscience, or the desire to do good, that the believer should be willing to submit to the ruling authority. It is because of this, the believer is to pay taxes. Taxes are not the direct topic of this discourse. Instead, this passage deals with the issue of a believer's relationship to secular government. The topic of taxes is a practical outworking of Paul's original command. Paul's elaborates here to say that the believer is to pay taxes out a desire to do good, as well as a desire to serve God. One could then conclude that this is a form of worship. Paul already established earlier in epistle that believers are "to present your bodies a living and holy sacrifice, acceptable to God, which is your spiritual service of worship."[447] In this way, obeying even an ungodly ruler is an act of worship directed towards the Lord. While these rulers do not knowingly serve

---

[445] Romans 8:28, NASB.
[446] Martin Luther, *Commentary on Romans,* (Grand Rapids, MI: Zondervan Publishing House, 1954), Reprint, Grand Rapids: MI: Kregel Publications, 181.
[447] Romans 12:1, NASB.

the Lord, Paul uses the word λειτουργοὶ because they are persons "who render special service" and are busily engaged in this endeavor.[448] To put this simply, they are unwilling and unknowing instruments in the hands of God to bring about a believer's sanctification. Paul concludes this section discussing the wider practical implications beyond the issues of taxes. The issue of taxes has already been discussed at length in all three synoptic gospels. Paul uses it here as a point for the believer to examine his own life. The believer is to pay taxes to whom they are due, but in addition to this, they are to pay custom or revenue to whom it is due, to respect and finally honor to whom these are due. Respect and honor are important because they move "away from the realm of taxes and indicate a proper regard for those in high places."[449] It is more than just about giving a denarius to the government, but a life lived in humble submission to all authorities. To Paul, it is about more than a coin, it is about the attitude of heart, which is exemplified in giving due respect and honor.

Conclusion

The believer's responsibility towards the governing authorities has always been, and likely will remain an important issue as the Day of the Lord approaches. Having focused on this single passage, one must conclude that Paul was not concerned with revolutionizing the government. This passage stands in direct opposition to modern liberation theology or the social gospel. Instead, it focuses on one principle, which speaks very broadly on the matter. The believer is to live in humble submission to the rulers placed

---

[448] Johannes P. Louw and Eugene Albert Nida, vol. 1, *Greek-English Lexicon of the New Testament: Based on Semantic Domains*, electronic ed. of the 2nd edition. (New York: United Bible Societies, 1996), 460.
[449] Leon Morris, *The Letter of James*, Pillar New Testament Commentary, (Grand Rapids: William B. Eerdmans Publishing Company, 1988), 466.

over them by God. This is an act of obedience and by extension worship to God. The believer is to do this because God has enthroned rulers, even evil ones, and He is sovereignly using them for his own purposes. The only notable exception to this rule is when a civil law goes against one His direct commands. Even then, revolution is not the answer, but submission to the penalty imposed by the state as Paul exemplified time and again. Shadrach, Meshach and Abednego provide great examples concerning a believer's responsibility to a pagan, ungodly authority.

CASE STUDY:

TIMOTHY KELLER

As one of the co-founders of *The Gospel Coalition*, Keller has played a major role in new Calvinism. What is important to note here is the possible influence of postmodernism on his form of Calvinism. While this does not necessarily characterize every new Calvinist, it may be part of a larger overall trend. Many within new Calvinism seem more aware of the implications of some of Keller's theological statements. Despite this, the work he has done through *The Gospel Coalition* greatly impacted the new Calvinist movement as they seek to impact the world.

Keller is also known for founding Redeemer Presbyterian Church in New York City. Since there is little on which Redeemer Presbyterian Church stands theologically, it is possible to reproduce its core values in their entirety. It is interesting that this is where they have chosen to take their stances theologically.

Redeemer Presbyterian Church's Core Values

1. Gospel

The 'gospel' is the good news that through Christ the power of God's kingdom has entered history to renew the whole world. When we believe and rely on Jesus' work and record (rather than ours) for our relationship to God, that kingdom power comes upon us and begins to work through us.

2. Changed People

The Gospel changes people from the inside out. Christ gives us a radically new identity, freeing us from both self-righteousness and self-condemnation. He liberates us to accept people we once excluded, and to break the bondage of things (even good things) that once drove us. In particular, the gospel makes us welcoming and respectful toward those who do not share our beliefs.

3. City

We believe that nothing promotes the peace and health of the city like the spread of faith in the gospel. It renews both individual lives and reweaves the fabric of whole neighborhoods. We believe that nothing moves Christians to humbly serve, live with, and love all the diverse people of the city like the gospel does.

4. Community

The gospel creates a new community which not only nurtures individuals but serves as a sign of God's coming kingdom. Here we see classes of people loving one another who could not have gotten along without the healing power of the gospel. Here we see sex, money, and power used in unique non-destructive and life-giving ways.

5. Movement

We have no illusions that our single church or our Presbyterian tradition is sufficient to renew all of New York City spiritually, socially, and culturally. We are therefore committed to planting (and helping others plant) hundreds of new churches, while at the same time working for a renewal of gospel vitality in all the congregations of the city.

6. Serving

Though we joyfully invite every person to faith in Jesus, we are committed to sacrificially serving our neighbors whether they believe as we do or not. We do this by using our gifts and resources for the needs of others, especially the poor. And more than merely meeting individual needs, we work for justice for the powerless.

7. Renewing

We believe that the gospel has a deep, vital, and healthy impact on the arts, business, government, media, and academy of any society. Therefore we are highly committed to support Christians' engagement with culture, helping them work with excellence, distinctiveness, and accountability in their professions.[450]

This document is a manifesto of a church that has wholeheartedly embraced postmodernism. It appears that they have shaped their thinking and practices in an effort to be relevant to the world around them. In *Deconstructing*

---

[450] Redeemer Presbyterian Church, "Core Values," http://www.redeemer.com/about_us/vision_and_values/core_values.html, (Accessed September 5, 2013).

Defeater Beliefs, Keller denies the sinful heart of man in praxis by espousing a rationalistic presentation of the gospel. He sees that the mind, and not the heart, is the issue preventing people from coming to a saving faith in Christ. He says; "Christianity is disbelieved in one culture for totally opposite reasons it is disbelieved in another."[451] This is a denial of the essence of Calvinist soteriology. He replaces a bold proclamation of the gospel with one that must be loving, attractive and non-offensive. This is what he refers to as the sandwich approach to the gospel. It is more of a bait-and-switch technique than a presentation of the gospel. One major issue, "the word of the cross is foolishness to those who are perishing."[452] The gospel is offensive. Paul says, "but if I, brothers, still preach circumcision, why am I still being persecuted? In that case the offense of the cross has been removed."[453] The cross and the gospel by their very nature are offensive and exclusive.

This is a fundamental flaw, which runs throughout the theology of Keller and Redeemer Presbyterian Church is connected to a misunderstanding of hamartiology. Romans 3 explains, the issue preventing people from coming to a saving faith in Christ is primarily a heart issue. There is not one unregenerate person who would desire to follow God even if the gospel was presented in the most attractive way possible. This is truly the Reformation and Calvinistic understanding of the depravity of the human heart. All the contextualization in the world could not help save a single

---

[451] Timothy Keller, "Deconstructing Defeater Beliefs: Leading the Secular to Christ," Jan 1, 2000, http://www.case.edu.au/images/uploads/03_pdfs/keller-deconstructing-defeater.pdf, (Accessed September 5, 2013). Accessed through The Gospel Coalition at http://thegospelcoalition.org/resources/entry/Deconstructing-Defeater-Beliefs-Leading-the-Secular-to-Christ.
[452] 1 Corinthians 1:18ff, NASB.
[453] Galatians 5:11, ESV.

soul. Keller does not outright deny important doctrinal matters, but in postmodern fashion he does not appear to hold them absolutely. This is part of the paradigm shift in new Calvinism.

Mission over theology

One of the dangers that led to such a divergence from traditional reformed theology is the emphasis placed on the mission of the church over and above theology. Notice the absence of the doctrines of grace in Redeemer's core values. The openness in theology allows for a diversity of new Calvinist pastors and theologians to maintain a close-knit fellowship. If one self-identifies as a Calvinist, then other doctrines are seemingly insignificant. What is truly important is the missional nature of the church. There is theological indifference as long as one self-identifies as a Calvinist. This corresponds with the postmodern mindset: we are to be tolerant and not to judge others. Redeemer Presbyterian Church's theology is so open one can hypothetically reject central tenants of the Nicene Creed and still be in line with their core values. For example, although it mentions Jesus as redeemer, it does not mention His divinity. It also fails to mention a biblical vision of salvation mentioning "Christ gives us a radically new identity, freeing us from both self-righteousness and self-condemnation." It does not mention that this new identity frees man from condemnation and the penalty of sin. It subtly replaces biblical terminology with modern philosophical and liberal concepts. The postmodern man can say a lot without saying anything. This is exemplified in Redeemer's Core Values. This is why new Calvinism has been able to produce such ecumenicity. In speaking on doctrinal distinctives, Keller states:

> the 'already' of the New Testament means more boldness in proclamation. We can most definitely be

> sure of the central doctrines that support the gospel. But, the 'not yet' means charity and humility in non-essentials beliefs. In other words, we must be moderate about what we teach except when it comes to the cross, grace and sin. In our views, especially those that Christians cannot agree on, we must be less unbending and triumphalistic.[454]

One can see Ladd's influence once again manifest itself. The already/not yet paradigm is expressed in ways beyond eschatology.

What is more important than theology is authentically living out Christianity. It views Christianity through a philosophical lens, the best possible religious system to live by, and not as absolute truth. This is why they are so concerned with living out the faith and minimally concerned with standing for the true faith doctrinally. Hypocrisy is what stands in the way of postmoderns in New York City, where Keller pastors. They need to overcome this obstacle in order that souls can be saved. If only they had seen a church and a people living authentically, then they would see the beauty and majesty of Christ's plan at work and be compelled to believe. One problem, many churches will more characteristically resemble the Corinthian church than the utopian ideal of Redeemer. It is the biblical gospel that has the answer. Man is sinful. This is why the church appears hypocritical. This is where the gospel starts, with universal guilt and universal condemnation. That is why the gospel is such good news. It is the message of salvation to those who are perishing. Keller does not see sin in its proper biblical definition. He chooses instead to read his understanding back into sin, thereby contextualizing sin

---

[454] Tim Keller, "The Centrality of the Gospel," http://download.redeemer.com/pdf/learn/resources/Centrality_of_the_Gospel-Keller.pdf, (Accessed September 5, 2013).

improperly. He states that "the root of every sin is a failure to believe the gospel message that Jesus, and Jesus alone, is our justification, righteousness, and redemption."[455] How does the root of sin apply to Adam or to anyone prior to the coming of Christ?

Keller perverts the gospel. It is no longer a proposition: believe and be saved. The best way that Keller's false gospel can be defined is a God-empowered change mechanism. This is what it is to him. Jesus is the redeemer; the believer is to be an agent of redemption, the gospel concerns redemption. This is not the biblical understanding of redemption. Observe the following statements concerning Keller's view of the gospel:

> The gospel is to be applied to every area of thinking, feeling, relating, working, and behaving.[456]

> The main problem, then, in the Christian life is that we have not thought out the deep implications of the gospel, we have not "used" the gospel in and on all parts of our life.[457]

> the key to continual and deeper spiritual renewal and revival is the ***continual re-discovery of the gospel***" (emphasis original)[458]

> Paul used the gospel on racism[459]

---

[455] Timothy J. Keller, *Center Church: Doing Balanced, Gospel-Centered Ministry in Your City,* (Grand Rapids, MI: Zondervan, 2012), Kindle Edition. Loc. 1755-1756.
[456] Tim Keller, "The Centrality of the Gospel."
[457] Ibid.
[458] Ibid.
[459] Ibid.

> We have seen that the gospel is the way that anything is renewed and transformed by Christ--whether a heart, a relationship, a church, or a community.[460]
>
> All problems, personal or social come from a failure to use the gospel in a radical way.[461]

This final statement claims that the root of all the world's problems is not sin, but a failure to use the gospel. This is not biblical. It is surprising that more within Reformed circles are not raising their voices against this kind of theology. This is what happens when a movement embraces postmodernism and emphasizes spirituality over doctrine. It inevitably abandons true religion.

In succumbing to the postmodern mindset, he refuses to believe there is any non-contextualized gospel. He believes that all gospel presentations are contextualized; even those recorded in Scripture. While these are based in actual events, he goes to great lengths to show that Paul in one place is sharing the gospel to Jewish persons and in another place sharing it with Greeks. He emphasizes the discontinuity between these two gospel presentations over and above their continuity. This is because, in his thinking, the church has failed to properly contextualize the gospel. He never goes so far as denying the historicity of the gospel, but he does deny that the gospel can be expressed in a non-contextualized way. This is of great importance as it provides the grounds for the practical outworking of his theology. He claims to be a Calvinist, but it is difficult to see Calvin or the doctrines of grace being understood in his theology. He states:

---

[460] Ibid.
[461] Ibid.

> contextualization is not — as is often argued — 'giving people what they want to hear.' Rather, it is giving people the Bible's answers, which they may not at all want to hear, to questions about life that people in their particular time and place are asking, in language and forms they can comprehend, and through appeals and arguments with force they can feel, even if they reject them.[462]

While Keller frequently quotes Luther, this statement is an outright denial of Luther's thesis in *Bondage of the Will*. This work was perhaps the most important work of the Reformation and a great foundation upon which to understand the grace of God. A person's rejection or acceptance of the gospel has nothing to do with the way it is presented. This does not mean that the church should not care about how the gospel is presented; it most definitely should. What Keller is arguing is that the properly contextualized gospel yields the best results. He states explicitly "our ministry will be unfruitful because we have failed to contextualize well."[463] He also says:

> it is possible to subscribe to every orthodox doctrine and nevertheless fail to communicate the gospel to people's hearts in a way that brings about repentance, joy, and spiritual growth.[464]

The reason this is certainly true is due to the hardened heart of the hearer and not the ineffectiveness of the communicator. There is a break between the ears and the heart. It is only God who can accomplish these ends.

Social Justice

---

[462] Timothy J. Keller, *Center Church,* Loc. 2250-2253.
[463] Ibid, Loc. 2259.
[464] Ibid, Loc. 1847-1848.

There is an ever-pressing concern within new Calvinism, and in the theology of Keller, for social justice to be enacted. There is this aurora about the new Calvinists that they are the only group with a real concern for the poor. While the church carries a message, it is an offer of reconciliation toward God and it has nothing to offer other than the true message of the gospel. If the church abandons this message, then what good will food or clothes do for those in need? The church should be concerned for those in need, but Scripture explains that the church is to do this as a service for the Lord. As Paul says, if you abandon the true gospel you have believed in vain. All social work is in vain apart from the true propositional gospel.

What Keller and others have proposed is a larger vision of the gospel that includes social action and racial reconciliation. It is as if those who believe only in the propositional aspect of the Gospel do not care about social responsibility or racism. Keller in describing the Christian life states, "this kind of life (activism) reflects the character of God."[465] Activism is a part of the Christian life, but this fails to take into account Paul's teaching in Romans 13 or Peter's in 1 Peter 2. While Christians in America are given the privilege of participating in government, most Christians live under authoritative governments. These same Christians are not given the freedom to participate in social activism, and must submit to their governments as God-ordained authorities.

Keller then couples social activism with a lordship view of salvation whereby, "true grace always results in changed lives of holiness and justice."[466] It is one of Keller's contributions to new Calvinism to add the phrase "and

---

[465] Timothy Keller, *Generous Justice: How God's Grace Makes Us Just*, Kindle Edition, Loc. 361.
[466] Timothy J. Keller, *Center Church,* Loc. 387.

justice" to a lordship understanding of salvation. He goes on to say in another work, "the implication is that if you do not actively and generously share your resources with the poor, you are a robber. You are not living justly."[467] Apparently, you are not a Christian if you do not share generously with the poor. This is a misunderstanding of the lesson of Ananias and Sapphira. It is not surprising, but it is still shocking, to see him claim, "if you are not just, you've not truly been justified by faith."[468] This thinking is not biblical. Scripture goes to great lengths to show that there is no one good except God. In the same way, there is no one who is just except God alone. Keller's beliefs could be a logical outworking of lordship salvation. It is easy to see that when one begins to add a single requirement to salvation, it is much easier to adding requirements. Personal salvation is not enough. What must be done, according to Keller, "we must retell the culture's story in Jesus."[469] This is something he refers to as gospel renewal. There is a major issue with this concept of the big gospel, which is becoming increasing popular today. Perverting the gospel is a serious matter. So serious in fact that Paul states unequivocally "as we have said before, so I say again now, if any man is preaching to you a gospel contrary to what you received, he is to be accursed!"[470] Keller claims that the church in general has abandoned or forgotten about the social aspect of the gospel. If the biblical gospel truthfully does includes these social elements, as Keller claims, then is the church apostate and accursed? ἀνάθεμα would need to be pronounced on those who Keller is speaking out against. There are two gospels being proposed. Only one can be the gospel; the other gospel is false and Paul pronounces ἀνάθεμα on it. Stallard explains,

---

[467] Timothy Keller, *Generous Justice: How God's Grace Makes Us Just*, Loc. 346.
[468] Ibid, Loc. 1205-1206.
[469] Timothy J. Keller, *Center Church,* Loc. 3523-3524.
[470] Galatians 1:9, NASB.

the intermingling of the biblical gospel with the social gospel, "can easily lead to a lack of clarity in the giving of gospel invitations and to a lack of evangelism in the work of Christians."[471]

In his magnum opus on practical ecclesiology, *Center Church,* Keller exhorts the contemporary church to not only pursue the redemption of individuals but society as well. He speaks of the church's approach to its current practices in unflattering terms saying:

> many Christians resist the idea that social systems need to be dealt with directly. They prefer the idea that 'society is changed one heart at a time,' and so they concentrate on only evangelism and individual social work. This is naïve.[472]

One looks in vain for biblical support for this statement. Keller's theological justification is laughable and his biblical support is imaginary. He develops his own conclusion of the Good Samaritan parable saying:

> social reform moves beyond the relief of immediate needs and dependency and seeks to change the conditions and social structures that aggravate or cause that dependency. Imagine a sequel to the Good Samaritan parable. The months go by and every time he makes his trip from Jerusalem to Jericho he finds another man in the road, beaten and robbed. Finally the Samaritan says, "How do we stop the violence?[473]

---

[471] Mike Stallard. "Gospel Centeredness, Jesus and Social Ethics" *Journal of Ministry and Theology* 15:2 (Fall 2011): 6.
[472] Timothy Keller, *Generous Justice: How God's Grace Makes Us Just*, Loc. 1491-1492.
[473] Ibid, Loc. 1472-1475.

He also looks to Israel and the provisions made in the Mosaic Law for the poor. He says, "Israel was charged to create a culture of social justice for the poor and vulnerable because it was the way the nation could reveal God's glory and character to the world."[474] This is eisegesis. God made the provision for the poor in light of the sinfulness of man. This is the same with the provision for the King in the Pentateuch. It is true that provision was made in the Law for a king, but this was not God's desire for Israel It was created with the foreknowledge of Israel's disobedience. It is the same way for the protection of the poor. It is a protection from man and not a mandate to eliminate poverty. Keller would have great difficulty reconciling this belief with Jesus' rebuke of Judas when Judas protested that Christ's feet should not have been anointed with expensive oil.[475] The question of Judas has a modern twist in Keller's proposal. This is not to say that the church is to be indifferent about society, but it is a reminder to keep a proper perspective about social injustice being only a temporal issue. Eternal issues are of much graver concern for the church. This is why the epistles to the church are not concerned with social transformation. In fact, Paul writes to submit to the government even though he was frequently imprisoned for his faith in an empire that was egregiously unjust. His desire was never to reform society.

Overall, Keller's anthropology is reminiscent of postmillennialism. He even makes the claim, "God is distressed that the unity of the human family has been broken and declares his intention to take down the walls of racism and nationalism that human sin and pride have put there."[476] This is the heart of postmillennial thought. He mainly sees the goodness in man and not the true depth of his sinfulness

---

[474] Ibid, Loc. 260-262.
[475] Matthew 26:6-13, Mark 14:3-9, John 12:1-10.
[476] Timothy Keller, *Generous Justice: How God's Grace Makes Us Just*, Loc. 1430-1431.

and depravity. He pays lip service to the doctrine of total depravity, but in reality it is denied in the outworking of his beliefs.

The city itself plays an important role in Keller's practical theology. This is not too surprising given that he is a pastor in New York City. This is important to him because "the city is humanity intensified — a magnifying glass that brings out the very best and worst of human nature — it has a dual nature."[477] The biblical doctrine of depravity denies this dual nature in man before regeneration. It is true that cities can be a special place for the gospel, but this is because of the concentration of humanity that occurs there. The gospel does work powerfully in cities but its uniqueness is found against the backdrop of a city's utter darkness. In the dark places the light can burn brighter. This is not to say that the suburbs or country are any better; they too have their own distinct issues. What is necessary is to break down the romanticized notion of Keller's that God works especially in cities and to protest the concept that the city as an entity plays a pivotal role in the arc of redemptive history."[478]

Total Depravity

Keller claims for himself the title of Calvinist, but he does not truly hold to the doctrine of total depravity. What this means is that in his attempts to reach the lost, Keller does not see the true nature of the unregenerate person's heart and mind. Part of this stems from an over-value placed on reason. This is also seen in his estimation of the problem

---

[477] Keller, Timothy J. *Center Church*, Loc. 3684-3685.
[478] Ibid, Loc. 3693.

of evangelism; "gospel preaching that targets some sins but not the sins of oppression 'cannot possibly work among the overwhelming majority of people in the world.'"[479] There is a touch of liberation theology in this, but more importantly it makes the response of man to the gospel contingent upon the contextualization of the one presenting the gospel. Thank the Lord this is not true.

Keller has often sought to avoid the issues that have plagued the church growth movement, but all too often his thinking still aligns with it. Keller pastors a very large church that he planted. It is not surprising then to see that he views God as working in a special way in his specific church. He readily admits that this is not because of any specific methodology that he has employed, but due to his church's fidelity to the gospel. They take the beliefs of the church growth movement, "try this method and a church will grow," and simply replace it with "follow Scripture, as we see it, and a church will grow." It repeats the heart of the church growth movement's belief that churches produce growth, not the Spirit. Keller even suggests that the pastor is to be judged based not on numerical growth (as in the church growth movement) or in his faithfulness (which is a naïve dead orthodoxy) instead he "came to the conclusion that a more biblical theme…(for evaluation is) fruitfulness."[480] Obedience in ministry will inevitably result in quantifiable fruit; otherwise the minister is ineffective. In one statement, he even says, "if gospel ministry was going to be productive…"[481] The productiveness of gospel ministry, as he sees it, is dependent upon the work of man. This is far from the truth. It is only God who can produce fruit in ministry, whether it is through the pastor or even in spite of

---

[479] Timothy Keller, *Generous Justice: How God's Grace Makes Us Just*, Loc. 759-760.
[480] Keller, Timothy J. *Center Church*, Loc. 96.
[481] Ibid, Loc. 131.

him. While he derides the church growth movement for claiming to know the secret behind growth, he essentially instructs others to follow his method because it is more biblical. Keller's thesis behind *Center Church* is that what is needed by church today is a gospel vision: a vision for the full gospel that reaches the cities and renews the world. The church needs a proper contextualization of the gospel that reaches the postmodern world. He says, "our ministry will be unfruitful because we have failed to contextualize well."[482] He completely ignores that it is God and only Him who makes ministry fruitful.

One area that explicitly denies the depraved nature of man's mind and heart is Keller's approach to evangelism. In his sandwich approach to evangelism, he says:

> first, the gospel must be presented briefly but so vividly and attractively (and so hooked into the culture's base-line cultural narratives) that the listener is virtually compelled to say *'It would be wonderful if that were true, but it can't be!'* Until he or she comes to that position, you can't work on the implausibility structure! The listener must have motivation to hear you out. That is what defeaters do – they make people super impatient with any case for Christianity. Unless they find a presentation of Christ surprisingly attractive and compelling (and stereo-type breaking) their eyes will simply glaze over when you try to talk to them.[483]

This ignores the nature of an unregenerate man's heart. A depraved heart is enslaved to its own sinful desires, and the gospel will not appear attractive to the unregenerate man.

---

[482] Ibid, 2259.
[483] Timothy Keller, "Deconstructing Defeater Beliefs: Leading the Secular to Christ."

Somehow, the response of man to the gospel is best accomplished through Keller's technique of presenting the wonderful things about being a Christian and then only later explaining to them the implications of becoming a Christian. It is as if becoming a Christian can be solely achieved by human means. It seeks to manufacture the work of the Spirit artificially. One hopes that the theological world will recognize the missional nature of new Calvinism for what it is, postmodernism.

CHAPTER 5

CONTINUATIONISM

At first, it may appear that the new Calvinism's continuationist beliefs are an ancillary issue, especially in regards to their soteriology. This is certainly true to an extent. This is one reason for the placement and length of this section of the dissertation. The doctrine of continuationism does still bear some importance in understanding the movement of new Calvinism. Specifically, the reason for new Calvinism's openness or affinity for the contemporary use of the sign gifts may be due to the influence of the charismatic tradition. Some within the movement even refer to their theology as "charismatic with a seatbelt."[484] It is forgotten that the charismatic tradition is not known for its strict adherence to the doctrine of justification by faith alone. Charismatic theology usually asserts that true believers will be endowed with certain gifts. Typically these gifts include things like prophecy, healing, tongues, et cetera. Following this, one new Calvinist states that at conversion, "the Holy Spirit brings with him at least one ability to do ministry like Jesus. It's a supernatural enablement to do ministry like Jesus."[485] The last portion of this definition is most startling. Modern charismatic-reformed theology differentiates itself from the more traditional Pentecostal charismatics in that it

---

[484] Mark Driscoll, "Spiritual Gifts Part I," August 6, 2006, http://marshill.com/media/1st-corinthians/spiritual-gifts-part-i, (Accessed September 5, 2013)
[485] Ibid.

does not look for tongues to be present by necessity in the true believer. Instead, some say that one is not living the full or complete Christian life if they are not graced with these gifts. With this, new Calvinism's charismatic background tends to see justification as being accompanied by Spirit-filling and the use of supernatural gifts like tongues. Accordingly, one new Calvinist estimates "about 20 percent of the elders in (his) church have the gift of tongues."[486] Others have the supernatural ability to teach like Jesus, heal like Jesus, or to prophesize like Jesus. If one is not gifted with a supernatural ability to do ministry like Jesus, should salvation be called into question? If held with consistency, why not inspect for spiritual gifts? In addition, some new Calvinists view eternal security in much the same way as other charismatics. All deny eternal security. This is detailed more above, but charismatics, whether reformed or not, do not truly hold that a person may know with certainty that they will go to heaven. Their soteriology may be better classified as Pentecostal instead of reformed. While they believe in predestination, they replace assurance with conditional security. For the Arminian-Pentecostal, salvation is determined by an individual's remaining in the faith until their death and assurance are based upon being filled with the Spirit. For the reformed-charismatic, salvation must persevere, or it is not true salvation and assurance is based upon a person's subjective experience of holiness.

      Continuationism is a major issue for new Calvinism. It is of such great importance that it makes the short-list of essential doctrines. Although described as generally continuationist, they leave little room for cessationists. This shows their doctrinal shallowness. This is a core part of who they are, but it is still negotiable. Notice this extreme statement, "I believe God is at work in the Vineyard Movement-as in hundreds of other movements today. Oh,

---

[486] Ibid.

that we may be on the Move with God in Minneapolis."[487] What is striking is that no one has yet mentioned why they have felt the need to be open, but cautious when it comes to the uses of the sign gifts in the church. This is because their doctrine shows no real understanding of any objective pneumatology. Even Grudem's *Systematic Theology*, which spends a great deal of time defending the doctrine of continuationism, devotes little space to understanding the Spirit's work today. Instead, their doctrines are derived from subjective experience. They are even defended using the inaugurated eschatology of Ladd. Notice what the faculty of Fuller Theological Seminary asserts; "since the rule of God has indeed come in Jesus Christ, should we not assume that the same healing miracles would be regularly performed in the ongoing ministry of the contemporary church?"[488]

It has yet to be answered, why continuationism is so important? Instead, attacks are made on the worldly cessationists, betraying a total lack of understanding of their position. This is the caricature of cessationists: "some say, God doesn't heal anymore, he used to do that. God doesn't do miracles anymore, he used to do that."[489] This is plainly false. No cessationist would make such a claim. Instead, the heart of the cessationist position is that God no longer equips people with these abilities because they are no longer necessary. They were always intended to be foundational. After all, Scripture is sufficient to equip the man of God for

---

[487] John Piper, "The California Conference on Holiness: Kudos and Cautions," February 19, 1990, http://www.desiringgod.org/resource-library/taste-see-articles/the-california-conference-on-holiness-kudos-and-cautions, (Accessed September 5, 2013).
[488] Lewis B. Smedes, ed., *Ministry and the Miraculous: A Case Study at Fuller Theological Seminary,* (Pasadena, CA: Fuller Seminary Press,1987), 16.
[489] Mark Driscoll, "Spiritual Gifts Part II," August 6, 2006, http://marshill.com/media/1st-corinthians/spiritual-gifts-part-ii, (Accessed September 5, 2013).

every good work.[490] God still performs the miraculous, but He simply does not equip certain people with these abilities to perform these actions in a normative sense. It is repeated time and again that God does not change and, therefore, the sign gifts are still functioning. This betrays a complete ignorance of the fact that God's dealing with man certainly changes. The sacrificial system is no longer in place, but the Judaizers are repeatedly repudiated in the New Testament epistles for making the same claim that God does not change, referencing the need to obey the Mosaic Law. This is a straw man argument through and through. A *Desiring God* conference speaker attacks the cessationist gospel as "an anemic diluted deficient destructive Gospel."[491] This is a startling and inflammatory statement.

Most of the responses concerning continuationism have come from those within the reformed church. Horton echoes this sentiment saying, the "Calvinism-Charismatic bridge goes in both directions and his view of continuing prophecy has contributed to a curious hybrid that in my view cannot survive in the long run."[492] Simply put, the reformed church states: continuationism is not Calvinism. In turn, the traditional reformed Church is referred to derogatorily as "sectarian reformed."[493]

New Calvinism's theology of spiritual gifts is more descriptive than prescriptive. It tells the following about the movement. First, it is postmodern. Its theology is a "pick and

---

[490] Cf. 2 Timothy 3:16-17.
[491] Tope Koleoso, "How Should a Reformed Pastor be Charismatic?" Desiring God National Conference for Pastors 2013, http://www.youtube.com/watch?v=1cmdWLJF3Dw, (Accessed June 22, 2013).
[492] Michael Horton, "Reformed and Charismatic?" August 22, 2011, http://www.whitehorseinn.org/blog/2011/08/22/reformed-and-charismatic/, (Accessed June 20, 2013).
[493] Lewis B. Smedes, ed., *Ministry and the Miraculous,* 52.

mix."[494] Its hermeneutic approach is described as "community-based."[495] For those not familiar with this, it essentially is a mob mentality. The majority is correct in determining doctrine. Since the culture is predominantly open but cautious when it comes to the sign gifts, then so is new Calvinism. This may not be true with other doctrines, but it certainly is true when it involves continuationism. The movement has also lost some reverence for God. It does not fear the Lord, but desires the miraculous working of God to be normative for all. An article in Spurgeon's *Sword and Trowel* explains this well:

> the new *Calvinism with the new* Calvinists constantly extol the Puritans, but they do not want to worship or live as they did. One of the vaunted new conferences is called *Resolved*, after Jonathan Edwards' famous youthful *Resolutions* (seventy searching undertakings). But the culture of this conference would unquestionably have met with the outright condemnation of that great theologian.[496]

Finally, it takes unbiblical stances to re-interpret Scripture in light of the testimony of experience. It is said speaking in tongues "oftentimes accompanied with the gift of interpretation."[497] Paul says:

---

[494] Carl Trueman, Phone Conversation, June 18, 2013.
[495] Robert L. Thomas, "The Hermeneutics of Non-Cessationism," *The Master's Seminary Journal* 14/2 (Fall 2003): 296. 387-310.
[496] Peter Masters, "New Calvinism, the Merger of Calvinism with Worldliness," *Sword and Trowel,* Metropolitan Tabernacle, Dec. 2009, http://www.metropolitantabernacle.org/Sword-And-Trowel/Evangelical-Magazine-Sword-and-Trowel-Articles/New-Calvinism-Merger-of-Calvinism-and-Worldliness, (Accessed June 23, 2013).
[497] Mark Driscoll, "Spiritual Gifts Part V," August 6, 2006, http://marshill.com/media/1st-corinthians/spiritual-gifts-part-v, (Accessed September 5, 2013).

if anyone speaks in a tongue, *it should be* by two or at the most three, and *each* in turn, and one must interpret; but if there is no interpreter, he must keep silent in the church; and let him speak to himself and to God.[498]

There is a great difference between oftentimes and must. Prophecy likewise is "personal revelation from the Holy Spirit....not necessarily free from error."[499] Peter explains, "no prophecy was ever made by an act of human will, but men moved by the Holy Spirit spoke from God."[500]

CASE STUDY:

MARK DRISCOLL

There are many who believe that a dissertation discussing the theological merits of new Calvinism would focus extensively on its most controversial figure Mark Driscoll. This would not at all be surprising to many because of Driscoll's ability to upset large segments of people. His unilateral statements and sensationalistic teaching/preaching is frequently intended to ruffle the feathers of Christians. His theology is not discussed in greater detail because, upon an examination of new Calvinism, he is not found to be the theological backbone of new Calvinism. He is not even really the theological backbone of his own books.[501] Driscoll is certainly theological, but he expresses neither the depth nor

---

[498] 1 Corinithians 14:27-27, NASB.
[499] John Piper, "The New Testament Gift of Prophecy: Definition, Theses and Suggestions," March 26, 1990 http://www.desiringgod.org/resource-library/taste-see-articles/the-new-testament-gift-of-prophecy, (Accessed September 5, 2013).
[500] 2 Peter 1:21, NASB.
[501] Most of Driscoll's books are co-authored by Gerry Breshears. This is not intended to be a dig at the recent charges of plagiarism made against Driscoll.

the breadth of others within new Calvinism. Rooted in lordship salvation, Driscoll, in his postmodern version of a systematic theology, asserts:

> the first thing we are to do in response to God's revelation is repent (vv.36-38). Repentance is the Spirit-empowered acknowledgement of sin that results in a change of mind about who and what is lord in our life...the second response is to accept the revealed message about Jesus by Spirit-empowered faith."[502]

He also states, "the conversion of a Christian is in fact a conversion to both Jesus and Jesus' mission...a conversion to Jesus' mission above every other mission in life."[503]

One of Driscoll's greatest contributions to new Calvinism is in the field of practical ministry. Other new Calvinists have duplicated his approach to ministry. Driscoll's praxis has become normative for many young churches planted in the likeness of Mars Hill Church.[504]

Most are familiar with Driscoll's background. He emerged into prominence from a movement known as the emerging church, alongside of other notable men like Brian McLaren and Rob Bell. Although he has, in the recent past, stood in opposition to the extremes of the emerging church, what is glossed over is that he only objected to the extremes of their theology and not their overall approach to ministry. Since taking his stand in opposition to the emerging church, new Calvinism has adopted him as one of their own and quickly assimilated him into its ranks. A product of this

---

[502] Mark Driscoll and Gerry Breshears, *Doctrine: What Christians Should Believe,* (Wheaton, IL: Crossway, 2010), 317.
[503] Mark Driscoll and Gerry Breshears, *Vintage Jesus: Timely Answers to Timeless Questions,* (Wheaton, IL, Crossway, 2007), 223.
[504] Mars Hill refers to the church that Driscoll pastors.

merger has been a breed of Calvinism that follows the ministry practices of the emerging church. It is viewed as being the best of both worlds by far too many. His rock star status and persona drawing legions of emulators have helped to drive the expansion new Calvinism beyond the *Acts 29 Network*.

For the benefit of the reader, it is important to discuss what Driscoll sees as the difference between new Calvinism and old Calvinism.

> 1. Old Calvinism was fundamental or liberal and separated from or syncretized with culture. New Calvinism is missional and seeks to create and redeem culture.
>
> 2. Old Calvinism fled from the cities. New Calvinism is flooding into cities.
>
> 3. Old Calvinism was fearful of the Holy Spirit and generally cessationist (i.e., believing the gifts of the Holy Spirit such as tongues and prophecy had ceased). New Calvinism delights in the Holy Spirit and is generally continuationist with regard to spiritual gifts.
>
> 4. Old Calvinism was fearful and suspicious of other Christians and burned bridges. New Calvinism loves all Christians and builds bridges between them.[505]

In these first two statements, one can see a great deal of Keller's philosophy of ministry involving a focus on cities and the redemption of culture. The third statement is the openness to the sign gifts has been articulated by Grudem

---

[505] Mark Driscoll, "Time Magazine Names New Calvinism 3rd Most Powerful Idea."

and adopted by most new Calvinists. Driscoll's forth point is an apt description of postmodernism. It is an open, inclusive environment. While Driscoll stays truer to orthodoxy in his theology, it is not drastically different from that taught by McLaren and Bell. The difference between Driscoll and the emerging church is simply a matter of degree. The influence of the emerging church remains present.

Inclusive or Exclusive?

Perhaps the most difficult thing to determine, in regards to Driscoll and the *Acts 29 Network* of churches, is whether they are doctrinally inclusive or exclusive. At times, they seem to be almost as inclusive as the emergent church. For example, Mars Hill Church does not have a written doctrinal statement posted on their website. Acts 29, on the other hand, is very specific in its theology. For example, one cannot be a dispensationalist and be involved in the *Acts 29 Network*. It is said in their doctrine section:

> We are not eschatological Theonomists or Classic Dispensationalists (e.g. Scofield) and believe that divisive and dogmatic certainty surrounding particular details of Jesus Second coming are unprofitable speculation, because the timing and exact details of His return are unclear to us.[506]

One wonders in vain why there is such a negative attitude against dispensationalists, even those who are very Calvinistic. At the same time, in their doctrinal statement, there is no stance taken in regards to paedobaptism. They desire not to be dogmatic, but in truth are dogmatic about a few theological stances. It is said:

---

[506] Acts 29 Network, "Pastor Training Program Frequently Asked Questions," http://www.acts29network.org/ptp-faq/, (Accessed September 5, 2013).

> we are not fundamentalists who retreat from cultural involvement and transformation, but rather missionaries faithful both to the content of Scripture and context of ministry.[507]

Those who contend for the fundamentals of the faith lack a passion for the salvation of souls. One need only look at the ministry of D.L. Moody to see that this is not the case. It is often repeated that Acts 29 churches are "first Christians, second Evangelicals, third Missional, and fourth Reformed."[508] As long as one holds to the five points of TULIP, and earnestly desires to advance God's kingdom by engaging the world, theology is an issue of secondary importance to be decided within the confines of the local church.

At times, it even seems that there is willingness to dialogue with anyone who pastors a megachurch. This may be one reason why Rick Warren, a natural antagonist of new Calvinism, has been given a great deal of respect. His ministry is worthy of fellowship, despite the fact that he is not in the mainstream of reformed theology. Nowhere has this become more evident than in James MacDonald's open fellowship with T.D. Jakes. Their thinking goes, if one serves as pastor of a megachurch, this is a sign of God's blessing, and the body of Christ should be willing to learn from their ministries. Walker states that many new Calvinists hold "something that works (the numbers being the evidence) must be worthy, must be right…if they are bigger, then by definition they have something to teach us."[509]

All too often, Driscoll and Acts 29 portray the church as coldly orthodox. They view the traditional church as a

---

[507] Ibid.
[508] Ibid.
[509] Jeremy Walker, *New Calvinism Considered: A Personal and Pastoral Assessment,* (Darlington, England: EP Books, 2013), Kindle Location 629, 638.

caricature. It is the fundamentalists who do not really care about the poor and marginalized, and do not really have a heart for evangelism. As many have grown up in the era of seeker-sensitive churches, new Calvinism appears to be a reaction to this. The negative aspects of traditional churches are focused upon and stereotyped. In this, there really is a divisive spirit in the movement as a whole stemming from a desire to do things differently. What they seek is a paradigm shift. This is not necessarily a bad thing. The reformers did the same thing. One must ask a pointed question: is the pattern that has been put forth by the church truly something that needs to change? Must all pastors grow long beards and get tattoos in order to be relevant?[510]

In an effort to cast a net over a wider audience, Driscoll's writings have introduced laypersons to the field of theology. It is evident that this has motivated him to paint broad strokes in his written works. What is surprising is that there are times when no alarm has raised by other reformed pastors and theologians when displaying gross tendencies towards the emerging church. Nowhere is this more evident than in Mars Hill Church's website which states:

> Jesus is a good friend. We've all been a bad friend at some point....maybe we've taken advantage of friends or been short with them or simply not been there when needed. And we've probably experienced that as well. But Jesus is a good friend. In fact, he's a perfect friend. And even when we're horrible friends to him, he's always a good friend to us.*[511]*

This is a core part of how Mars Hill Church presents the gospel on its site, but it is simply not true.

---

[510] This is in large part a debate between the normative and regulative principles of worship. New Calvinism unquestionably holds to an unadulterated normative principle of worship.

New Calvinism's Approach to Ministry

What it is that draws lay people to Driscoll and does not cause suspicions to be aroused in seasoned theologians by someone who has been so connected to the emergent church? The answer can be found in his charisma and practical theology. This is where a great deal of current criticism lies. A recent work summarized the points of concern within the movement of new Calvinism. Some of his concerns are:

> a willingness to use professional non-Christians in worship
>
> a commercial attitude towards 'doing church'
>
> an ugly showmanship of overly dramatic, sickly cultured preaching
>
> a large ministry revolving around one prominent figure
>
> something called ecclesiastical franchising (planting satellite campuses without a present preacher)[512]

The contemporary church has caused new Calvinists to be disheartened by what Keller derogatorily calls the "indifference" of those who are theologically orthodox.[513] It

---

[511] Mars Hill Church, "Jesus," http://marshill.com/jesus, (Accessed September 5, 2013).
[512] Jeremy Walker, *New Calvinism Considered: A Personal and Pastoral Assessment.*
[513] Timothy Keller foreword to *Unfashionable,* (Colorado Springs, CO: Multnomah Books, 2009), xv.

is the emergent (missional) methodology of ministries like Driscoll's that speak to people like Tchividjian who asserts:

> "]Christians make a difference in this world by being different from this world; they don't make a difference by being the same...only by being properly unfashionable...only then will we be redemptively different and serve as God's cosmic change agents in a world yearning for change.[514]

This type of thinking is more reminiscent of Arminianism than Calvinism. It is traditionally the Arminian who supposes that man affects God's cosmic plan. It is as if what has been discovered is that the proper contextualization of one's ministry is responsible for spiritual growth, salvation of souls, church growth, et cetera.

Much of this theology is connected to a doctrinal understanding that sees Christ's active obedience imparted to the believer. This is Christ's vicarious law-keeping given to believers. This may seem like quite a stretch but, in fact, it is not. As Kauffman observes in regards to Tchividjian's work, *Jesus + Nothing = Everything*:

> Tchividjian conflates justification and sanctification—and unfortunately, the work of the Second and Third Persons of the Trinity—by teaching that the holiness of our sanctification has already been accomplished on the Cross by Jesus. As he himself summarizes the book, 'The Christian life is not about my transformation; it's about Christ's substitution.' To the contrary, *justification* is about Christ's substitution, but *sanctification is about my transformation*.[515]

---

[514] Tullian Tchividjian, *Unfashionable*, 9-10,18.
[515] Timothy F. Kauffman, "Sanctification, Half Full: The Myopic

What Kauffman is attempting to explain is that not only has Jesus died for you as a substitute, He has also lived and imparted His righteous life to you as a substitute. This builds upon the reformed system, which sees believers as remaining under the Law. Believers are instructed to follow the Law in all its depth like Jesus; it just no longer has the same penalties. McClain refutes this concept, pointing to Galatians 4:8. He claims this passage makes Christian living simply:

> "weak and beggarly' legalism...[which] ultimately moves in the direction of theological disaster, bringing and compounding confusion into our views of sin, of salvation, of the work of Christ, and even the doctrine of God.[516]

When accompanied with perseverance, as articulated so clearly by Steele:

> whereas we previously emphasized the *preservation* of the saints, we must also emphasize the *perseverance* of the saints in faith and holiness. Too many people have been led to think that if they have ever made a profession of faith, or ever prayed a 'sinner's prayer,' or were baptized and joined a church, they can rely on having been 'once saved, always saved.' Insufficient emphasis is given to God's requirement that *we must persevere to the end in a life that seeks after holiness*.[517]

Hermeneutic of the 'Grace' Movement," Trinity Foundation, http://www.trinityfoundation.org/journal.php?id=282, (Accessed September 5, 2013).

[516] Alva J. McClain, *Law and Grace: A Study of New Testament Concepts as They Relate to the Christian Life*. (Winona Lake, IL: BMH Books, 1954), 54.

[517] David N. Steele, et al, *The Five Points of Calvinism: Defined, Defended, and Documented,* Second Edition, (Philipsburg, NJ: P & R Publishing, 2004), 148.

It completely misses the mark of man's spiritual abilities and quest for holiness. Thankfully not all Calvinists ascribe to the perseverance of the saints, choosing instead to see the biblical doctrine of preservation or, more precisely, eternal security. Steele's argument is correct in asserting that not all who claim the name of Christ are saved, but making perseverance a condition of salvation has led to other doctrinal errors. Anderson astutely observes, "it turns the Christian life into a 'have to' life rather than a 'thank you' life."[518]

---

[518] David R. Anderson, *Free Grace Soteriology,* (Xulon Press, 2010), ix.

CHAPTER 6

CONCLUSION AND FUNDAMENTAL ISSUES

If one were to summarize the issue with new Calvinism in one sentence, it might look something like this; new Calvinism is a perversion of the gospel of grace. It redefines the gospel and does not truly understand the nature of God's grace. In so doing, they have perverted this foundational doctrine of Scripture.

The Biblical Words for Grace

Grace is understood as both a biblical word translated from a number of Greek and Hebrew roots as well as a theological concept. Because of this, it is important to begin with an understanding of not only the biblical words translated as grace, but also to mention the origin of the concept of divine grace, even when specific words are not utilized. In addition to this, grace is a characteristic of God Himself and any understanding of grace must be based in the fact that God's character is the ultimate standard upon which to judge any definition of grace. It is important to remember Ryrie's admonition, "if grace is in a Person, the doctrine of grace, though built on a word study, may extend beyond that."[519] In its most simplistic form, grace can be defined as unmerited favor. This means partiality is shown to someone when it is not deserved. It is this undeserved element that is

---

[519] Charles C. Ryrie, *The Grace of God* (Chicago, IL: Moody Press, 1963), 9.

most crucial to understanding the biblical doctrine of grace. It is also important to see that grace can occur prior to an explicit mention of grace, mercy or favor. For example, grace is shown when Adam is not put to death at the time of his sin. In fact, based on the foreknowledge of God of the fall, one can even say that God graciously made man knowing that they would rebel against Him. Grace, being an attribute of God, therefore, preceded creation. After all, it is said Christ was the lamb slain from the foundation of the world (cf. Rev. 13:8)

Salvation by Grace

In order for the biblical gospel to truly be good news, it must be the grace of God that makes it good news worthy of proclamation. Works are said not to play a part in salvation lest they give one grounds to boast. They also have no part in salvation because the gospel would cease to be good news. Therefore, the biblical gospel must always be according to grace and grace alone. As Chafer says, "an act is in no sense gracious if under any condition a debt is incurred."[520] What needs to now occur is an assimilation of the biblical definitions of grace and gospel so that one may understand what it is precisely that Paul refers to as τὸ εὐαγγέλιον τῆς χάριτος τοῦ θεοῦ (the gospel of the grace of God).[521]

Grace is a part of the character of God, but it must be measured against His justice. The depth of His grace cannot be measured because it is inexhaustible, but it is not limitless. This is because it is limited by His personal sense of justice.

Grace has always been an eternal part of the plan of God. Redemption is not an afterthought but has always been

---

[520] Lewis Sperry Chafer, *Grace*, 6.
[521] Acts 20:24.

part of God's sovereign plan, even in permitting the fall. Knowing full well that Adam would pervert the freedom given to him, God still made man. He knew that man would fall, and His sense of justice would demand the sacrifice of His Son. It should be amazing to the reader that God decided to make man at all. Not only was Adam made with a complete freedom of will, more than likely he was also given a positive inclination towards righteousness so that he could make decisions, otherwise he would have been unable to choose between right and wrong. Given this, as well as the perfect conditions of creation in Eden, Adam did not choose to serve God. It is remarkable that God would graciously create man with freedom of will, knowing that man would not choose to serve Him. Why then did God permit the fall? Man will never know the full reason for this, but all of creation is meant to bring glory to the Lord. It must not be forgotten that creation is temporal. God has raised it up, provided for it, and will bring it to its.

Soli Deo Gloria

To God be the glory alone. All evangelicals share this common desire to ascribe to God all the glory and honor that is due Him. More often than not this is a point of commonality between different theological systems within Protestantism. This great doctrine of the Reformation is represented in the *Disputation of Martin Luther on the Power and Efficacy of Indulgences.* In Luther's refusal to ascribe to the Pope glory that is due to God alone, he states "the true treasure of the Church is the Most Holy Gospel of the glory and the grace of God."[522] The Reformation was sparked by Luther's understanding that the gospel. It is about what God has done for man, and not about what the church has to offer in terms of indulgences.

---

[522] Martin Luther, *95 Theses,* 62.

Some within New Calvinism have attempted to ascribe all the glory to God in the process of salvation, fearing that any part played by man somehow robs God of the glory due to Him. They are very quick to lay the charge of semi-Pelagian or synergism. Scripture affirms that man does play a crucial role in his conversion, even if salvation itself is a gift from God. New Calvinism's understanding of salvation is often mechanistic, describing the process of salvation as being accomplished by the decrees of God in eternity past. One writer in Sproul's *Festschrift* states, "effectual grace is grace sufficiently powerful to bring us, kicking and screaming and struggling otherwise, to God Himself and to keep us there."[523] While God's omnipotence is sufficiently strong to accomplish salvation, this is not how conversion occurs.

For new Calvinism, man's role or responsibility to have faith is removed because faith is a gift from God. Free grace theology asserts that man's faith is primarily accomplished through God's working in the will of man, not exclusively through decree of God. God works through the will of man, bringing him necessarily to faith but not in a way whereby he acts under compulsion. Luther thoroughly dismisses the claim that man can, of himself, will to be saved. In *The Bondage of the Will,* Luther shows that there is no one who seeks after God, no one who desires to be saved. God works in the heart of man, wooing them to Himself. In this, God is the author of salvation but he accomplishes it through man, contrary to the opinion of many new Calvinists. God never pulls man kicking and screaming into heaven against his will. Instead, God works within man to draw them to Himself. Paul affirms this working of God within man to will when he asserts, "for it is God who is at work in you, both to will and to work for *His* good pleasure."[524]

---

[523] Paul Helm, "The Many Shades of Calvinism" in *Tabletalk Magazine,* 12.

Calvin affirms, stating, "the Lord draws men by their own wills; wills, however, which he himself has produced."[525]

Calvin is always careful to distinguish between that which happens as a result of necessity and that which comes about as a result of compulsion. He distinguishes that even when God foreknows things, they are not known contingently nor do they come about out of a sense of compulsion due to His foreknowledge. Assuredly, what God foreknows must come about, but that does not deny that the manner in which these actions come about is voluntary. Calvin expounds upon this idea in one of the greatest parts of his *Institutes* saying:

> man, since he was corrupted by the fall, sins not forced or unwilling, by a most forward bias of the mind; not by violent compulsion, or external force, but by the movement of his own passion; and yet such is the depravity of his nature, that he cannot move the act expect in the direction of evil....for this necessity is in a manner voluntary.[526]

This has too often been forgotten especially among young Calvinists. In an attempt to defend their system philosophically, they have not allowed this seeming paradox to remain. In the end Isaiah's words must be remembered, "'for My thoughts are not your thoughts, Nor are your ways My ways,' declares the LORD."[527] This does not rob God of his glory. Neither does viewing all actions as being accomplished through God's decrees ascribe Him more glory. If anything, it shows more of the greatness of His

---

[524] Philippians 2:13, NASB.
[525] John Calvin, *Institutes of the Christian Religion,* Book 2, III:13.
[526] Ibid, Book 2, III:5.
[527] Isaiah 55:8, NASB

power to work through the sinful hearts of unregenerate man rather than by forcing man to act out of compulsion.

Is Unconditioned

A great deal of time and energy has been wasted discussing the function of non-meritorious good works for justification. It is said that perseverance in goods works and others conditions must be met in order to determine whether one's faith is saving type of faith. There are few who deny that works do not merit favor from God. In attempting to make works a necessary and inevitable outgrowth of saving faith and regeneration, it has all too often been said that justification is conditional. For example, Seifrid says, "Paul declares that justification is contingent upon obedience, and specifically upon 'doing the law.'"[528] While it is true that eternal life is conditioned sole upon fulfilling the condition of belief, it is non-meritorious because nothing is done but to believe. The free gift of grace is received. It does not merit. Chafer says, "a benefit cannot be called a gift if it is paid before, at the time, or after...salvation is never conditioned on human faithfulness, or on the promise of human faithfulness."[529] The irony is to be observed that the same people who claim that making salvation the gift of God in Ephesians 2:8-9, is synergism or semi-Pelagianism, are also those who make saving faith dependent upon fulfilling certain conditions, namely perseverance in good works.

Grace: the sole means of justification

Grace is the sole means whereby a believer is justified. It is completely apart from not only merit but works as well. If conditions are fulfilled, then it gives the believer

---

[528] Mark A. Seifrid, *Christ, Our Righteousness: Paul's Theology of Justification,* New Studies in Biblical Theology Series, ed. by D.A. Carson, (Downers Grove, IL: InterVarsity Press, 2000), 147.
[529] Ibid.

grounds for boasting. The believer cannot boast because they know that they could not believe apart from God opening their eyes and an awareness of the tremendous grace they have been shown negates any boasting.

Sola Fide

This is most important doctrine of the Reformation. The basis for justification is faith alone. Luther stated that this is "the article upon which the church stands or falls (*articulus stantis et cadentis ecclesiae*)."[530] This is the primary doctrine of the Reformation and the one on which all Protestants were judged to be anathema by the Roman Catholic Church at the Council of Trent. Calvin articulates this idea well when he states:

> a man will be *justified by faith* when, excluded from the righteousness of works, he by faith lays hold of the righteousness of Christ, and clothed in it appears in the sight of God not as a sinner, but as righteous. Thus we simply interpret justification, as the acceptance with which God receives us into his favour as if we were righteous; and we say that this justification consists in the forgiveness of sins and the imputation of the righteousness of Christ.[531]

Although many ardently defend this, it is all but abandoned by most in practice. The rallying cry of the Reformation, "man is justified by faith alone", is almost always held to be "man is justified by faith alone.*" There always seems to be an asterisk placed on *Sola Fide* which desires to say "faith is by justification alone…but justifying faith is never alone." This is despite the fact that in Sproul's observation; Calvin

---

[530] Martin Luther qtd. In R.C. Sproul, *Faith Alone: The Evangelical Doctrine of Justification*, electronic ed. (Grand Rapids: Baker Books, 2000), 18.
[531] John Calvin, *Institutes of the Christian Religion,* Book 3, XI:2

"made it 'superabundantly clear' that justification in its *completion* as well as its *initiation* should be ascribed to faith."[532] Works always seem to become a necessary and sufficient condition of saving faith.

There is an ever-present claim made by some that works are non-meritorious but a necessary condition of salvation. This is the heart of the gospel of the grace of God. It was due to the charges of antinomianism made by the Roman Catholic Church that the reformers themselves failed to hold to *Sola Fide* completely and consistently. They knew "sin is lawlessness" and wanted desperately to avoid charges of antinomianism.[533] Calvin believed that it is "by the intervention of faith alone [Jesus] reconciles them to himself...without the aid of works."[534] *Sole Fide* for Calvin and Luther meant, in justification, works do not aid faith. This does not totally eliminate the role of works. Calvin goes on to state:

> We dream not of a faith which is devoid of good works, nor of a justification which can exist without them: the only difference is, that while we acknowledge that faith and works are necessarily connected, we, however, place justification in faith, not in works.[535]

This dichotomy, between faith that is alone and is also not alone, is present in the Augsburg

Confession, which states:

---

[532] R.C. Sproul, *Faith Alone: The Evangelical Doctrine of Justification*, 124.
[533] 1 John 3:4.
[534] John Calvin, *Institutes of the Christian Religion*, Book 3, XVII:3.
[535] Ibid, Book 3, XVI:1.

> also they teach that men cannot be justified before God by their own strength, merits, or works, but are freely justified for Christ's sake, through faith, when they believe that they are received into favor, and that their sins are forgiven for Christ's sake, who, by His death, has made satisfaction for our sins. This faith God imputes for righteousness in His sight.[536]

It also asserts:

> they teach that this faith is bound to bring forth good fruits, and that it is necessary to do good works commanded by God, because of God's will, but that we should not rely on those works to merit justification.[537]

This is why it is being argued that standing by the doctrine of *Sola Fide* necessarily means departing at certain points from not only the reformers themselves but also the reformed confessions. The heirs of the Reformation are those who truly follow *Sola Fide* and not those whose theology most closely resembles Calvin, Luther, the Westminster Confession, the Canons of Dordt, et cetera.

Justification must be viewed as completely separate from sanctification despite the fact that there is an aspect of sanctification (positional sanctification) that has been accomplished at justification. Within reformed theology, there has traditionally been a close relationship between justification and experiential sanctification. These must be viewed as related but distinct. By this, it is meant that justification is by faith only and that while it may correlate with (experiential) sanctification it is improper to relate these concepts conditionally. It is also problematic to confuse the

---

[536] Augsburg Confession, Article IV.
[537] Ibid, Article VI.

believer's ultimate sanctification with experiential sanctification by seeing that they must reach some necessary degree of experiential righteousness in this life. When this mistake is made, all too often it sees the carnal believer as not holy enough to have been justified. Works do not matter except in that works proceed from justification; to assert otherwise would be to abandon the principle of *Sola Fide*.

CONCLUSION

The need for this academic assessment of new Calvinism is justified by the sheer influence that the movement is having in, not only the academic world, but in local churches as well. The movement known as new Calvinism has garnered a great deal of attention recently. Most of the reaction to this movement has been positive; after all, what is wrong with being conservative in doctrine and liberal in practice, focusing on missions, social responsibility, et cetera? Overall, the movement deals with issues of great importance theologically, but its theology has been given little attention publically. The importance of a critical theological analysis can be seen in several factors. To begin, Wayne Grudem's *Systematic Theology* has sold over 300,000 copies, a best-seller by theological standards. In volume alone, its influence is widespread. Perhaps more important than sheer numbers, Grudem's *Systematic Theology* is pointedly influencing the younger generation of conservative pastors and academics. This is greatly reflected in the age demographics of new Calvinism. In addition to this, in the larger religious sphere, there is a tremendous battle being waged in the Southern Baptist Convention over the issue of Calvinism. The future of the nation's largest denomination is significantly intertwined with whatever the future holds for new Calvinism.

The postmodern world has caused so many to become disillusioned with creedal Christianity. Even the great confessional traditions of reformed theology have been abandoned. Many movements have truly failed to define themselves. Progressive dispensationalism is one of the most notable perpetrators of this and has for more than 25 years remained undefined. New Calvinism is no different. A robust, systematic understanding of theology is needed due to the interdependence of the various fields of theology. Eschatology, for example, may seem insignificant, but it is greatly affected by hermeneutics, soteriology, the doctrine of the kingdom, et cetera. Baptism, the covenants/dispensations, sign gifts and other similar issues need to be defined by new Calvinism because, the old adage goes, if you do not stand for anything, you will fall for anything. While the world may love bite-sized theology and empty platitudes, the last thing it needs is another hipster pastor. May the gospel of the grace of God be proclaimed to all.

"What is today a matter of academic speculation begins tomorrow to move armies and pull down empires"[538]

---

[538] J. Gresham Machen, "Christianity and Culture" in *Princeton Theological Review,* Vol. 11 (1913), 7.

APPENDIX 1

REPENTANCE AND THE 2014 TOGETHER FOR THE GOSPEL CONFERENCE

Recently, *Together for the Gospel* convened for their bi-annual conference. This conference was especially significant for this dissertation. While many issues were discussed, it is the panel discussion on sanctification that pertains most to this present work. Many statements made during this panel concern material already presented. It therefore serves an affirming role, verifying the accuracy of the way their views have been portrayed. For example, new Calvinism has a marked antagonism towards dispensationalism. Derek Thomas, professor of Systematic Theology at Reformed theological Seminary, referred to antinomianism/easy-believism as a virus infecting the church.[539] Additionally, Piper continues to propagate his view about a future aspect of justification, saying, "election is unconditional, glorification is conditional…it is all over the Bible, you must become something to pass muster at the last judgment." Statements of this nature should not surprise the reader at this point because these beliefs have been well established above.

While an exhaustive treatment of biblical repentance is not within the scope of this work, the issues to be discussed in this appendix involve a misunderstanding of repentance, repentance's relationship to faith, and repentance's connection to the federal headship of Adam. Since it is John Piper's comments at the *Together for the*

---

[539] All quotations were taken from the Panel Session at the 2014 Gospel Coalition Conference unless otherwise noted. The speakers present included: Derek Thomas, John Piper, Kevin DeYoung and Matt Chandler. The Panel Session was entitled "Preaching Sanctification." A video can be found at Together for the Gospel's website at http://t4g.org/media/2014/04/preaching-sanctification/.

Gospel conference that instigated this discussion, his views will be discussed more pointedly. Therefore, Piper will be acting as the representative head of new Calvinism.

Prior to the convening of the *Together for the Gospel* Conference, Piper publically defined repentance. His definitions:

> The basic meaning of repent is to experience a change of the mind's perceptions and dispositions and purposes.[540]

> Repentance is the change of attitude or behavior that results from the feeling of remorse over the sin.[541]

> Repentance in Jesus' message is not behavior but the inner change that gives rise to new God-centered, Christ-exalting behavior…The first demand of Jesus' public ministry was, 'Repent.' He spoke this command indiscriminately to all who would listen. It was a call for radical inward change toward God and man.[542]

There is a subtle change within the definition of repentance to include not just a change of mind, but a change in the mind's perceptions or feelings and a practical change in life. Instead of seeing one who changes his mind as repentant,

---

[540] John Piper, "Thoughts on Jesus' Demand to Repent: Letters from Cambridge #2," April 19, 2006, Desiring God Ministries, http://www.desiringgod.org/articles/thoughts-on-jesus-demand-to-repent (Accessed May 20, 2014).

[541] John Piper, "The Good End of Godly Regret," December 30, 1984, Desiring God Ministries, http://www.desiringgod.org/sermons/the-good-end-of-godly-regret, (Accessed May 20, 2014).

[542] John Piper, "Thoughts on Jesus' Demand to Repent: Letters from Cambridge #2," April 19, 2006, Desiring God Ministries, http://www.desiringgod.org/articles/thoughts-on-jesus-demand-to-repent (Accessed May 20, 2014).

true repentance must include sorrow for sin and a new desire to stop sinning. This should not be surprising given the teaching of new Calvinism on lordship salvation.

At the *Together for the Gospel* conference, there was a vivid display of new Calvinist soteriology. This teaching makes salvation virtually unattainable. Piper said, "salvation may be imperiled by unrepentant sin." He also told two stories about giving pastoral counsel. He stated:

> I looked at a girl in the face one time, who was living with her boyfriend, and I said if you don't stop that, you'll go to hell...If you don't get out of that relationship, you are gonna go to hell'

The counsel he suggested giving to someone addicted to pornography: "Tear out your eye, or you will go to hell." All this was said in front of a group of 7,000 pastors and church leaders and was met with cheers and applause. Concerned with charges of legalism, Derek Thomas asks, "How much effort can you give to bearing fruit before it becomes legalism?" Piper's responded: "You can't give too much." He explains, "as a saved person you are now a good tree that bears good fruit. It is legalism which says to the bad tree, start bearing good fruit and you can go to tree heaven." It is said that an unregenerate sinner is a bad tree, while a regenerate believer is a good one. The old nature is exchanged for the new. The biblical justification for this is taken from the Sermon on the Mount. Piper mentions Matthew 7:17, "so every good tree bears good fruit, but the bad tree bears bad fruit" (NASB). This passage talks about identifying false prophets, not salvation. One commentator explains, Matthew was teaching that "the test of the prophet is his conformity to Scripture" and not about the relationship between good works and salvation.[543] How can *Together for*

---

[543] Charles F. Pfeiffer and Everett Falconer Harrison, eds., *The Wycliffe*

the Gospel support this definition of repentance, yet in its core doctrines "deny that salvation can be separated from repentance toward God and faith in our Lord Jesus Christ"?

It is also significant to question how the concept of repentance can be held in this way while simultaneously defending federal headship.[544] Paul explains in Romans 5:12 that sin entered into the world through Adam, and because of this, sin spread to all men. It is because of this sin that man is born condemned (v. 16). It is said that sin is imputed to man. If holding to federalism, Adam sinned as a representative of man. Therefore, man today is born condemned because of Adam's sin. This is nothing new. Now combine this with the new Calvinist understanding of repentance: one must experience a "change of attitude or behavior that results from the feeling of remorse over the sin."[545] Since unrepentant sin leads to eternal damnation, the inevitable conclusion is that one must repent of not only Adam's sin, but also the sin nature imputed to them. One must feel remorse for Adam's sin, but how can one be sorry for something that he has been given, namely his Adamic nature. It must then be asked of a potential convert, have they truly repented over the sin that condemned them? This is a vain attempt to get around the simple truth that death spread to all men because all sinned in Adam, the doctrine of seminal headship.

Bible Commentary: New Testament (Chicago: Moody Press, 1962), Mt 7:15.

[544] It is likely that the support of federal headship is connected to the new Calvinism's complementarianism. If one believes in federal headship, it is easy to support complementarianism. This connection is not biblical. It is possible to be a complementarian and hold to seminal headship. It is also possible, as in many reformed churches, to hold to federal headship and egalitarianism.

[545] John Piper, "The Good End of Godly Regret," December 30, 1984, Desiring God Ministries, http://www.desiringgod.org/sermons/the-good-end-of-godly-regret, (Accessed May 20, 2014).

APPENDIX 2

NEW CALVINIST REVIEWS OF *FUTURE GRACE*

The following are reviews of John Piper's *Future Grace* by other new Calvinists.[546]

"There have been two or three books outside of the Bible that have profoundly shaped how I see and understand my relationship with God. When I first read *Future Grace* in the summer of 1999, it sent my head spinning and my heart soaring. I couldn't be more excited about this revision."
—*Matt Chandler, lead pastor, The Village Church*

"Over a decade ago, I gave each of my three teenage daughters their own copy of *Future Grace.* As a father I was committed to providing them with a solid theological foundation and a rich understanding of the grace of God, and *Future Grace* was a key addition to their fledgling libraries. Now, I am thrilled to give this revised edition with even further "Christ-centered clarification" to my teenage grandson, and I eagerly anticipate the future grace of *Future Grace* in his heart and life."
—*C.J. Mahaney, president, Sovereign Grace Ministries*

"In *Future Grace* John Piper encourages believers to understand the present struggles of the Christian life in terms of the surpassing grace of God in Christ—a grace that calls us to exult in God's future work in us, even as we experience God's present grace and rest in the assurance of God's grace to us in the past. In this new edition, Piper serves the church by showing us a mind at work as he wrestles with some of the most crucial issues of the Christian life. This book is deeply biblical, passionately practical, and Christ-centered."

---

[546] The reviews included are actually contained in *Future Grace,* 2012 edition.

—*R. Albert Mohler Jr., president, The Southern Baptist Theological Seminary*

"*Future Grace* gave wonderful encouragement to my heart when it first came out in 1995, and now it has done so again in this new edition. I think John Piper is faithful to Scripture when he explains that the Bible does not motivate us to obedience by appealing to our gratitude for salvation, but by calling us to believe that God will empower us, help us, and draw us near to Himself in this present life, if we are obedient to the conditions found in His many promises in Scripture. This book provides a much-needed key that will help every Christian understand just how to live a joy-filled life that is pleasing to God."
—*Wayne Grudem, research professor, Phoenix Seminary*

"Few books have sharpened my theological thinking, opened my exegetical eyes, and so consistently fed my soul as this one. Of all of John Piper's 'big books,' *Future Grace* has had the biggest impact on my life and ministry."
—*Kevin DeYoung, pastor and author*

"*Future Grace* is one of the fundamental building blocks for John Piper's distinctive message. Here he emphasizes that saving faith, founded on the work of Christ in the past, is directed toward God's promises for our future. That is a profoundly moving and motivating message, and I commend it to Christians today. The new edition clarifies some problems and presents the message more fully at various points."
—*John Frame, professor, Reformed Theological Seminary*

245

APPENDIX 3

ORIGINS OF NEW CALVINISM

Very few people have attempted to give a thorough understanding of the origins of new Calvinism. Because of the limited extent of this work, it is possible to include here exhaustively. The most important of these is likely the work of Bryers and Challies. Below is a summary of their findings:

The New Calvinism: Where did these New Calvinsts come from?

A Visual History by Josh Byers & Tim Challies[547]

Pre-History

1986- *Desiring God* by John Piper
 Chosen by God by R.C. Sproul
 The Cross of Christ by John Stott

1987- Council on Biblical Manhood and Womanhood: Wayne Grudem founds an organization dedicated upholding both equality and differences between men and women in marriage and the church

1989- The Danvers Statement is published in *Christianity Today:* CBMW's statement defines and defends complementarian gender roles

1993- Albert Mohler is appointed president of Southern Baptist Theological Seminary: Mohler reverses the

---

[547] This is a recreation of the chart found at https://s3.amazonaws.com/Challies_VisualTheology/new-calvinism-timeline.html. It has been recreated in order to make it readable in word format.

slide towards liberalism and re-establishes Reformed theology

1994- Jon Piper and Jon Bloom found Desiring God

Systematic Theology by Wayne Grudem: Grudem's theology will become the unofficial textbook of the movement

The Alliance of Confessing Evangelicals: James Boice convenes a group of Reformed leaders to revive a passion for "the truth of the Gospel" within the church

Evangelicals and Catholics Together: Charles Colson and Richard John Neuhaus attempt to bridge Catholics and Protestants. Most Reformed Christians reject the statement.

The Discipline of Grace by Jerry Bridges: Bridges teaches us how and why to preach the gospel to ourselves

1995- *The Purpose-Driven Church* by Rick Warren: The book becomes the textbook for church growth principles

1996- *The Cambridge Declaration:* The declaration reaffirms the doctrine of the Reformation in contrast to Roman Catholicism and modern challenges

1997- *Nine Marks of a Healthy Church* by Mark Dever: Mark Dever provides the ecclesiology of the movement

Hip-Hop group The Cross Movement releases their first studio album, *Heaven's Mentality:* An aggressive focus on the glory of God is a response to mainstream rap's focus on the glory of man

The inaugural Passion Conference: It mobilizes the 268 generation and gives John Piper a voice to the youth

1998- Mark Driscoll & David Nicolas found Acts 29: Church planting will be the movement's primary means of evangelism

1999- Hip-Hop artist The Ambassador releases his first solo album *Christology: In Layman's Terms:* "Lyrical Theology" is established as a category in people's minds

2000- *Indelible Grace* by Indelible Grace: They usher in a retuned hymn movement

Passion One Day One 2000: John Piper preaches his iconic message *Boasting Only in the Cross* which later becomes the book *Don't Waste Your Life*

2001- The *ESV Bible* is published: It will become the unofficial Bible translation of the movement

In Christ Alone by Keith Getty and Stuart Townsend: The song ushers in a new age of hymn writing

A New Kind of Christian by Brian MacLaren: The book established him as a Christian leader and thinker

9/11 shakes our world and drives us to ask for deeper and better answers to suffering and evil

2002- *The Purpose-Driven Life* by Rick Warren: Christians are divided ove the book and its approach to the Christian life

The Cross-Centered Life by C.J. Mahaney: Mahaney uses the "cross-centered" terminology that would soon morph into "gospel-centered"

Rob Bell debuted his *Nooma* films: The film's look and feel resonate with a crowd disenchanted with the tired flannelography of their youth

2003- Tim Challies registers Challies.com: This blog and other new media will play a significant role in new Calvinism

Sovereign Grace Ministries is founded (renamed from People of Destiny International)

Jonathan Edwards by George Marsden is published: The New Calvinists look back to the puritans

Word Press is founded and Blogger is purchased by Google: The blog has hit the mainstream

Blue Like Jazz by Donald Miller: Miller gives a voice to a disillusioned generation

2004- *The Radical Reformission* by Mark Driscoll: Mark Driscoll spans the gap between Emergent and Calvinist

The Passion of the Christ by Mel Gibson

Merriam-Webster declares "blog" their word of the year: The people have, and will, maintain a voice

The End of Faith by Sam Harris: Where Christians want answers to suffering and evil, atheists assure us there are none

Reach Records is founded by Lecrae & Ben Washer: This brings an unexpected connection between Reformed theology and hip-hop

Justin Taylor founds his blog *Between Two Worlds*

Total Truth by Nancy Pearcey is published

C.J. Mahaney voluntarily hands the senior pastor position at Covenant Life Church to Joshua Harris

2005- The Gospel Coalition is founded by Timothy Keller & D.A. Carson

Apple introduces iTunes podcasts: it allows church to easily publish sermons and lets users listen to sermons from all over the world which incidentally helps create the "celebrity pastor"

2006- Desiring God National Conference features David Wells, Timothy Keller, John Piper, D.A. Carson & Mark Driscoll: This conference is an endorsement of Mark Driscoll and the bringing together of two generations

Voice Raps at Bethlehem Baptist Church: John Piper's endorsement causes it to explode in popularity

Richard Dawkins' *The God Delusion:* As Reformed theology surges, so too does the New Atheism

The inaugural Together for the Gospel Conference is held in Louisville, Kentucky and draws 2,800 church leaders: Conferences will be held in 2008, 2010, 2012, and 2014, with numbers rising each time

Christianity Today publishes Collin Hansen's article "Young, Restless, Reformed" : The article was subtitled "Calvinism is making a comeback-and shaking up the church." The "young, restless and reformed" terminology will stick.

The Reform &Resurge Conference features Timothy Keller, Mark Driscoll, Matt Chandler, Joshua Harris, Ed Stetzer, Darrin Patrick &Eric Mason: This shows the breadth of the movement and identifies new leaders within it

2007- Douglas Wilson & Christopher Hitchens begin a series of debates via *Christianity Today:* In 2008 they would go on the road together, and in 2009 release *Collision*

Mark Dever publishes a 10-part blog series titled "Where did all these new Calvinists come from?"

The inaugural Gospel Coalition Conference, a private event, draws 500 church leaders: Keller preaches "Gospel-Centered Ministry" which anticipates Center Church. Conferences are held in 2007, 2009, 2011, 2013, eventually drawing up to 5,500

2008- *The Reason for God* by Timothy Keller: The book establishes him as a bestselling author and a modern equivalent of C.S. Lewis

Rebel by Lecrae: The album includes Piper-inspired track "Don't Waste Your Life." Lecrae quickly becomes the most popular Christian rapper

Why We are Not Emergent by Kevin DeYoung & Ted Kluck: The book marks the beginning of the end of the emergent church

The *ESV Study Bible* is published

Thabiti Anyabwile is introduced as one of the T4G speakers: He speaks boldly on race and signifies this movement will transcend race

Johnny Hunt is elected president of the Southern Baptist Convention after Albert Mohler withdraws from consideration due to health concerns: Hunt begins a time of peacemaking in the convention

2009- *TIME* magazine lists The New Calvinism as one of the "10 Ideas Changing the World Right Now"

Matt Chandler is diagnosed with a malignant brain tumor: This reinforces suffering as a theme of the movement

2010- *Radical* by David Platt: The book goes on to sell more than a million copies and establishes Platt as a major voice in the movement

Phillip Ryken is named President of Wheaton College: This shows that Reformed theology has begun to enter the mainstream

2011- John MacArthur writes a series of blog posts to the Young, Restless and Reformed where he tells them to "Grow up, Settle down. Keep reforming.": Some of the younger people in the movement begin to stop listening to his voice

Love Wins by Rob Bell: Calvinist's reaction to the book inadvertently propels it to the bestseller list. Bell resigns from his church and his influence soon wanes.

2012- "Why I Hate Religion, But Love Jesus" by Jefferson Bethke debutes on YouTube and receives over 20,000,000 views: He popularizes gospel-centered theology and the thinking of some of Calvinism's leaders

    The Elephant Room Round 2 features T.D. Jakes and leads to an outcry: James MacDonald and Mark Driscoll soon withdraw from the council of the Gospel Coalition

    Matt Chandler becomes the president of ACTS 29

    The inaugural Gospel Coalition conference for women: the conference draws 3,600

    Covenant Life Church leaves Sovereign Grace Ministries: the family of church declines in the face of difficulties

2013- Greg Thornbury is named president at The King's College

    John MacArthur's *Strange Fire* book & conference: MacArthur warns of making too little of distinctions between charismatics and cessationists

    Russell Moore is named President of the Southern Baptist Ethics & Religious Liberty Commission

    Ligon Duncan is appointed chancellor of Reformed Theological Seminary

2014- The inaugural CROSS conference: The Conference provides and explicit emphasis on student missions and gives it a pointed theological edge[548]

---

[548] Josh Byers and Tim Challies, "The New Calvinism: Where Did All

The next important work was done by Mark Dever, a 10-part series of messages delivered at Capitol Hill Baptist Church in Washington, DC. He traces the major influences fueling the rise of new Calvinism.[549]

1. Charles Spurgeon
2. Martyn Lloyd-Jones
3. Banner of Truth Trust
4. Evangelism Explosion
5. The Inerrancy Controversy
6. Presbyterian Church in America (PCA)
7. J.I. Packer
8. John MacArthur and R.C. Sproul
9. John Piper
10. Reformed Rap
11. Influential parachurch ministries
12. The rise of secularism and the decline of Christian nominalism

Finally, the following is the historical chart representing the history of New Calvinism as proposed by Paul M. Dohse Sr.[550] Although this work does not agree with the conclusions reached here, Dohse's work is included here because it is one of the only sources found that has attempted to trace the historical origins of New Calvinism.

---

the New Calvinists Come From? A Visual History," March 11, 2014, Challies.com-Informing the Reforming, https://s3.amazonaws.com/Challies_VisualTheology/new-calvinism-timeline.html (accessed March 18, 2014).
[549] Mark Dever qtd. in Matt Smethurst, "Where Did All the New Calvinists Come from?", The Gospel Coalition, October 24, 2013, http://thegospelcoalition.org/blogs/tgc/2013/10/24/where-did-all-these-calvinists-come-from/ (accessed March 18, 2014).
[550] Paul M. Dohse Sr., Paul's Passing Thoughts, http://paulspassingthoughts.com/2012/02/20/new-calvinist-flow-charts/, (Accessed September 5, 2013).

254

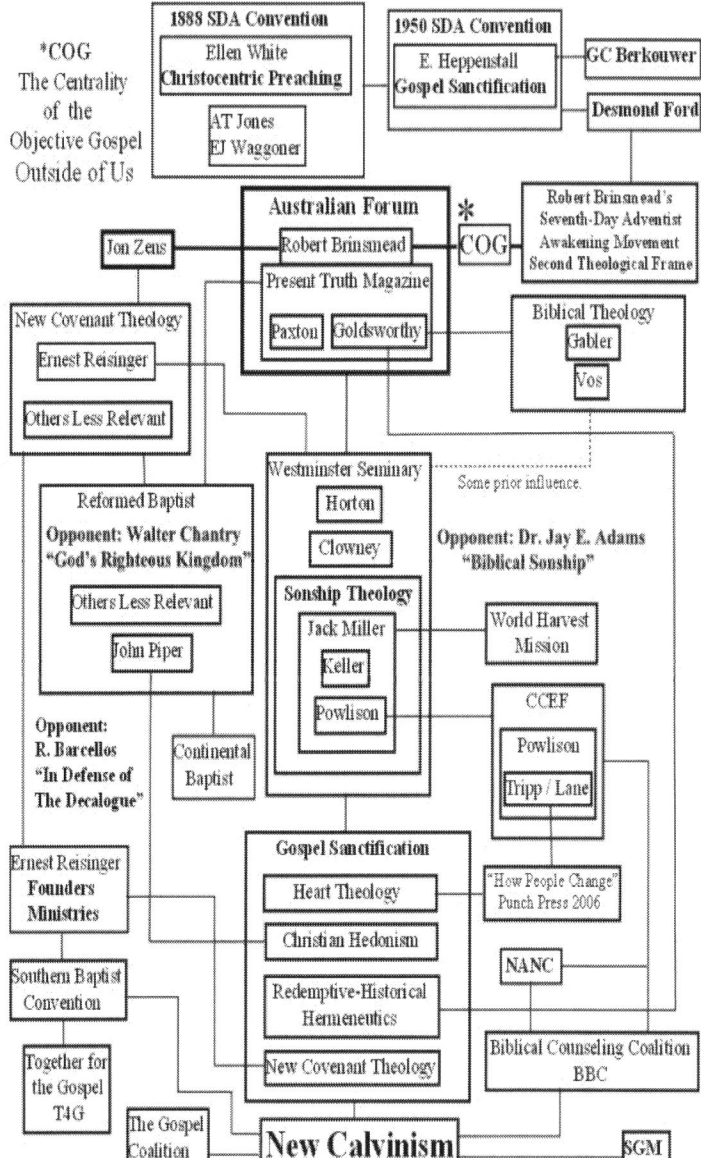

The real reason the "scandalous gospel" is scandalous.

BIBLIOGRAPHY

Acts 29 Network. "Doctrine: What We Believe and Why We Believe It." http://www.acts29network.org/about/doctrine/. (Accessed September 5, 2013).

_____. "Pastor Training Program Frequently Asked Questions,"

http://www.acts29network.org/ptp-faq/. (Accessed September 5, 2013).

Anderson, David R. *Free Grace Soteriology.* Xulon Press, 2010.

Andrews III, Reditt. *Sin and the Fall.* The Gospel Coalition Booklet. 2009.

Arndt, William Frederick W. Danker and Walter Bauer. *A Greek-English Lexicon of the New Testament and Other Early Christian Literature.* 3rd ed. Chicago: University of Chicago Press, 2000.

Beasley, Michael J. *The Fallible Prophets of New Calvinism: An Analysis, Critique and Exhortation Concerning the Contemporary Doctrine of "Fallible Prophecy."* The Armoury Ministry, 2013.

Beeke, Joel R. "Does Assurance Belong to the Essence of Faith? Calvin and the Calvinists." *The Master's Seminary Journal* 5/1 (Spring 1994), 43-71.

Beeke, Joel R. and Mark Jones. *A Puritan Theology.* Grand Rapids, MI: Reformation Heritage Books, 2012.

Beilby, James K. et al. ed. *Justification: Five Views.* Spectrum Multiview Books Series. Downers Grove, IL: IVP Academic, 2011.

Beougher, Timothy. *Richard Baxter and Conversion: A Study of the Puritan Concept of Becoming a Christian.* Mentor, 2008.

Berkhof, Louis. *Systematic Theology.* Grand Rapids, MI: Wm. B. Eerdmans Publishing Co., 1941.

Bigalke Jr., Ron J. Editor. *Progressive Dispensationalism: An Analysis of the Movement and Defense of Traditional Dispensationalism.* Lanham, MD: University Press of America, 2005.

Bird, Michael F. "What is There Between Minneapolis and St. Andrews? A Third Way in the Piper-Wright Debate." *Journal of the Evangelical Theological Society* 54:2 (Jun 2011): 299-309.

Blum, Edwin A. "Augustine: The Bishop and Theologian." *Bibliotheca Sacra* 138, no. 549 (1981).

Boice, James Montgomery. *Whatever Happened to the Gospel of Grace?: Rediscovering the Doctrines That Shook the World.* Wheaton, IL: Crossway Books, 2009.

Buchanan, James. *The Doctrine of Justification*: An Outline of its History in the Church and of its Exposition from Scripture. Kindle Edition. Titus Books, 2013.

Byers, Josh and Tim Challies. "The New Calvinism: Where Did All the New Calvinists Come From? A Visual History." March 11, 2014. Challies.com- Informing the Reforming.

https://s3.amazonaws.com/Challies_VisualTheology/new-calvinism-timeline.html. (Accessed March 18, 2014).

Bryson, George. *The Dark Side of Calvinism: The Calvinist Caste System.* Santa Ana, CA: Calvary Chapel Publishing, 2004.

Calvin, John. *Calvin's Commentaries.* Galaxie Software, 2002.

Calvin, John. *Institutes of the Christian Religion.* Bellingham, WA: Logos Bible Software, 1997.

Chafer, Lewis Sperry. *Grace.* Chicago: Moody Press, 1947.

_____. *Salvation: God's Marvelous Work of Grace.* 1917; Reprinted Grand Rapids, MI: Kregel Publishing, 1991.

_____. *Systematic Theology.* 8 Volumes. 1947; Reprinted Grand Rapids, MI: Kregel, 1976.

Challies, Tim. "John Piper: 12 Features of the New Calvinism." Challies.com-Informingthe Reforming." http://www.challies.com/quotes/john-piper-12-features-of-the-new-calvinism. (Accessed March 18, 2014).

Chandler, Matt and Jared Wilson. *The Explicit Gospel.* Wheaton, IL: Crossway Books, 2012.

Clark, R. Scott, ed. *Covenant, Justification, and Pastoral Ministry: Essays by the Faculty of Westminster Seminary California.* Phillipsburg, NJ: P & R Publishing, 2007.

Clark, R. Scott "The History of Covenant Theology," *Tabletalk Magazine.* October 2006 (Lake Mary, FL: Ligonier Ministries, Inc., 2006

Congdon, Philip F. "John Piper's Diminished Doctrine of Justification and Assurance." *Journal of the Grace Evangelical Society.* Vol. 23:44 (Spring 2010), 59-74.

Cowan, Steven B. "Common Misconceptions of Evangelicals Regarding Calvinism." *The Journal of the Evangelical Theological Society*, 33/2 (June 1990) 189-195.

Dabney, Robert L. *Systematic Theology.* Carlisle, PA: Banner of Truth Trust, 1985.

Desiring God Ministries. "Affirmation of Faith." http://www.desiringgod.org/about/our-distinctives/affirmation-of-faith. (Accessed September 5, 2013).

Dever, Mark. *Proclaiming a Cross-Centered Theology.* Together for the Gospel Series. Wheaton, IL: Crossway Books and Bibles. 2009.

DeYoung, Kevin and Greg Gilbert. *What is the Mission of the Church? Making Sense of Social Justice, Shalom, and the Great Commission.* Wheaton, IL: Crossway, 2011.

Dohse Sr., Paul M. Paul's Passing Thoughts. http://paulspassingthoughts.com/2012/02/20/new-calvinist-flow-charts/. (Accessed September 5, 2013).

_____. *The Truth About New Calvinism: Its History, Doctrine, and Character,* Volume 1. Second Edition. (Zenia, OH: TANC, 2011)

Driscoll, Mark and Gerry Breshears. *Doctrine: What Christians Should Believe.* Wheaton, IL: Crossway, 2010.

Driscoll, Mark. *A Call to Resurgence: Will Christianity Have a Funeral or a Future?* Carol Stream, IL: Tyndale House Publishers, 2013.

_____. "Augustine on Theology." The Resurgence. http://theresurgence.com/2009/03/17/augustine-on-theology. (Accessed November 19, 2013).

_____. "Four Points of the Movement." The Resurgence. http://theresurgence.com/2011/07/25/four-points-of-the-movement. (Accessed September 5, 2013).

_____. "Spiritual Gifts Part I." August 6, 2006, http://marshill.com/media/1st-corinthians/spiritual-gifts-part-i. (Accessed September 5, 2013).

_____. "Spiritual Gifts Part II." August 6, 2006, http://marshill.com/media/1st-corinthians/spiritual-gifts-part-ii. (Accessed September 5, 2013).

_____. "Spiritual Gifts Part V." August 6, 2006, http://marshill.com/media/1st-corinthians/spiritual-gifts-part-v. (Accessed September 5, 2013).

_____. "Time Magazine Names New Calvinism 3rd Most Powerful Idea." *The Resurgence.* http://theresurgence.com/2009/03/12/time-magazine-names-new-calvinism-3rd-most-powerful-idea. (Accessed September 5, 2013).

_____. *Vintage Jesus: Timely Answers to Timeless Questions.* Wheaton, IL, Crossway, 2007.

Enns, Paul P. *The Moody Handbook of Theology*. Chicago, IL: Moody Press, 1989.

Evans, William B. "Deja Vu All Over Again? The Contemporary Reformed Soteriological Controversy in Historical Perspective." *Westminster Theological Journal* 72:1 (Spring 2010): 135-151.

_____. *Imputation and Impartation,* Studies in Christian History and Thought Series. Eugene, OR: WIPF & Stock, 2008.

Ferguson Sinclair B. and J.I. Packer. *New Dictionary of Theology*. Electronic edition. Downers Grove, IL: InterVarsity Press, 2000.

Frame, John M. *Salvation Belongs to the Lord: An Introduction to Systematic Theology*. Kindle Edition. Phillipsburg, NJ: P & R Publishing, 2006.

Geiger, Eric, et al. *Transformative Discipleship: How People Really Grow*. Nashville, TN: B & H Publishing Group. 2012.

Gerstner, John H. *Jonathan Edwards: A mini-theology*. Wheaton, IL: Tyndale House Publishers, 1983.

Greear, J.D. *Stop Asking Jesus into Your Heart: How to Know for Sure You Are Saved*. Nashville, TN: B & H Publishing Group, 2013.

Grenz, Stanley J. "Postmodernism and the Future of Evangelical Theology: *Star Trek* and the Next Generation." *Evangelical Review of Theology* 18/4 (October 1994).

Grudem, Wayne. *Politics According to the Bible: A Comprehensive Resource for Understanding Modern*

Political Issues in Light of Scripture. Grand Rapids, MI: Zondervan, 2010.

_____. *Systematic Theology: An Introduction to Biblical Doctrine.* Grand Rapids, MI: Zondervan, 2000.

Hannah, John D. An *Uncommon Union: Dallas Theological Seminary and American Evangelicalism.* Grand Rapids, MI: Zondervan, 2009.

Hansen, Colin. *Young Restless, Reformed: A Journalist's Journey with the New Calvinists.* Wheaton, IL: Crossway, 2008

Helm, Paul. "Many Shades of Calvinism." in *Tabletalk.* June 1, 2010. http://www.ligonier.org/learn/articles/many-shades-calvinism/. (Accessed September 5, 2013)

Hewitson, Ian A. *Trust and Obey: Norman Shepherd & The Justification Controversy at Westminster Theological Seminary.* Minneapolis, MN: NextStep Resources, 2011.

Hodge, Charles. *Romans*. Crossway Classic Commentaries. Wheaton, IL: Crossway Books, 1993.

_____. *Systematic Theology.* 3 Volumes. Peabody, MA: Hendrickson Publishers.

Holcomb, Justin. "A Tale of Two Theologies: The Dutch and Scottish Reformed Theologies." http://theresurgence.com/2012/07/18/a-tale-of-two-theologies-the-dutch-and-scottish-reformed-traditions. (Accessed September 5, 2013).

_____. "Two Major Streams of Reformed Theology." September 24, 2012. http://thegospelcoalition.org/blogs/tgc/2012/09/24/tw

o-major-streams-of-reformed-theology/. (Accessed September 5, 2013).

Horton, Michael. *The Christian Faith: A Systematic Theology for Pilgrims on the Way."* Grand Rapids, MI: Zondervan, 2011.

_____. "Reformed and Charismatic?" August 22, 2011, http://www.whitehorseinn.org/blog/2011/08/22/reformed-and-charismatic/. (Accessed June 20, 2013).

Hughes, R. Kent. *Acts: The Church Afire.* Preaching the Word. Wheaton, IL: Crossway Books, 1996.

Johnson, Gary L.W. et al. *By Faith Alone: Answering the Challenges to the Doctrine of Justification.* Edited by Guy P. Waters. Wheaton, IL: Crossway, 2007.

Kauffman, Timothy F. "Sanctification, Half Full: The Myopic Hermeneutic of the 'Grace' Movement." Trinity Foundation, http://www.trinityfoundation.org/journal.php?id=282 (Accessed September 5, 2013).

Keller, Timothy J. *Center Church: Doing Balanced, Gospel-Centered Ministry in Your City.* Grand Rapids, MI: Zondervan, 2012.

_____. *Generous Justice: How God's Grace Makes Us Just.* New York: Riverhead Trade, 2012.

_____. "Deconstructing Defeater Beliefs: Leading the Secular to Christ." Jan 1, 2000. http://www.case.edu.au/images/uploads/03_pdfs/keller-deconstructing-defeater.pdf. (Accessed September 5, 2013).

Kendall, R.T. *Calvin and English Calvinism to 1649.* Studies in Christian History and Thought Series. Eugene, OR: WIPF & Stock, 1997.

Kevin D. Kennedy, "Hermeneutical discontinuity between Calvin and later Calvinism,"Scottish Journal of Theology *64.3 (Aug 2011): 299-312.*

Koleoso, Tope. "How Should a Reformed Pastor be Charismatic?" Desiring God National Conference for Pastors 2013. http://www.youtube.com/watch?v=1cmdWLJF3Dw. (Accessed September 5, 2013).

Ladd, George Eldon. *Jesus and the Kingdom.* Waco, TX: Word Books, 1964.

Lane, A.N.S. "Calvin's Doctrine of Assurance." *Vox Evangelica* 11(1979): 32-54.

Larsen, David. Phone Conversation. June 13, 2013.

Lenski, R. C. H. *The Interpretation of the Acts of the Apostles.* Minneapolis, MN: Augsburg Publishing House, 1961.

Lightner, Robert. *Sin, Savior and Salvation.* Nashville, TN: Thomas Nelson Publishers, 1990.

Louw, Johannes P. and Eugene Albert Nida. Volume 1. *Greek-English Lexicon of the New Testament: Based on Semantic Domains.* Electronic edition of the 2nd edition. New York: United Bible Societies, 1996.

Luther, Martin. *Bondage of the Will.* Grand Rapids, MI: Fleming H. Revell, 1957.

_____. *Commentary on Galatians.* Oak Harbor, WA: Logos Research Systems, Inc., 1997.

_____. *Commentary on Romans,* Translated by J. Theodore Mueller. Grand Rapids, MI: Kregel Publications, 1954.

_____. *Tabletalk.,* Translated by William Hazlitt. Ross-shire, Great Britain: Christian Focus Publications, 2003.

_____. *A Treatise on Good Works.* Kindle Edition

Lybrand, Fred R. *Back to Faith: Reclaiming Gospel Clarity in an Age of Incongruence.* Xulon

Press, 2009.

MacArthur, John. "Grow Up Advice for YRR (Part 2)." July, 25, 2011. http://www.gty.org/blog/B110725. (Accessed September 5, 2013).

_____. *Hard to Believe: The High Cost and Infinite Value of Following Jesus.* Nashville, TN: Thomas Nelson Publishers, 2003.

_____. "Keep Reforming." August 29, 2011. http://www.gty.org/blog/B110829. (Accessed September 5, 2013).

_____. *The Gospel According to Jesus: What is Authentic Faith.* Revised and Expanded. Grand Rapids, MI: Zondervan, 2008.

_____. "The MacArthur New Testament Commentary." 29 Volumes. Chicago: Moody Press, 1985-2011.

_____. *The Truth about the Lordship of Christ.* Nashville, TN: Thomas Nelson, 2012.

Machen, J. Gresham. "Christianity and Culture" in *Princeton Theological Review.* Volume 11 (1913): 1-15.

Marsden, George. Personal Correspondence. July 27, 2013.

Mars Hill Church. "Jesus." http://marshill.com/jesus. (Accessed September 5, 2013).

Masters, Peter. "New Calvinism, the Merger of Calvinism with Worldliness." *Sword and Trowel.* Metropolitan Tabernacle. Dec. 2009, http://www.metropolitantabernacle.org/Sword-And-Trowel/Evangelical-Magazine-Sword-and-Trowel-Articles/New-Calvinism-Merger-of-Calvinism-and-Worldliness. (Accessed September 5, 2013).

Merriam-Webster Inc. *Merriam-Webster's Collegiate Dictionary.* Eleventh edition. Springfield, MA: Merriam-Webster, Inc., 2003.

Milton, Michael A. "The Once and Future Calvin," at http://www.monergism.com/thethreshold/articles/onsite/Once&FutureCalvin.pdf. (Accessed September 5, 2013): 1-18.

Moody, Josh. *No Other Gospel: 31 Reasons from Galatians Why Justification by Faith Alone is the Only Gospel.* Wheaton, IL: Crossway, 2011.

McClain, Alva J. *Law and Grace: A Study of New Testament Concepts as They Relate to the Christian Life.* Winona Lake, IL: BMH Books, 1954.

Morris, Leon. *The Letter of James.* Pillar New Testament Commentary. Grand Rapids: William B. Eerdmans Publishing Company, 1988.

Moyer, R. Larry. *Free and Clear: Understanding & Communicating God's Offer of Eternal Life.* Grand Rapids, MI: Kregel Publications, 1997.

Muller, Richard A. *Calvin and the Reformed Tradition: On the Work of Christ and the Order of Salvation.* Grand Rapids, MI: Baker Academic, 2012.

Murphy, Martin. "Total Depravity" in *After Darkness Light: Essays in Honor of R.C. Sproul.* Edited by R.C. Sproul Jr. Phillipsburg, NJ: P & R Publishing, 2003.

Murray, Iain H. *Spurgeon Vs. The Hyper-Calvinists: The Battle for Gospel Preaching.* Carlisle, PA: Banner of Truth Trust, 1995.

Murray, John. *Redemption: Accomplished and Applied.* Kindle Edition.

Nimmo, "Paul T. Schleiermacher on Justification: A Departure from the Reformation?" *Scottish Journal of Theology* 66.1 (Feb 2013): 50-73.

Olson, C. Gordon. *Beyond Calvinism & Arminianism: An Inductive, Mediate Theology of Salvation.* Third Edition. Lynchburg, VA: Global Gospel Publishers, 2012.

Owen, John. *The Doctrine of Justification by Faith.* Kindle Edition. Monergism Books, 2012.

Palmer, Edwin H. *The Five Points of Calvinism.* Grand Rapids, MI: Baker Books, 1972.

Piper, John. "Act the Miracle: Future Grace, the Word of the Cross, and the Purifying Power of God's Promises." September 30, 2012. http://www.desiringgod.org/resource-library/conference-messages/act-the-miracle-future-grace-the-word-of-the-cross-and-the-purifying-power-of-god-s-promises. (Accessed October 10, 2012).

_____. "Adam, Christ, and Justification, Part 4." August 20, 2000. http://www.desiringgod.org/resource-library/sermons/adam-christ-and-justification-part-4. (Accessed September 5, 2013).

_____. "Are We to Continue in Sin That Grace Might Increase?" September 10, 2000. http://www.desiringgod.org/resource-library/sermons/are-we-to-continue-in-sin-that-grace-might-increase. (Accessed September 5, 2013).

_____, *Counted Righteous in Christ: Should We Abandon the Imputation of Christ's Righteousness?* Wheaton, IL: Crossway Books, 2002.

_____. *Future Grace: The Purifying Power of the Promises of God.* Revised Edition. Colorado Springs, CO: Multnomah Books. 2012.

_____. "God Abides in the One Who Loves and the One Who Confesses." May 19, 1985. http://www.desiringgod.org/resource-library/sermons/god-abides-in-the-one-who-loves-and-the-one-who-confesses. (Accessed September 5, 2013).

_____. "God Sanctifies His People Palm Sunday." April, 22, 1992. http://www.desiringgod.org/resource-library/sermons/god-sanctifies-his-people. (Accessed September 5, 2013).

_____. "Is God Less Glorious Because He Ordained that Evil Be?" July 1, 1998 at Jonathan Edwards Institute. http://www.desiringgod.org/resource-library/conference-messages/is-god-less-glorious-because-he-ordained-that-evil-be. (Accessed November 12, 2013).

_____. "Justification and the Diminishing Work of Christ," November 14, 2007 at Evangelical Theological Society Annual Meeting. http://www.desiringgod.org/resource-library/conference-messages/justification-and-the-diminishing-work-of-christ (Accessed September 5, 2013).

_____. "Make your Mouth a Means of Grace." October 12, 1986. http://www.desiringgod.org/resource-library/sermons/make-your-mouth-a-means-of-grace. (Accessed September 5, 2013).

_____. "Olympic Spirituality Part 1." August 2, 1992. http://www.desiringgod.org/resource-library/sermons/olympic-spirituality-part-1. (Accessed September 5, 2013).

_____. "Sustained by the Faithfulness of God." January 17, 1988. http://www.desiringgod.org/resource-library/sermons/sustained-by-the-faithfulness-of-god. (Accessed September 5, 2013).

_____. "The California Conference on Holiness: Kudos and Cautions." February 19, 1990, http://www.desiringgod.org/resource-library/taste-see-articles/the-california-conference-on-holiness-kudos-and-cautions. (Accessed September 5, 2013).

_____. "The Danger of Being Merely Human." February 21, 1988. http://www.desiringgod.org/resource-library/sermons/the-danger-of-being-merely-human. (Accessed September 5, 2013).

_____. "The Full Assurance of Hope," February 9. 1992. http://www.desiringgod.org/resource-library/sermons/the-full-assurance-of-hope. (Accessed September 5, 2013).

_____. "The Full Assurance of Hope to the End." October 20, 1996. http://www.desiringgod.org/resource-library/sermons/the-full-assurance-of-hope-to-the-end. (Accessed September 5, 2013).

_____. *The Future of Justification: A Response to N.T. Wright.* Wheaton, IL: Crossway Books, 2007.

_____. "The Justification Debate: A Primer." Compiled by Trevin Wax. *Christianity Today.* June 2009: 34-37.

_____. "Living by Faith in Future Grace." November 12, 2012. http://www.desiringgod.org/resource-library/sermons/living-by-faith-in-future-grace. (Accessed September 5, 2013).

_____. "The New Testament Gift of Prophecy: Definition, Theses and Suggestions." March 26, 1990 http://www.desiringgod.org/resource-library/taste-see-articles/the-new-testament-gift-of-prophecy. (Accessed June 30, 2013).

_____. *The Passion of Jesus Christ.* Wheaton, IL: Crossway Books, 2004.

_____. "The Unmerited, Conditional Grace of God." February 2, 1994. http://www.desiringgod.org/resource-library/taste-see-articles/the-unmerited-conditional-grace-of-god. (Accessed September 5, 2013).

_____. "What Do You Have to Believe About Creation in Order to be an Elder at Bethlehem. "June 26, 2009. http //www.desiringgod.org/resource-library/ask-pastor-john/what-do-you-have-to-believe-about-creation-in-order-to-be-an-elder-at-bethlehem. (Accessed September 5, 2013).

_____. "Whatever is Not From Faith is Sin." August 24, 1980, http://www.desiringgod.org/resource-library/sermons/whatever-is-not-from-faith-is-sin. (Accessed September 5, 2013).

_____. "What Happens When You Die? All Appear Before the Judgment Seat of Christ." August 1, 1993. http://www.desiringgod.org/resource-library/sermons/what-happens-when-you-die-all-appear-before-the-judgment-seat-of-christ. (Accessed September 5, 2013).

_____. "What We Believe About the Five Points of Calvinism." March 1, 1985. http://www.desiringgod.org/resource-library/articles/what-we-believe-about-the-five-points-of-calvinism. (Accessed September 5, 2013).

Polhill, John B. vol. 26, *Acts*, The New American Commentary. Nashville: Broadman & Holman Publishers, 1995.

Pratt, Jr., Richard L. et al. in *Tabletalk Magazine, June 2010: The New Calvinism*, ed. Burk Parsons, Lake Mary, FL: Ligonier Ministries, 2010.

Radmacher, Earl. *Salvation*. Nashville, TN: Word Publishing, 2000.Redeemer Presbyterian Church. "Core Values." http://www.redeemer.com/about_us/vision_and_values/core_values.html. (Accessed September 5, 2013).

Robbins, John W. "Pied Piper," *Trinity Review*. June, July 2002.

Robertson, A.T. *Word Pictures in the New Testament*. 6 volumes. Nashville, TN: Broadman Press, 1933.

Rogers Jack B. and Donald K. McKim. *The Authority and Interpretation of the Bible: An Historical Approach*. San Francisco: Harper & Row, 1979.

Ryrie, Charles C. *A Survey of Bible Doctrine*. Chicago: Moody Press, 1972.

_____. *Balancing the Christian Life*. Chicago: Moody, 1994.

_____. *Basic Theology*. Wheaton, IL: Victor Books, 1986.

_____. *Dr. Ryrie's Articles*. Bellingham, WA: Logos Research Systems, Inc., 2010.

_____. *So Great a Salvation*. Wheaton, IL: Victor Books, 1989.

Salmond, S. D. F. translator, *The Ante-Nicene Fathers, Volume V: Fathers of the Third Century: Hippolytus, Cyprian, Novatian, Appendix*. Edited by. Alexander

Roberts, James Donaldson and A. Cleveland Coxe. Buffalo, NY: Christian Literature Company, 1886.

Schaff, Philip. *The Nicene Fathers*. Electronic edition. 10 Volumes. Garland, TX: Galaxie Software, 2000.

Seifrid, Mark A. *Christ, Our Righteousness: Paul's Theology of Justification*. New Studies in Biblical Theology Series. Edited by D.A. Carson. Downers Grove, IL: InterVarsity Press, 2000.

Showers, Renald E. *There Really Is a Difference!: A Comparison of Covenant and Dispensational Theology*. Bellmawr, NJ: The Friends of Israel Gospel Ministry, Inc., 1990.

Smedes, Lewis B. Editor. *Ministry and the Miraculous: A Case Study at Fuller Theological Seminary*. Pasadena, CA: Fuller Seminary Press, 1987.

Smethurst, Matt. "Where Did All the New Calvinists Come from?" The Gospel Coalition. October 24, 2013. http://thegospelcoalition.org/blogs/tgc/2013/10/24/where-did-all-these-calvinists-come-from/. (Accessed March 18, 2014).

Spence-Jones, H. D. M. ed. *The Pulpit Commentary*. 52 Volumes. London; New York: Funk & Wagnalls Company, 1909.

Spicq, Ceslas and James D. Ernest. *Theological Lexicon of the New Testament*. 3 Volumes. Peabody, MA: Hendrickson Publishers, 1994.

Sproul, R.C. *Chosen by God*. Wheaton, IL: Tyndale House Publishers, 1986.

_____. *Do We believe the Whole Gospel?* December 1, 2010, http://www.ligonier.org/learn/articles/do-we-believe-whole-gospel/. (Accessed September 5, 2013).

_____. *Essential Truths of the Christian Faith.* Wheaton, IL: Tyndale House, 1992.

_____. *Grace Unknown: The Heart of Reformed Theology.* Electronic edition. Grand Rapids, MI: Baker Books, 2000.

_____. Interview with Mark Driscoll. Video Recording. Available at The Resurgence. http://theresurgence.com/2009/11/30/what-is-the-biggest-upcoming-theological-battle. (Accessed September 5, 2013).

_____. *Lifeviews: Make a Christian Impact on Culture and Society.* Electronic Edition. Old Tappan, NJ: Revell, 1986.

_____. *Roman: The Righteous Shall Live by Faith.* The St. Andrews Expositional Commentary Series. Wheaton, IL: Crossway Books and Bibles, 2009.

_____. *Truths We Confess: A Layman's Guide to the Westminster Confession of Faith.* 3 Volumes. Phillipsburg, NJ: P &R Publishing, 2007.

Stallard, Mike. "Gospel Centeredness, Jesus and Social Ethics" *Journal of Ministry and Theology* 15:2 (Fall 2011): 5-24.

_____. "Justification by Faith or Justification by Faith Alone?" *Conservative Theological Journal* 3:8 (April 1999): 53-73.

Straub, Jeffrey P. "The Emerging Church: A Fundamentalist Assessment." *Detroit Baptist Seminary Journal* 13:1 (Fall 2008): 69-91.

Steele, David N. et al. *The Five Points of Calvinism: Defined, Defended, and Documented.* Second Edition. Philipsburg, NJ: P & R Publishing, 2004.

Stegall, Thomas L. *The Gospel of Christ: A Biblical Response to the Crossless Gospel Regarding the Contents of Saving Faith.* Milwaukee, WI: Grace Gospel Press, 2009.

Stewart, Kenneth J. "The Points of Calvinism: Retrospect and Prospect." *Scottish Bulletin of Evangelical Theology* 26: 2 (2008): 187-203.

Storms, Sam et al. *For the Fame of God's Name: Essays in Honor of John Piper.* Edited by Justin Taylor. Wheaton, IL: Crossway, 2010.

Strong, Augustus Hopkins. *Systematic Theology.* Philadelphia: American Baptist Publication Society, 1907.

Swanson, James. *Dictionary of Biblical Languages With Semantic Domains: Greek (New Testament.* Electronic edition. Oak Harbor: Logos Research Systems, Inc., 1997.

Sweeney, Douglas A. and Allen C. Guelzo, Editors, *The New England Theology: From Jonathan Edwards to Edwards Amasa Park.* Grand Rapids, MI: Baker Academic, 2006.

_____, et al, *Jonathan Edwards and Justification,* Electronic Edition. Edited by Josh Moody. Wheaton, IL: Crossway Books, 2012.

Tchividijan, Tullian. *Unfashionable: Making a Difference in the World by Being Different.* Colorado Springs, CO: Multnomah Publishers, 2009.

Thorson, Stephen. "Tension in Calvin's View of Faith: Unexamined Assumptions in R.T. Kendall's Calvin and English Calvinism to 1649." *Journal of the Evangelical Theological Society* 37/3 (September 1994) 413-426.

Thomas, Robert L. Electronic Mail Message. (June 21, 2013).

_____. "The Hermeneutics of Non-Cessationism." *The Master's Seminary Journal* 14/2 (Fall 2003): 387-310.

Trueman, Carl. Phone Conversation. June 18, 2013.

Vance, Laurence M. *The Other Side of Calvinism.* Revised Edition. Pensacola, FL: Vance Publications, 1999.

Waldron, Samuel E. "John Calvin Versus Norman Shepherd on Sola Fide." *Reformed Baptist Theological Review* 02:2 (Jul 2005): 87-106.

Walvoord, John F. "The Augustinian-Dispensational Perspective." in *Five Views on Sanctification.* Grand Rapids, MI: Zondervan, 1986.

_____. *Jesus Christ Our Lord: A Handbook of Bible Doctrine.* Chicago: Moody Press, 1969.

Warfield, B.B. *Biblical Doctrines.* Carlisle, PA: Banner of Truth Trust, 1988.

Walker, Jeremy. *New Calvinism Considered: A Personal and Pastoral Assessment.* Darlington, England: EP Books, 2013.

Wells, David F. ed. *Reformed Theology in America: A History of its Modern Development.* Grand Rapids, MI: William B. Eerdman's Publishing Company, 1985.

Whaldron, Samuel F. *Faith Obedience and Justification: Current Evangelical Departures from Sola Fide.* Reformed Baptist Dissertation Series #1. Palmdale, CA: Reformed Baptist Academic Press, 2006.

Wilson, Jared C. "The Gospel-Driven Church: Gospel-Centeredness for the Cause of Gospel Wakefulness." The Gospel Coalition. http://thegospelcoalition.org/blogs/gospeldrivenchurch/2013/12/18/re-mark-driscoll/. (Accessed December 20, 2013).

Wilson, Sandy. *Christ's Redemption.* The Gospel Coalition Booklets. 2009.

Woods, Andy. "Romans 7 and Sanctification." *Chafer Theological Seminary Journal* 14:2 (Fall 2009).

Zeller, George. Phone Interview. June 26, 2013.

_____. "What is the Gift of God: A Study of Ephesians 2:8-9." (revised 5/07). http://www.middletownbiblechurch.org/reformed/godgift.htm. (Accessed September 5, 2013).

Printed in Great Britain
by Amazon